International Economic Integration in Historical Perspective

International economic integration is perceived as one of the paramount forces shaping the modern world. Many organizations, both public and private, are trying to combine economic activities across international borders. The European Union and the North American Free Trade Area are two examples of government-managed international economic integration. Private organizations include various criminal groups as well as international churches.

International economic integration is not a recent phenomenon; its roots can be traced back to the Roman Empire. *International Economic Integration in Historical Perspective* departs from the conventional short-term analysis and takes a long-term view of the process, offering perspectives that are both detailed and diverse. Dennis M. P. McCarthy examines seven types of organizations that exemplify international economic integration, such as colonial empires, merchant associations, religious empires, criminal empires, free trade areas, customs unions and common markets. Representative examples of each type are analysed in a comparative framework. An introduction defines key terms and concepts; a retrospective summarizes the main insights that emerge from the book. Endnotes and a detailed bibliography offer readers ways to pursue topics further.

This timely and unique book demonstrates that international economic integration is an economic and political process that also involves political economy. *International Economic Integration in Historical Perspective* will prove indispensable to students and general readers who wish to gain a firm understanding of international economics and the processes that shape the world today.

Dennis M. P. McCarthy is Associate Professor Emeritus of History, Iowa State University, Ames, USA.

Routledge explorations in economic history

1 **Economic Ideas and Government Policy**
Contributions to contemporary economic history
Sir Alec Cairncross

2 **The Organization of Labour Markets**
Modernity, culture and governance in Germany, Sweden, Britain and Japan
Bo Stråth

3 **Currency Convertibility**
The gold standard and beyond
Edited by Jorge Braga de Macedo, Barry Eichengreen and Jaime Reis

4 **Britain's Place in the World**
A historical enquiry into import controls 1945–1960
Alan S. Milward and George Brennan

5 **France and the International Economy**
From Vichy to the Treaty of Rome
Frances M. B. Lynch

6 **Monetary Standards and Exchange Rates**
M. C. Marcuzzo, L. Officer and A. Rosselli

7 **Production Efficiency in Domesday England, 1086**
John McDonald

8 **Free Trade and its Reception 1815–1960**
Freedom and trade: Volume I
Edited by Andrew Marrison

9 **Conceiving Companies**
Joint-stock politics in Victorian England
Timothy L. Alborn

10 **The British Industrial Decline Reconsidered**
Edited by Jean-Pierre Dormois and Michael Dintenfass

11 **The Conservatives and Industrial Efficiency, 1951–1964**
Thirteen wasted years?
Nick Tiratsoo and Jim Tomlinson

12 **Pacific Centuries**
Pacific and Pacific Rim economic history since the 16th century
Edited by Dennis O. Flynn, Lionel Frost and A. J. H. Latham

13 **The Premodern Chinese Economy**
Structural equilibrium and capitalist sterility
Gang Deng

14 **The Role of Banks in Monitoring Firms**
The case of the crédit mobilier
Elisabeth Paulet

15 **Management of the National Debt in the United Kingdom, 1900–1932**
Jeremy Wormell

16 **An Economic History of Sweden**
Lars Magnusson

17 **Freedom and Growth**
The rise of states and markets in Europe, 1300–1750
S. R. Epstein

18 **The Mediterranean Response to Globalization Before 1950**
Sevket Pamuk and Jeffrey G. Williamson

19 **Production and Consumption in English Households 1600–1750**
Mark Overton, Jane Whittle, Darron Dean and Andrew Hann

20 **Governance, The State, Regulation and Industrial Relations**
Ian Clark

21 **Early Modern Capitalism**
Economic and social change in Europe 1400–1800
Edited by Maarten Prak

22 **An Economic History of London, 1800–1914**
Michael Ball and David Sunderland

23 **The Origins of National Financial Systems**
Alexander Gerschenkron reconsidered
Edited by Douglas J. Forsyth and Daniel Verdier

24 **The Russian Revolutionary Economy, 1890–1940**
Ideas, debates and alternatives
Vincent Barnett

25 **Land Rights, Ethno Nationality and Sovereignty in History**
Edited by Stanley L. Engerman and Jacob Metzer

26 **An Economic History of Film**
Edited by John Sedgwick and Mike Pokorny

27 **The Foreign Exchange Market of London**
Development since 1900
John Atkin

28 **Rethinking Economic Change in India**
Labour and livelihood
Tirthankar Roy

29 The Mechanics of Modernity in Europe and East Asia
The institutional origins of social change and stagnation
Erik Ringmar

30 International Economic Integration in Historical Perspective
Dennis M. P. McCarthy

International Economic Integration in Historical Perspective

Dennis M. P. McCarthy

LONDON AND NEW YORK

First published 2006
by Routledge
2 Park Square, Milton Park, Abingdon, Oxon OX14 4RN

Simultaneously published in the USA and Canada
by Routledge
711 Third Avenue, New York, NY 10017

Routledge is an imprint of the Taylor & Francis Group, an informa business

First issued in paperback 2012

Typeset in Times by Wearset Ltd, Boldon, Tyne and Wear

British Library Cataloguing in Publication Data
A catalogue record for this book is available from the British Library

Library of Congress Cataloging in Publication Data
A catalog record of this title has been requested

ISBN13: 9-780-415-51463-7 (pbk)
ISBN13: 9-780-415-77027-9 (hbk)
ISBN13: 9-780-203-08672-8 (ebk)

Harry A. Miskimin, Jr.
1932–95
Ars longa, vita brevis.

Contents

Preface

This book originated in my fascination with international economic integration as one of the most important global forces of our time. My motivation for writing it drew strength from my conviction that a phenomenon so central to our daily lives deserves study in all its present facets and in its many historical dimensions.

Ideally, this work should exhaustively analyze all those present facets and many historical dimensions. Realistically, here I can make only a beginning. So I present a basic book that can be profitably read by anyone interested in the major issues of the day. The work is not a textbook, but it lends itself as supplementary reading to students taking courses in various subjects. These include courses in globalization, political economy, international economic relations, international economic history, international business history, international trade, international organizations, global economics and poverty, international economic integration and, of course, the history of international economic integration.

There is an extensive literature on international economic integration as a contemporary phenomenon. But this literature greatly needs a book that takes a very long-term view of the process and offers historical perspectives that are detailed and diverse. The present work is thus timely and unique, as no other book offers the rich historical perspectives on international economic integration that this one does.

Every author travels his or her own distinctive path. I would never have written this book, had I not gone to the Yale Graduate School to study economic history. The university had an interdisciplinary program in the subject, which required that students complete advanced degrees in both economics and history. This experience continues to shape my intellectual interests.

I would never have gone to graduate school, had three scholars not influenced me to study economic history in the first place. I would never have survived the Yale Graduate School without the timely counsel and intervention of a fourth scholar. I pay tribute to them all here. I honor one of them in the title of this book and another in the dedication.

David J. Loschky, William N. Parker, and Alexander Gerschenkron all stimulated my early interest in economic history. Loschky taught me US and European economic history when I was an undergraduate at Boston College. He was then a doctoral candidate at Harvard and introduced me to Alexander Gerschenkron. Professor Gerschenkron had a formidable set of intellectual skills, ranging from econometrics to literary criticism. His combination of technical competence and intellectual cosmopolitanism was reassuring. After meeting him when I was a senior at Boston College, I realized I could study economic history and keep my personality.

David Loschky had a relaxed teaching style highlighted by his openness to alternative approaches. He was also a great facilitator. Besides introducing me to Professor Gerschenkron, he told me about William N. Parker at Yale. Like Gerschenkron, Professor Parker blended academic rigor with a wide-ranging outlook. William Parker excelled at writing and speaking about dry subjects with great lucidity and wry humor.

Last but not least in this honored quartet is Harry A. Miskimin, Jr. He gave advice and support that got me through the Yale Graduate School. He kept me focused on "the big picture": if you want to be a university academic, you must get a doctorate. He had a great sense of humor, with flashes of exquisite understatement. I am blessed to have benefitted from his counsel.

In 1962 Alexander Gerschenkron published *Economic Backwardness in Historical Perspective*. I have never been comfortable with the concept of economic backwardness, as it reeks of ethnocentrism, but I like the idea of a book that provides an "historical perspective" on a central topic. International economic integration surely is a dominant subject of our times; hence, the title of this book.

I began my research in connection with vignettes I wrote on international economic integration in different parts of the world for my book, *International Business History: A Contextual and Case Approach* (Praeger, 1994). I also gave two papers to the Business History Conference that advanced my understanding of international economic integration. The first was published as "International Business and Economic Integration: Comparative Business Strategies Past and Present," *Business and Economic History*, Second Series, Volume Twenty-one, 1992, pp. 237–46. The second appeared as "International Economic Integration and Business Cultures: Comparative Historical Perspectives," *Business and Economic History*, Volume Twenty-five, No. 1, Fall 1996, pp. 72–80.

A single-author work is that in name only. Numerous people have helped me and deserve listing in the "credits" for this production. I thank John Ingham, Rondo Cameron, Naomi Lamoreaux, Mary Yeager, Diana Davids Olien, Todd Christopher Doorenbos, Barbara A. McCarthy, Timothy J. McCarthy, Chris Stockman, Edwin Krafsur, Jason Thein, Fred Carstensen, colleagues in an Iowa State History seminar called "the Vigilantes," and students in my own course in the History of International Economic Integration at Iowa State University.

Robert Langham, the senior economics and finance editor at Routledge, played a special role. He encouraged me every step of the way. I am greatly indebted to him and the entire Routledge team. I am privileged to work with a first-class organization that treats its authors with great collegiality. All the outside reviewers contributed mightily to the improvement and maturation of my manuscript.

Finally, as Professor Arthur M. Schlesinger, Jr., wrote: "once again, may I say that I will greatly welcome corrections or amplifications of anything I have written in this text (*The Politics of Upheaval*, Boston, Massachusetts, 1960, p. x)."

Dennis M. P. McCarthy
Ames, Iowa, USA

Introduction

International economic integration as economics, politics, and political economy

International economic integration is a major force in the world today. The European Union continues to add new members. In the western hemisphere the North American Free Trade Area of Canada, Mexico, and the United States is a well-established organization that may serve as a building block for a Free Trade Area of the Americas. Other free trade areas, such as that sponsored by the Association of South East Asian Nations, are emerging in Asia and the western Pacific. And in most regions of Africa, despite formidable hurdles, some type of economic integration is developing.

But international economic integration is not just a modern occurrence. It has a long history that reaches back thousands of years. Nor is international economic integration the exclusive preserve of governments.

The resulting historical tableau is extraordinarily rich and diverse. Glimpses at a few parts of this canvas reveal the Roman Empire, the colonial empires wrought by European countries, merchant associations fashioned by traders from around the world, the United States itself, as well as the examples mentioned above.

A phenomenon so influential deserves an appropriate framework. Frameworks contain the essentials an author wants a reader to know right away. They can explain such items as definitions, hypotheses, arguments, classifications, and rationales.

My framework poses four questions. What is international economic integration? What is the best way to study international economic integration? What kinds of organizations are involved in international economic integration? And why did I select those I did for analysis in this book? These can be summarized as the problems of definition, method, classification, and selection.

I will first consider the problems of definition and method together, because they are so closely connected.

International economic integration: the problems of definition and method

Defining international economic integration immediately encounters the promise and problem of academic categories. These offer promise, because specialized illumination can cast shafts of bright light on complicated topics. But they also present hurdles, because academic compartmentalization simply cannot adequately explain certain subjects. International economic integration is a classic example of the latter.

A word in our central topic – economic – has predisposed many to entrust international economic integration to the care of economists and indeed to regard it as primarily an economic process. To be sure, economic integration on all spatial levels – from the household, through the nation-state, and reaching international or cross-border cooperation – involves combining in some way the processes economists study. These include how goods are produced, distributed, and exchanged. Economics greatly helps us understand them in their material dimensions.

But combining these processes results from human decisions, taken singly or in organizations. And where there are people and organizations, there is politics, which contemporary economics is ill equipped to analyze. After all, it was in the later nineteenth century that economics split from political economy, as it was then known, economists believing that in separation and specialization lay the path to greater rigor.

If international economic integration were primarily an economic process, the incapacity of economics to analyze politics would not matter much. But international economic integration is much more than an economic process. *It is an economic and a political process that also involves political economy. This is the main argument of my book.* As such international economic integration needs illumination from economics, politics, and from the modern version of political economy.

It would be easier to entitle this introduction as "international economic integration as political economy" and to posit political economy as the all-encompassing rubric. But that would be wrong.

Modern political economy does have much to offer to our study of international economic integration in historical perspective. It is refreshing that a discipline acknowledges and builds upon the interactions between economics and politics in human organizations, including governments.

A contemporary definition of political economy has it focused on "the interrelationships between political and economic institutions and processes." Political economists study how governments "affect the allocation of scarce resources." They also analyze how "the economic system" and personal "economic interests" influence the laws and policies of governments.[1]

The pivotal word in the above definition is "interrelationship." This implies reciprocity, which is a two-way relationship, each side doing something for or to the other. But there are two types of interrelations: those that already exist and those that may develop in the future.

Of course, economics and politics are related in every grouping involved in international economic integration. This relation originates in the nature of bureaucracy, which automatically adds politics to whatever an organization claims to be doing.

But not every relation is automatically an interrelation, in fact or in promise. This is why I see essential ongoing roles for economics and politics as separate disciplines in our analysis. What if economics and politics are related but not yet interrelated in an organization?

If decision-makers want to interrelate politics and economics in their organizations more effectively or at all, they should know as much as possible about each force in its own terms. They then can take realistic steps to bring them together in whatever manner they decide. Economics and politics as specialized disciplines, along with the modern version of political economy, are all invaluable searchlights as we study international economic integration in both the past and present.

International economic integration: the problems of classification and selection

In defining international economic integration I have offered what I strongly believe is the most insightful way to study the subject. In dealing with the problem of classification, I take a panoramic approach, because international economic integration can arise from the actions of governments, private businesses, or public–private combinations.

Our classification is based on the kinds of organizations that pursue international economic integration. It features two general categories: government and non-government or, as some would prefer, public and private. These are not exclusive dichotomies. Some private associations have performed governmental functions and are, therefore, quasi-public in certain respects. They would occupy a middle ground between public and private.

In this book I examine four kinds of organizations that clearly belong in the government category. These are colonial empires, free trade areas, customs unions, and common markets. I analyze three types that may be private or may occupy a middle ground between public and private. These are merchant associations, religious empires, and criminal empires. Some merchant associations are private, but others have acted on behalf of governments. Most religious groups that operate across international boundaries are private; but one, the Roman Catholic Church, operates as a government today and had more extensive governmental responsibilities in the past.

Most international criminal organizations would like to remain private, even undetected. But some have fulfilled governmental functions and continue to do so in the present.

These seven types do not exhaust the range of organizations that are involved in international economic integration. Space limitations have led to omissions that please no one, especially the author. I have left out international organizations such as the United Nations and regional associations such as the African Union. Some specialized agencies of the United Nations certainly deserve study as agents of international economic integration in their own right. NGOs, or non-governmental organizations, can be agencies of international economic integration, depending on their mission and whether they operate across international borders. There are thousands of NGOs and I am but one scholar.

My most salient omission is a type of private business. While I consider the Roman Catholic Church and the Mafia as multinational corporations and devote chapters to them in this book, I still have not given adequate attention to all the roles multinational corporations play in international economic integration. Some will regard no penance as sufficient for this lacuna. But in my previous publications I made a beginning. I refer readers to my 1992 paper in *Business and Economic History* and my 1994 book *International Business History: A Contextual and Case Approach*. So in the present book I chose the seven kinds of organizations I did for one reason. They expand the range of my publications on the kinds of organizations involved in international economic integration.

I challenge those disappointed with my omissions and presentations in this book to do better. I hope all the shortcomings of this book will stimulate research and publication that will enrich the field of international economic integration.

There is no consensus classification for government-managed international economic integration. I use the most elementary one, which features three types of groups. These are, in ascending order of greater economic integration, the "free trade area," the "customs union," and the "common market." After I define these three, I will consider other government classifications.

A free trade area pursues internal *trade liberalization*. This term means reducing every kind of internal trade barrier. A customs union is a free trade area with one additional feature: a common external tariff wall. Participants in a customs union strive not only for internal trade liberalization but also for a common tariff front towards outsiders.

Of the three types, a common market bonds members the most intensively. A common market is a customs union with two more features. First, members work for cross-border mobility of their labor and capital. Workers can seek jobs wherever they can find them within the common market. Investors likewise can operate free from national restrictions anywhere in the market. The second feature concerns the law: participating countries endeavor to fashion a set of laws that apply to the entire common market. Achieving complete mobility of capital and labor and producing community laws in every area are very difficult goals that may never be totally realized, even after decades of work.

Some organizations involving countries are difficult to compartmentalize as exclusively a free trade area, or a customs union, or a common market. In practice, country groups move along a spectrum of international economic integration, which this three-term classification cannot completely elucidate. Indeed, all organizations considered in this book proceed along their own spectra of international economic integration.

International economic integration is a process whose goals depend on the kind of group. For a free trade area, customs union, and common market, the theory is classic and conventional. Such groups can have two goals. The first is removing internal barriers to business and economic activity. Barriers include tariffs and quotas. Tariffs are taxes on commodities crossing borders. Quotas are numerical limitations on how much of a particular good can enter a country in a certain time period.

The rationale for reducing obstacles to exchange is well documented. Falling barriers can energize all kinds of business and economic activity. The incomes of many people will rise. Their spending and saving will help others. And their local and national economies will strengthen.

A second goal for a free trade area, customs union, or common market may be closer political relationships among participants. Every group originates in politics, I have argued, and must advance in politics. Members talk and negotiate with one another as human beings, not merely as the sums of their material wealth. As a group becomes more integrated economically, political struggles intensify, because the greater cohesion of the whole usually requires more sacrifices from participants.

The goals for other kinds of groups come from particular organizations within a group. Consider, for example, colonial empires, which we study in Chapter 1. While all colonial empires originate in imperialism, each colonial empire faces its own mix of economic, financial, and survival considerations. Each structures itself and its relations with the outside world accordingly.

Scholars have refined the most elementary classification of government-managed international economic integration. The late Bela Balassa was a leader in this endeavor. He proposed a five-step ladder. This starts with the elementary three, but adds two steps higher than the common market: an economic union and complete economic integration.

For Balassa, "an economic union, as distinct from a common market, combines the suppression of restrictions on commodity and factor movements with some degree of harmonisation of national economic policies..." The fifth and highest step, complete economic integration, "presupposes the unification of monetary, fiscal, social, and countercyclical policies and requires the setting-up of a supranational authority whose decisions are binding for the Member States."[2] Other scholars have built on Balassa's work.[3]

I welcome attempts at greater sophistication. These may eventually clarify the spectrum of international economic integration along which government groups move. But Balassa's steps, as well as our elementary three, are akin to stages. If used as mandates, stages can dogmatize a process.

Consider Balassa's fifth step, complete economic integration. Step 5 "requires the setting-up of a supranational authority whose decisions are binding for the Member States." "Supranational authority" here is vague but surely includes a court of last resort.

Both the European Union and the United States, which we compare and contrast as common markets in Chapter 7, had courts of last resort in place well before they became even partial common markets in practice. Balassa's "supranational authority" thus makes a belated and misleading appearance in Step 5 and should actually be in Step 3, a common market.

To be sure, the elementary three is not immune to scholarly straitjacketing. But I use them not as a rigid trichotomy but as flexible guidelines. And I view them from the perspective of political economy. This means that greater economic integration is not in itself necessarily better. In other words, a common market is not inherently superior to a free trade area for every group.

Some organizations face political constraints that may make it unrealistic for them to go much beyond a free trade area. This is not a reason to feel inferior but a cause for great celebration: a free trade area is a major accomplishment. As readers will see, politics and economics must advance together and form interrelations in an organization pursuing cross-border economic integration.

Where one gets too far ahead of the other or where the proper political foundations have not been laid for the greater cohesion of a group, there will be trouble.

Even with the elementary three of free trade area, customs union, and common market, there are still problems. Sometimes there is no question for me in what category a particular organization belongs. The *Zollverein* was a customs union and *Mercosur* approximates one and they are properly studied in Chapter 6. The United States of America and the European Union are indubitably common markets and they belong in Chapter 7. Some who follow Balassa suggest that the EU may be an economic union. But for me the EU is, not may be, a common market and I will treat it as such.

Many other government groups now aspire to closer forms of international economic integration. Some even embody their hopes in the name of their organization. But, practically, they are free trade areas or close to that classification.

Moreover, there is today a customs union that emerged from a free trade area and a free trade area that has historical roots in a customs union. In Chapter 5 on free trade areas I consider the Latin American Free Trade Association and the Andean Community. The Andean Community is a customs union that emerged from the old Latin American

Free Trade Association. I also review the old and new versions of the East African Community. The old EAC was a customs union; the new EAC is trying to become a free trade area and more.

Historical experience has a way of showing that there is more than one path forward. Indeed, the ladder of international economic integration, or stages through which a group progresses, may not be appropriate metaphors. Organizations should choose and adapt what works best for them from a wealth of historical insights that are not dogmatically ranked. I hope the examples in the following seven chapters will give life to some of these insights.

Finally, international economic integration in itself has neither heart nor soul. Those in charge must ensure that its positive features dominate and, where it causes harm, they must repair the damage.

International economic integration truly has a dark side: economic disintegration. Colonial empires imposed their own versions of international economic integration upon their subject territories. In so doing, they inflicted great economic disintegration on the land and the indigenous people living on it, which readers will soon see in Chapter 1. As many chartered companies carried out the mandates of their government charters, they too inflicted disintegration on the environments they were trying to manipulate, a theme of Chapter 2. Organized religion and organized crime, the topics of Chapters 3 and 4, also created their own forms of disintegration as they sought the kind of international economic integration that would best promote their own self-interests. And all the types of government-managed international economic integration can have drawbacks. Readers encounter these principally in Chapter 5, which evaluates several controversial free trade agreements.

1 Colonial empires

Imperialism and colonialism: types, causes, and forms

Many colonial empires have come and gone over the last 2,000 years. Colonial empires are associated with colonialism, which is directly related to imperialism. Imperialism is a broad term that encompasses whatever leads some people to dominate others. Imperialism pertains to an empire as a whole, whereas colonialism focuses on the individual colonies that an empire possesses. Colonies are the territories seized by an empire and can become administrative units of it.

Imperialism has many causes. The drive to acquire power, money, wealth, or territory can be rooted in economic, business, political, religious, social, psychological, and cultural considerations. An empire usually runs on several sources of motivation and particular empires have their own distinctive mixes of these factors.

The term empire can refer to a number of situations. Many empires throughout history have developed a strong bureaucratic or administrative dimension. In many cases the dominating country maintained physical control over its subject lands and peoples by setting up administrations in their territories. Civil servants or military personnel or both could run these bureaucracies. The colonial empires of Great Britain, France, Germany, and Portugal followed this pattern. Japan wanted its own colonies in the twentieth century and maintained a military occupation of Korea from 1910 to 1945.

Administrative empires need not be associated only with governments. Religious and criminal empires are creations of people not in government. But they exhibit the essential characteristic of empire building: a core group wants to extend its power and influence over other people and places. These empires develop their own organizations that cross international borders and, in this sense, they are administrative empires.

Empires need not be administrative or even formally organized. In this regard the notions of informal imperialism, economic imperialism, economic colony, and sphere of influence are all important. Formal imperialism is usually associated with governments creating their own bureaucracies to administer their individual colonies. Informal imperialism designates a spread of power and influence that does not take shape in official or government organization. Informal imperialism can prepare the way for formal imperialism by setting in motion a dynamic that will compel a government to extend its administrative apparatus outside its national borders. But a crucial point is that informal imperialism does not inevitably produce formal imperialism. Whether or not that transformation occurs depends on the particular techniques employed by those engaged in a specific case of informal imperialism.

Governments or private groups can pursue economic imperialism. This kind of imperialism is based on trying to dominate or manipulate international trading and investment flows. It may be informal imperialism, if it is practiced by a government but does not yet involve the official structures of that government in an up-front manner. Economic imperialists, whether they are countries, businesses, or people, strive to create conditions that will yield them more wealth. Their main concern is self-acquisition, not the betterment of their trading or investment partners. Economic imperialism has frequently been self-aggrandizement at the expense of others: the imperialist gains by inflicting losses on others.

Sometimes this behavior is so concerted and widespread that it creates an economic colony. Formal colonies, those established by imperial governments, can be economic colonies, but an economic colony does not necessarily become a formal one. An economic colony is a territory or group that has become dependent on outsiders, usually but not exclusively the dominating economic imperialists. Dependent means excessively reliant on those outsiders for the sources of one's own survival and well-being. This excessive reliance entrenches a crucial harm: the loss of local decision-making about one's economic present and future.

The concept of economic colony is not the sole domain of governments. Private businesses can create their own economic colonies, both outside the borders of their home countries as well as within them. Sometimes the economic colonies developed by businesses have included large regions within another country or territory. The areas of the world that have been colonized both by government and business have truly been doubly victimized.

Sphere of influence, in international relations, designates an area on land or sea over which a particular government exerts its presence, sometimes with military force. Sphere of influence can also have an economic dimension. A country, business, or individual entrepreneur can create an economic sphere of influence by investing substantial amounts of capital or other resources in a location. An economic sphere of influence can be a prelude to an economic colony. When an investment presence reaches such levels that it not only dominates but also starts to exclude competitors, conditions are ripe for transforming an economic sphere of influence into an economic colony.

These terms – formal and informal imperialism, economic imperialism, economic colony, and economic sphere of influence – help one analyze imperialism and colonialism in their economic and business dimensions. These are not the only aspects of imperialism and colonialism. While we focus on economic and business matters, cultural imperialism and epistemological imperialism are as important for understanding the impact of government and business in foreign lands.

Cultural imperialism exports one culture and imposes it on others. Culture has many definitions, but they are all based on how people think and act in a society. These actions include the production and appreciation of literary and artistic works. But culture embraces more: it embodies the distinctiveness of the ways all people think and act in a given group. Countries have their own cultures; so do businesses and other organizations. Cultural imperialism proclaims two commandments: our ways are better than yours; and you should renounce your ways and follow ours. These attitudes can lead to the establishment of cultural spheres of influence and cultural colonies.

Akin to cultural imperialism is epistemological imperialism. Some might regard it as a sub-set of cultural imperialism. Epistemology is the study of how one knows things. Epistemological imperialism maintains that one way of knowing something is the only correct way. In research and scholarship, for instance, a dogmatic insistence on one method that rejects others out of hand is epistemological imperialism. Today some scholars in the so-called "Third World" regard the dominance of "western paradigms" and "western modes of sequential reasoning" as examples of cultural imperialism.

International economic integration promotes cultural interaction, which can have different outcomes. The interaction may produce a genuine interpenetration that creates healthy cultural hybrids. But it can also result in a rising domination of one culture over another that unleashes escalating harms. These range from weakening parts of that other culture to destroying it completely.

Colonial empires and international economic integration

Not every colonial empire exhibited international economic integration. And some that created it may not have sought it as considered policy. But many did pursue some type of international economic integration and achieved it with varying degrees of success.

The Ottoman Empire

The Ottoman Empire, for example, did not develop any major international economic integration of its domains with its homeland. Osman I founded this empire in 1312. Its home base was Anatolia in the Near East. It expanded to include lands in the Middle East, North Africa, and Europe, particularly Greece and the Balkans. Its westward thrust into

Europe was stopped in Vienna in 1683. In 1922 Kemal Attaturk overthrew the Ottoman Empire and founded modern Turkey.

At its peak the Ottoman Empire had vast possessions. But these constituted neither a "unified economy" nor a "common market." The major factor working against imperial economic integration was the "high cost of transport."[1] Even if the cost of transport had not been so high, it is not clear that rulers of the Ottoman Empire would have pursued any significant international economic integration. Their main economic goal was financial: the maintenance of a tax system that yielded sufficient revenue to keep the empire going.

The Habsburg Empire

While the case of the Ottoman Empire is straightforward, that of the Habsburg Empire cannot be so simply put. The major questions are, what was the Habsburg (or Hapsburg) Empire? And was it a colonial empire?

The Habsburg dynasty has a long history covering centuries of political involvement in Europe. Its main base before 1918 was Austria-Hungary in central Europe. These two countries were more easily joined by a hyphen than unified by administration or equalized in economy. They were not the only parts of the homeland. In the west, besides Austria proper, there were the provinces of Bohemia and Moravia. The Habsburg dynasty produced rulers who sat on the thrones of other countries, such as Spain and the Netherlands in western Europe. And Habsburgs presided over the Holy Roman Empire, a more symbolic than bureaucratic grouping of central European states that lasted from either 800 or 962 until 1806. There were, then, greater and lesser territorial versions of the Habsburg Empire, depending on how one views empire. The family no doubt preferred the greater version. Possessions under control of a family member were part of the "empire," even if these had few other links with the dynasty's home base in Austria-Hungary.

The economic status of the two halves of the smaller territorial empire, Austria-Hungary, is why we include the Habsburg Empire in a discussion of colonial empires. Austria was much stronger economically than Hungary. This gross regional imbalance made Hungary in effect an economic colony of Austria.

The greater and lesser versions of the Habsburg Empire call for substantially different analyses with respect to international economic integration. The smaller territorial empire, Austria-Hungary, did experience one significant kind of international economic integration. In 1850 the customs frontier between Austria and Hungary was abolished: goods passing from one part to the other no longer paid customs or tariffs. Austria and Hungary now constituted a customs union.[2]

This union was protectionist: it had a high external tariff wall. Some earlier scholars argued that the customs union entrenched the colonial status of Hungary. But recent research suggests that the union did not substantially alter existing trade patterns.

Austria continued to export manufactured goods to Hungary, while Hungary sent agricultural products to Austria.[3] This relationship exemplifies the classic paradigm of an economic colony (Hungary) servicing the home country (Austria). One member sends manufactured goods, which embody more value than unprocessed agricultural commodities, to the other. The economic colony serves as a market for those manufactured exports but also ships agricultural products, usually unprocessed, to the home country.

The customs union may not have entrenched this colonial relationship, but it surely did not dissolve it. We are reminded once again that cross-border economic integration does not in itself promote regional economic equalization.

The smaller Habsburg Empire does reveal, therefore, one substantive attempt at international economic integration. But the same cannot be said for the larger Habsburg Empire. This was far more an example of dynastic than economic integration. The Habsburg Empire thus presents a mixed picture. In its greater version it belongs, along with the Ottoman Empire, in the category of empires that exhibited no significant international economic integration. But in its lesser, central European manifestation, the Habsburg empire belongs in our third group: colonial empires that sought some type of international economic integration and achieved it. This third group will receive attention after consideration of our second category: colonial empires that created international economic integration but may not have sought it as considered policy.

The Roman Empire

In the second category is the Roman Empire. This organization lasted over four hundred years, from the early years of the first century AD or CE until the middle of the fifth century AD or CE. Its home base, the city of Rome, was located on the Italian peninsula. But it expanded to embrace possessions in western and central Europe, including lands in the British Isles and territories in north Africa.

The Roman Empire created one of the first great trading littorals in global history: the Mediterranean littoral. A littoral is an ocean or sea with all the lands on it and around it. The Mediterranean littoral covers the Mediterranean Sea, its islands, and lands around it: in north Africa, the Near East, and southeastern, south central, and southwestern Europe. Rome founded strategic outposts, provided stability, spread a common language, Latin, and tried to enforce a growing body of law, Roman law.

All these elements – security, stability, language, and law – promoted the unity of the Mediterranean littoral as an arena for business. To be sure, all four factors were not present everywhere in the Mediterranean littoral. And when they came together, their impact was neither uniform nor continuous over time. But Rome did establish a framework for unifying the Mediterranean littoral as a venue where cross-border and cross-water business relationships of many kinds could develop. In so doing, the empire performed an inestimable service for international economic integration early in the first millennium. As one author put it, "for more than two centuries, the Roman peace more or less freed the inhabitants of the Roman world from major military disturbances; the Mediterranean was free of pirates, major roads were usually clear of brigands; tax burdens were by and large predictable."[4]

The Mediterranean littoral was a zone of increasing bilateral and multilateral trade relations during this period. Egypt and its western neighbor Cyrenaica became major exporters of grain and minor exporters of dates and cured fish to Italy and other areas of Europe. Egypt became a significant exporter of flax, a fiber used in the making of textiles, to many regions throughout the littoral. Egypt continued to export its manufactures – textiles, papyrus, glassware, drugs, ointments, perfumes, and *objets d'art* – in and around the littoral. In the later Roman period, some of these products, especially glassware, "encountered stiff competition" from the wares of Italy, Gaul, and Germany. As to its imports, Egypt remained an importer of metals – antimony, cobalt, silver, and tin – and such other commodities as timber, wine, and olive oil. While it imported an important list of products, Egypt never became dependent on imports from western Europe.[5]

The grain trade shows the increasing significance of the Mediterranean littoral for Rome itself. About 750,000 to one million people lived in the city of Rome in the early centuries of the empire. To meet their needs, the city had to import about 150,000 to 200,000 tons of grain every year.[6] A growing population dictated a search for sources of supply that over time reached more locations in and around the Mediterranean littoral. North Africa, which was a crucial provider of grain to the city during the preceding period of the Roman Republic, greatly increased that role under the empire. Other exporters of grain to Rome included Sicily, Sardinia, Gaul, the Chersonese, Spain, and Cyprus. Usually the city could sustain itself on Sicilian, Sardinian, Italian, and north African grain, with Egypt as the principal north African source.[7] The Mediterranean littoral, with threats to commerce greatly reduced under the *pax Romana*, truly cradled a thriving international business community.

The status of grain arriving in Rome from around the Mediterranean littoral brings to the fore the issue of what drove Roman expansion. That grain came from a number of sources. Some of it was state grain in the form of taxes paid in kind from the provinces of the empire. Some of it represented rents paid in kind by tenants of public land or imperial estates. Some of it was purchased from merchants or landowners at source and might be regarded as grain from the private sector.[8] The first two sources – state grain and state rents – suggest the importance of wide-ranging imperial structures for the food supply of the eternal city. Can one conclude from this evidence that "economic factors" were one of the main engines of Roman expansion? Not necessarily. The above evidence shows only that Roman expansion had economic consequences but it does not illuminate motivation or causation.

The related issues of motivation and causation are central to a continuing debate over the "ancient economy." The unresolved state of these questions is why the Roman Empire now appears in our second category: empires that created international economic integration but may not have sought it as considered policy.

A brief review of this controversy explains our classification. In the early 1970s Moses I. Finley, the renowned classical scholar, argued that an "ancient economy" did not exist in the Graeco-Roman world from 1000 BC to AD 500. He arrived at this conclusion by applying a contemporary definition of economy to the past. This definition was rooted in neo-classical economic analysis: an economy consists of interdependent markets governed by prices sensitive to conditions of supply and demand and driven by entrepreneurs and other players calculating the costs and benefits of their every move.

Not surprisingly, Finley, with his modernist approach, could find no evidence of an ancient economy. The ancients "lacked the concept of an 'economy,' and . . . lacked the conceptual elements which together constitute what we call 'the economy.' "[9] Finley was looking exclusively through contemporary lenses and not making enough of an attempt to see matters from the viewpoints of those then living. Projecting a modern definition back into the past without modifying it or revealing any sensitivity to local cognitions is not a valid historical method.

Such an approach led Finley to analyze the actions of Rome's builders in an intriguing fashion. He contended that Roman imperialism lacked substantial economic motivation: "not a single conquest by a Roman emperor was motivated by the possibility of imperial enrichment . . ." Yet on the very same page he observed, "for the Roman state, the provinces were a main source of revenue through taxes."[10] These taxes, as noted above, were sometimes paid in kind, not money; major amounts of grain came to the city of Rome in that manner. At first glance, these statements appear contradictory, unless one does not include revenue in the category of "imperial enrichment." For Finley, imperial enrichment as taxes or prestige or whatever did not cause Roman imperialism or expansion; they were consequences of those actions.

To suggest that Rome's leaders, when they contemplated or achieved their conquests, had no inkling at all that expansion could benefit them and the empire in *material* terms – and these are the stuff of any economy – is unrealistic. But classical scholars continue to dispute the meaning of the term "ancient economy," the precise roles agriculture did play in that economy, and what type of "economic person" existed if any in the ancient world.[11] In this situation one must remain content to underscore Rome's contribution to international economic integration without assigning cause or motivation. The Roman Empire created in the Mediterranean littoral one of the greatest commercial venues in world history.

In the third category are numerous examples of colonial empires that sought some type of international economic integration and achieved it with varying levels of success. Our treatment here is selective with respect to examples and focused with regard to theme. The Spanish, Portuguese, Belgian, and German colonial empires will be sketched, and then the British and French colonial empires will be analyzed in more detail. Emphasis is placed on the type of international economic integration each featured and its consequences.

Imperial sketches: Spain, Portugal, Belgium, and Germany

The Spanish Empire

Spain pioneered the transoceanic colonial empire. Starting in the early 1500s the Spanish built an empire that came to include lands in the Americas and Africa. Their most extensive possessions were in the western hemisphere, what exploring and colonizing Europeans called "the New World." In the sixteenth century they created two of the four viceroyalties or administrative subdivisions that would organize their "New World" lands. Founded in 1535, the Viceroyalty of New Spain was centered in Mexico City. Established in 1542, the Viceroyalty of Peru was based in both Lima and La Paz. The other two viceroyalties were not established until the eighteenth century: New Granada in 1717, with centers of administration at Caracas and Bogotá; and La Plata in 1776, headquartered in Buenos Aires. A viceroy appointed by Spain headed each of these subdivisions. He was responsible to the Spanish monarch and the Council of the Indies for the conduct of affairs in his region.

Our brief discussion of imperial organization suggests the importance Spain placed on increasing bureaucratization. Because the Spanish greatly prized the principle of administrative centralization, they had to create and maintain a heavy bureaucracy to run their American colonies. Its costs were enormous.

This was a bureaucracy founded on the vertical chain of command. While administrative subdivisions multiplied and bureaucrats increased in number, communication was usually up and down the chain of command. Information moved from remote overseas possessions back up to Spain itself, not as often between those on the same level of the chain but in different viceroyalties.

The vertical preoccupation of this chain of command carried over into imperial economic organization. Spain ordered that all exports from its colonies travel first to Spain itself. It prohibited trade between (bilateral) or among (multilateral) its "New World" colonies. Mexico, for example, could not legally export its textiles directly to Peru.

This was an exclusive vertical integration that did not permit any concomitant horizontal integration between or among the colonies themselves. There was smuggling: an "underground economy" moved goods illegally on land and sea. The British and others engaged in this illicit trading, both through Spain itself and direct to its colonies.[12] But since Spain had forbidden such commerce, it could not tax this "illegitimate trade" and so deprived its empire, under mounting stress during the 1600s and 1700s, of an important source of revenue.

The Spanish approach to empire contains salutary lessons. Early in its imperial run, Spain dominated several areas in Europe outside itself; it lost control over these locations by 1600. As its position as a major power in Europe eroded, Spain tried to stop the slide by leaning more heavily on its overseas territories for money. Among the major taxes levied on its colonies were those on internal sales and overseas commerce. These levies increased relentlessly throughout much of the seventeenth century and provoked much local discontent that on many occasions became rebellions. The strategy of abusing one part of an empire to maintain the overall edifice usually does not work, and Spain lost most of its "New World" empire by the early decades of the nineteenth century.

The kind of exclusive vertical economic integration the Spanish pursued was in the classic mercantilist vein. The colonies existed to serve the home country: it was the sun of their universe and they its satellites, by regulation and military force. That they could also help themselves by assisting each other was not part of a mercantilist world-view.

A vertical integration that permitted, even fostered, links among the colonies themselves would have better served the empire. A rigid verticality in any organization can stimulate a variety of creative responses. Spanish imperial economic organization invited an illegal activity that could not be repressed. Illicit trade continued, because "it was in the interests of too many Spaniards on both sides of the Atlantic."[13]

The Spanish case suggests a basic axiom. International economic integration that is so glaringly one-sided will promote actions, often illegal, designed to spread its benefits. Indeed, those running Spain's empire seemed to grasp this lesson, belatedly. They implemented major changes in the late eighteenth century, in the last decades for most of their American empire. Among these reforms was the abolition of restrictions on trade among Spanish colonies. And by 1789 licensed ships could sail direct to most ports in Spanish America.[14]

The Spanish imperial experience also raises an issue that appears in other situations of international economic integration. Some actions deemed illegal under a system could reveal directions that should in fact be taken by "official organization," because this "illegitimate" activity follows natural contours or is rational behavior. The Spanish prohibition on trade among its colonies assaulted timeless notions of both nature and rationality and, in the end, hurt the empire by for so long eliminating another source of revenue. The actions of the "illicit traders," in flouting imperial mandates but following natural trade patterns, filled in the gaps of the international economic integration the Spanish empire was promoting in an incomplete and distorted manner.

The Portuguese Empire

Portugal was a co-pioneer with Spain in constructing transoceanic colonial empires. In the history of European colonialism it began early and finished late. The Portuguese were in the first wave of global exploration and colonization. The Portuguese crossed the Atlantic Ocean and established settlements in South America. They journeyed down west Africa into southwest Africa, around the Cape of Good Hope and into southeastern Africa, and then across the Indian Ocean to the Indian subcontinent and beyond. Portugal's major colonies included Brazil, which became independent in 1822, and two African territories, Mozambique and Angola, which gained their independence in 1975.

Both the Spanish and Portuguese colonial empires were highly centralized. But while the Spanish cherished the principle of bureaucratic centralization, the Portuguese elevated it to the theory of administrative assimilation. Colonies were extensions of the European homeland: no constitutional distinctions were made between the metropolis (Portugal itself) and the colonies.

"Portugal Overseas" may have been constitutionally part of Portugal itself, but in economics and business the distinction between home country and colony still mattered greatly. As did the Spanish, the Portuguese operated on a crude top-to-bottom version of mercantilism, which was a set of policies that aimed to strengthen the evolving nation-state. Under mercantilism colonies existed to serve the home country exclusively, not each other. Mercantilism did not create colonialism but reinforced it.[15]

The Portuguese, like the Spanish, tried to carry a verticality of administration into imperial economic organization. This endeavor featured regulations and consequences similar to those found in the Spanish experience. Portugal restricted trade to Portuguese subjects, banned foreign ships from Brazilian and other colonial ports, and permitted only direct trade from the colonies to and from Lisbon.[16] Direct trade between Portuguese colonies or between a Portuguese colony and a non-Portuguese neighboring territory was thus outlawed.

As in the Spanish case, both nature and rationality, on their own, revised imperial law in practice. British and Dutch merchants, not Portuguese nationals, handled much of the Brazilian trade and purchased many of its products. Portuguese Africa was the scene of much illicit trade, including smuggling that flourished in spite of monopolies and rules against private trading. Even government officials, with blatant disregard for their own laws, promoted the interests of private enterprise.[17] Portuguese imperial economic integration, which also featured an unrealistic verticality, once again encouraged creative interpretation.

The Portuguese case is noteworthy, because many government bureaucrats assisted private and often illegal business activity. Government personnel, in effect, helped private entrepreneurs find and seize the "natural" and "rational" business opportunities which Portuguese imperial economic integration presented but then proscribed.

The Portuguese have been described as following an "uneconomic imperialism" in Africa, because their African colonies eventually drained their economic strength. A 1974 *coup* in Lisbon installed a government that granted independence to Portugal's African territories in the following year. Before this decision, the home government had been spending over half of its annual budget to finance wars against the independence movements in its African colonies. This was "uneconomic" imperialism in the end.

The Belgian Empire

The Belgian colonial empire, which consisted of the vast central African lands of the Democratic Republic of Congo (formerly Zaire), owes its foundation to one person.

King Leopold II of Belgium, constitutionally restrained at home, devoted much energy to building his own colony in Africa from the 1880s until he died in 1909. His intense desire to possess the Congo as his very own drove him to construct a hyper-centralized bureaucracy. He was most eager to exploit the human and natural resources trapped within those artificially drawn colonial boundaries. His special concern with bureaucracy led to the development of an international economic integration that formalized the roles of the favored as well as those of the oppressed with sharpness rare in the annals of colonialism.

Leopold II imposed a verticality of administration whose bureaucratization surpassed that of the Spanish and Portuguese. The chain of command was one of the most detailed and rigid in colonial history. A Governor-General in the Congo represented Leopold and had to clear almost every decision with Leopold himself. The country itself was divided into districts, the districts into zones, the zones into *secteurs*, and the *secteurs* into *postes*.

From Leopold at the top down to the *postes* there were six major administrative levels and numerous tiers within each level. This was "an arrangement," one scholar noted, "ideally contrived to multiply correspondence and to paralyze effective action."[18] This structure had one strength but also a fatal weakness. It would wear out most people who chose to protest within the system. But an organization, like a house, can be too insulated. Excessive levels of administration worked against the timely transmission of information about threats to bureaucratic rule from the ground level to top decision-makers.

This formalism of administration also pervaded a division of imperial labor that Leopold imposed on the Congo. Under his supervision the division of labor became a brutal partition of exploitation. He divided the country into economic spheres; each was under the primary control of himself, or the state, or business private or public. The line between the first two is artificial: Leopold II was the Congo Independent State. But he distinguished a sphere that he controlled personally (the *domaine de la Couronne*) from another that he managed as the head of the Congo Free State (the *domaine privé*). The *domaine privé* occupied about half of the Congo; almost all the country above the equator was closed to private traders. The *domaine de la Couronne* was a large territory around Lake Leopold II that became "the personal property of the King..."[19] The state exploited its lands either directly or through concessionary companies. These were so named because they received a permission or concession from the state to set up their own economic spheres of influence in the Congo and to perform certain undertakings within those designated areas.

One major illustration of this division of labor – direct or indirect state exploitation – came in Katanga, the southern part of the Congo that is rich in mineral resources. In the early 1890s the colonial government supposedly closed Katanga to private traders: it said it could not guarantee their safety. But the real story was different. In 1891 the government made an agreement with the *Compagnie du Katanga*, which gave each party its own economic sphere of influence within Katanga.[20] The company received about a third of the land the government claimed in the region, with a ninety-nine year concession to extract mineral wealth there. It also obtained a twenty-year preference to exploit any minerals it discovered on land in the government's economic sphere of influence in Katanga. Leopold created the *Compagnie du Katanga* and the colonial government was a major shareholder, along with the *Compagnie du Congo pour le Commerce et l'Industrie* and certain English interests.[21]

After Leopold's death in 1909, the Belgian government itself assumed control of the Congo and continued his pattern of close partnerships with business. Unilever, the Anglo–Dutch multinational, received five huge concessions from the colonial government after 1910. *Union Minière*, a major mining company, started to produce copper on a commercial scale in the Katanga region after 1911. Other companies worked gold, tin, and diamonds in other areas. While many smaller companies operated in the Congo, one major theme stands out: during its colonial period the economy of the Congo "was dominated by a few large companies."[22]

The Leopoldian period, from the mid-1880s until 1909, was an epoch of mental horror and physical abuse for thousands of Africans living in the Congo. Roger Casement, a British diplomat, toured the interior and published a report in February, 1904, which reinforced the conclusions of others: "in many districts the Africans were living under a system of forced labor, exacted from them by methods that sometimes involved murder and mutilation."[23] Edmund Morel, who headed the Congo Reform Association, was also instrumental in publicizing the atrocities in the country, especially those associated with the collection of rubber.[24] The mental and physical violence was widespread. Robert Harms casts a scholarly spotlight on this rampaging inhumanity in his study of the actions of one company – Abir – in the Maringa-Lopori Basin in the northern Congo from 1885 to 1903.[25]

The international economic integration Leopold established and Belgium entrenched in the Congo was extractive and favored the few. The Congo became a classic version of an "export economy." The formalized verticality of administration was matched by a systematic and ruthless verticality of extraction by, of, and for outsiders. This process collectivized the richest regions of the country in subordinate and often painful service to non-Africans – the colonial government and international businesses. Those non-Africans were the formally favored; they integrated what products and minerals they wanted with their own interests. Most Africans were the formally oppressed. As with a crude bottom-to-top version of mercantilism, the subjugated were forced to work for the favored and prevented by law and military force (the *Force Publique*) from advancing each other's economic interests. There was thus little horizontal economic integration between or among the regions in the Congo and no national economy linked those areas together.

The international economic integration Leopold II and Belgium fastened on the Congo promoted economic disintegration. Throughout the colonial period (1880s–1961) indigenous economies suffered. Leopold's forced labor was a frontal assault on local agricultural cycles and nutrition; people had little or no time to farm for themselves. And even when Belgium tried to eliminate Leopold's grossest abuses after his death, it still taxed the population in coin. This could only be legally obtained by selling something – either one's labor or one's produce – in a commercial situation that benefitted bureaucracy and expatriate business more than local Africans. Local economic disintegration and the absence of a national economy were two of the main factors that led to the break-up of the Belgian Congo during the civil war (1961–65) that tragically followed the achievement of formal independence in 1961.

The German Empire

While Portugal entered the business of transoceanic empires early and left late, Germany began late and finished early. Germany's late start came from the timing of its emergence as a unified nation-state in the 1860s and early 1870s. The man who forged German unification by a mixture of diplomacy, guile, and physical force was Otto von Bismarck of Prussia; his homeland was the base of a unified Germany. Bismarck's vision of Germany as a major European power with global aspirations influenced his decision to enter to the so-called European "scramble for Africa" in the 1880s. Germany's colonial empire, whose major possessions were in Africa but also included some Pacific territories, disintegrated as a result of Germany's defeat in World War I. From 1884 to 1919: Germany's colonial run lasted only three and a half decades.

Germany shares with Spain, Portugal, Leopold II, and Belgium a great dedication to the principle of bureaucratic centralization in managing colonial empires. But like the others, it implemented this approach in its own distinctive manner. Germany's African empire encompassed German East Africa, German South-West Africa, and two possessions in west Africa: Cameroon and Togo. The administration of this empire was highly centralized, though within each colony there were not as many levels of administration as existed in the Congo. And the empire exhibited a military ethos that was stronger in some territories than others. German East Africa, for instance, remained throughout its existence from the late 1890s until 1919 a military state. This territory was organized into military districts, administered by soldiers, not civilians.

Germany ruled ruthlessly. In German East Africa the Maji-Maji Rebellion (1905–07) was brutally suppressed, as were the Herero and Khoikhoi insurgencies (1904–07) in German South-West Africa. The German military openly pursued an "extermination strategy" in South-West Africa against the ethnic groups from which the rebels came. This genocide provided an early African preview of the Holocaust, during which Nazi Germany killed millions of Jews and untold numbers of other "misfits," like gypsies, gays, and lesbians.

While Germany increased the violence of its colonial administration, it did not originate any new approaches to international economic integration in the service of colonialism. But the crispness and literalness associated with a militarized chain of command rendered this version of mercantilism especially crude. There is a saying in Tanzania, an east African country that experienced both German and British colonial rule, which speaks volumes: "the Germans beat us, but at least the British used their courts."[26] The verticality of German extraction created an international economic integration that linked selected areas and commodities to foreign interests. And so were created "export economies" that featured roles for different kinds of businesses at different times during the empire's short run.

Chartered companies were active in the initial phases of German exploration and settlement. Concession and plantation companies, as well as banks, were involved throughout German colonial rule. Indeed, one such chartered company, the German East Africa Company (*Deutsch Öst-Afrika Gesellschaft*), created the conditions that compelled the German government itself to get involved in what was to become German East Africa. In the late 1880s and early 1890s the activities of this company, especially along the Indian Ocean or Swahili coast, incited a fierce resistance that the company could not quell by itself. The German government decided it had to intervene and dispatched troops to the area, the first step in deepening its own involvement in the territory.

In Germany's West African territories foreign businesses played strikingly different roles. In Cameroon expatriate companies were able to dominate economic activity, but in Togo the opposite outcome prevailed. The reasons are as much environmental as they are policy-oriented. In Togo the amount of arable land is small, since much of the country is an arid steppe. Concession and plantation companies there possessed only about 28,500 hectares of land, whereas in Cameroon the *Gesellschaft Süd-Kamerun* by itself controlled 50,000 square kilometers of land.[27]

Germany's fashioning of "export economies" – graphic illustrations of international economic integration of, by, and for the few – brought significant economic disintegration for the many. In Togo, two German banks, the *Deutsch-Westafrikanische Handelsgesellschaft* (DWHG) and the Dresdner Bank, formed another bank, the *Deutsch West-Afrikanische Bank* (DWB). The DWB, with an initial capitalization of one million German marks, provided banking services to foreign interests but not to indigenous African business people. The DWB financed "only European enterprises which promised substantial profits" and turned away African capitalists in Togo.[28] When these turned to other banks and the German government for help, they were similarly rebuffed. Deprived of sources of legal credit, many African businesses in Togo were stunted in their infancy. Stifling access to basic credit destroyed economic opportunity for African entrepreneurs and constituted economic disintegration of the most harmful sort. The group that wanted to integrate themselves into national and international economic relations was thwarted and a unifying source of a true national economy was denied.

Imperial case studies: Great Britain and France

The British Empire

The British Empire is the most global colonial empire in recorded history. It had significant possessions in Africa, Asia and its subcontinent, North and South America, and in the Atlantic and Caribbean. For centuries the sun truly never set on the British Empire.

The Empire still exists in three forms. The first consists of remnants of the administrative empire. On 1 July 1997, the British government handed over Hong Kong to the People's Republic of China. But in 2002 there were still thirteen "British Dependent Territories," as the colonies were officially renamed in the early 1980s. These include islands and archipelagoes in the Atlantic and Caribbean. Many inhabitants resent the colonial implications of the term "dependent territory."[29] The second form is the consultative assemblage of Great Britain and its former colonies and dominions called the British Commonwealth. And the third is the cultural empire of the English language and Anglo-Saxon customs and mores.

During its time the administrative empire worldwide came to be associated with five governing principles. The first is decentralization. Of all the colonial empires created by European countries, the British Empire exhibited the greatest degree of decentralization in its procedures. All organizations contain elements of centralization and decentralization – today this blend is called interdependence – and the most long-lived usually try to balance the two. The British Empire had a well-defined chain of command that reached from Whitehall in London down to the most local level in every colony.

But significant local decision-making autonomy existed at most times in most places. This was never independence from ultimate review from above. Rather, it meant daily opportunities to interpret central directives with flexibility and to implement them, as many colonial officers on the spot might say, with appropriate initiative and prudence.

The second governing principle is devolution, akin to decentralization but different from it. Whereas decentralization delegates power, devolution transfers it. Decentralization grants certain powers to levels of an empire conditionally. Devolution assigns those powers without condition and sometimes with finality: there is no reversing course. The history of British imperial decentralization contains more successes than failures. The record of British imperial devolution is marked by some spectacular failures. In Africa, the Federation of the Rhodesias and Nyasaland, which was an ill-considered attempt to transfer power to a white minority, collapsed in the early 1960s. In the Caribbean, the Federation of the British West Indies also ran aground in the 1960s. This was a more positive endeavor to organize many island nations, a number of which would otherwise face overwhelming economic challenges on their own.

Over its more than four centuries the British colonial empire also gained coherence from a third core principle. This is the conviction that every part of the empire should, to the best of its resources, "pull its own weight" in the imperial boat. The crew metaphor appears often in official colonial documents and reminds us that some colonial officers actually crewed when they were students at Oxford and Cambridge and many others would have loved to do so. The charming athleticism of the metaphor, however, meant something not so beguiling for the colonized: taxes, on more items, and often at rising levels. A colony "pulled its own weight" to the extent that it generated more revenue for both the local colonial bureaucracy and London itself.

This principle had some singularly drastic consequences, such as contributing mightily to the origins of the United States Revolution

(1775–81). Burdened by the costs of prosecuting the French and Indian War (also known in Europe as the Seven Years War from 1756–63), British officials in London decided to raise the tax burden on residents in their North American colonies. This decision, coupled with a serious attempt to enforce the Navigation acts that regulated colonial commerce, gave a biting financial immediacy to political and philosophical arguments for independence. More often "pulling one's weight" meant, as for Britain's African colonies, types and levels of personal and trade taxation that occasionally triggered riots but entrenched over the longer-term harmful consequences for economic activity.

The British colonial empire also developed a measured concept of administrative time best embodied in the phrase "in due course." This approach undergirded a fourth governing principal: change should be both gradual and incremental. The result was an emphasis on "small steps," taken one at a time and slowly, sometimes very slowly. "In due course" worked well as an administrative principle when there were no threatening discontents among a colonial population. But in the latter decades of British colonialism in Africa, for instance, "in due course" symbolized the unresponsiveness of a colonial system more and more under siege by African political parties seeking the immediate independence of their own countries.

The fifth and final principle that drove the British Empire was the one that contributed to the longevity of this organization most of all. The colonial service and indeed many other British nationals in and out of government deeply believed for a long time in the paramount importance of British administration for the rest of the world. A corollary of this principle was an abiding faith in the value of the constitutional arrangements Great Britain would create and eventually bequeath to its colonies and other dependencies. The fifth principle received vivid illustration in the movie *Gandhi.* During a pre-independence meeting with Mohandas K. Gandhi and other Indian leaders, a colonial official reportedly said, "With all due respect, Mr. Gandhi, where would India be without British administration?"

These five principles molded a unique imperial ethos and even culture. The British Empire shared with all other imperial organizations a vertical chain of command but its version was different. Not only was the chain of command decentralized, but it was also marked by a studied approach to decision-making and a pragmatic approach to action. Delegation (decentralization), responsibility ("pulling one's weight"), reflection ("in due course"), and pragmatism ("small steps") are the four hallmarks that in combination produced that imperial ethos and nurtured British imperial culture.

This colonial ethos and culture had profound and far-reaching influences on international economic integration in several senses: first of the empire itself and then of private business activities within its borders. The

British Empire was able to decentralize, in part because great emphasis was placed on standardizing administrative forms. These include all reports and memoranda through which administrators communicated with one another. This standardization was a companion phenomenon to a common administrative language and together both created necessary conditions for effective decentralization.

"Single currencies"

The standardization of administrative forms, an ongoing process, had crucial economic analogues. British colonial administrators sought a standardization of form in many areas of business and economic activity. One area was the money supply. They wanted, in today's language, a "single currency" (*unique monnaie*) for each colony. This would promote economic as well as administrative unity and so strengthen the power of the local colonial bureaucracy. In some cases, the "single currency" was both regional and territorial, as in British East Africa. The official money of east African shillings and cents circulated in all British territories in the region: Tanganyika, Zanzibar, Uganda, and Kenya. Only the "single currency" was legal tender. All other moneys were illegal, in government's eyes, and were suppressed right away or tolerated only for a prescribed period.

The drive to impose "single currencies" in the British colonies was central to an imperial economic integration that was itself decentralized in distinctive ways. The pound sterling, the "single currency" of the United Kingdom, has been a major global currency. It played, however, various roles in different parts of British Africa at different times. The usual imperial approach was to make the pound sterling the "normal colonial denomination."[30] This endeavor encountered strong local moneys already in place. These featured the Indian rupee and the Maria Theresa taler in east Africa, as well as indigenous African moneys on all parts of the continent. So the pound sterling may have been "the normal colonial denomination" in theory, but in practice it was one of a number of available local denominations.

For some, this policy ensured that most British possessions "had identical currencies with that of Britain."[31] But this was not a straightforward sameness. The Colonial Sterling Exchange Standard, as it evolved, illustrates this statement. It gave rise to regional currency boards that regulated the official money supply in west Africa from 1912, east Africa from 1919, and the Rhodesias and Nyasaland from 1940. Each region received its own special supply of coins minted in London. They all had British denominations and were supposedly convertible into sterling at face value, but were legal tender only in the colonies, not Britain itself. Identical denominations sometimes, but identical circulations never: this was monetary decentralization. The denominations had some standardization, but the appearance of the currency was regionally distinctive and the circulation legally localized.

The distinction between the extrinsic and intrinsic values of money helps demonstrate the refinement of colonial monetary decentralization. Intrinsic value refers to the metallic content of coinage. A coin with real silver in it can be melted down to yield its intrinsic value. Extrinsic value is whatever an organization, usually a government, says paper currency or coin is worth. The extrinsic value of a coin, for example, can be widely at variance with its intrinsic value. This divergence is known as debasement: the wider the difference, the grosser the debasement. The special silver coins minted for east and west Africa had intrinsic value until 1920. Thereafter silver alloy, sometimes called token coinage, replaced silver coinage in Great Britain and, at lagged intervals, in the colonies themselves.

Another variant of monetary decentralization occurred in different backings for token coinage in the colonies, on the one hand, and in Great Britain itself, on the other. Backing aimed to base the extrinsic value of that token silver coinage on more than the government's word. For its African currency regions, the British government insisted that every silver alloy coin issued be covered by a combination of British securities (90 percent) and bullion (10 percent). This procedure, regarded as the hallmark of the Colonial Exchange Standard until decolonization, was supposed to ensure a "sound currency" as it was then defined. But subsequent events left those African currency regions chained to unnecessarily rigid modes of currency backing. The British money supply at home no longer had a precious metallic cover by 1940 and was essentially a "fiduciary issue, partially covered by British government securities."[32]

Monetary decentralization highlighted the absence of something that independent states had and colonies did not: central banks with an ability to use monetary policy to promote economic growth and development. The Colonial Exchange Standard, as with so many things during the colonial era that began as well-meaning shields, turned into a yoke that bonded much of British Africa to a subservient and outmoded monetary past.

For all Africans, the drive to impose a "single currency" had more immediate meaning than the technical evolution of the Colonial Exchange Standard. The bureaucratic quest for a "single currency" became a daily reality for one compelling reason. Colonial bureaucracies usually required taxes be paid in their "single currency," not in kind or in another, unofficial money. The tax mix varied from one territory to another. But all colonial bureaucracies, finding the difficulties of collecting a personal income tax on Africans too daunting, levied taxes on African homes and on a wide spectrum of business activities.[33] One had to buy a government license to trade. Taxation also impinged on other economic activities: from processing, through transporting, and involved import and export fees. Tax demands thus figured prominently in African strategies with respect to the imposition of a "single currency." But there were other considerations as well. For an African business person, the preferred currencies of his or her customers and suppliers were major factors in determining how much of both official and unofficial moneys were needed.

African strategies with regard to a "single currency" receive illumination within a framework constructed from neo-classical economic theory and economic anthropology. Neo-classical economic theory clarified the demand for money under three rubrics: transactions, precautionary, and speculative. Economic anthropology, especially a type of cognitive anthropology known as ethnoeconomy, broadens the definition of the money supply to include both official and unofficial moneys. Ethnoeconomy can reveal how all peoples living in a given region perceived money. From economic anthropology we also learn that many societies associate four characteristics with money: portability, divisibility, durability, and homogeneity. A complete money supply thus recognizes both government and indigenous moneys. The universal economic logic that underpins the three-fold demand for money receives overwhelming corroboration in practice.[34]

Africans also showed an acute appreciation of the different attributes of all components of a territory's money supply. Their three demands for money took into account those four aforementioned attributes – portability, divisibility, durability, and homogeneity – as well as the difference between intrinsic and extrinsic value. For one thing, paper money was in extraordinary disfavor. It had no intrinsic value and, while portable, lacked durability: it was vulnerable to destruction by insects, fire, and flood. The backing associated with the Colonial Exchange Standard apparently applied to silver alloy coins, not paper. So if Africans needed yet another reason to eschew paper, the coin coverage of the Colonial Exchange Standard would have furnished it.

As to coinage, African approaches depended on the kind of coin, its denominational availability, how much intrinsic value it possessed, and in what particular metal that intrinsic value reposed. Elsewhere I have given detailed consideration to these approaches, coin by coin, in British East and West Africa.[35] It is worth underscoring, in light of the attention given above to the Colonial Exchange Standard, how Africans reacted to the withdrawal of silver coins and their replacement with silver alloy or token coinage. They treated silver alloy as the inferior coinage it was. Before silver could be repatriated to London, it had to be collected, and significant amounts of silver continued to disappear from circulation, thwarting repatriation. Gresham's law was confirmed in an African context: the inferior coinage drove the superior out of circulation.

But other important forces were at work. Repatriation emphasized the intrinsic value of silver and rendered those coins even more sensitive to the precautionary and speculative demands for money. The inferior status of silver alloy was confirmed by cross-media exchange rates that moved against the token coinage. More, and sometimes much more, silver alloy coinage was needed to receive the same amount of such non-government moneys as cowries or manillas, for example.[36]

African strategies with respect to the imposition of "single currencies" were based on a universal economic logic that colonialism so often ignored or sought to override. A bureaucratic logic drove the implementation of "single currencies," but wider economic results were not benign. A "single currency" that featured only the bureaucracy's money promoted a narrow version of monetary unification. It denied to a territory's residents the benefits that would have come from a richer menu of legal currency selections. More choices mean more opportunities for exchange and, if only a fraction of this potential had been realized, economic growth would have increased.

A "single currency" that accorded legal recognition to official coins and paper as well as to unofficial media that had territorial significance would also have contributed to the economic development of that territory. Whereas growth for an economist denotes annual increases in per person income, development embraces structural change in a positive sense. A cross-media "single currency" does not present an insurmountable design problem, but it does necessitate the abandonment of monetary bigotry. This required an intellectual cosmopolitanism beyond the reach of many, though not all, colonial administrators.

There are other topics besides money that show British imperial economic integration at work.

"Free trade: 'the Opobo matter'"

The British government, as it developed its presence on the African continent in the latter decades of the nineteenth century, claimed to be fighting for "free trade" on the local level. It tried to block efforts by African business people to create concentrations of economic power. At first glance, the British government was promoting "free trade." But the underlying questions are: "free trade" for whom, in what ways, and with what consequences?

A striking case study of this policy with troubling answers to those questions unfolded in southeastern Nigeria in the 1870s and 1880s. As we shall see, eliminating a powerful African middleman by questionable methods removed a home-grown obstacle to "free trade." But this let British merchants manipulate commercial opportunities for their own advantage without any countervailing indigenous checks. British business people had considerable organizational strength and the backing of British diplomats. And the Royal Navy, with a presence off the Atlantic Coast of Nigeria, was the ultimate guarantor of British "freedom to trade."

Our story takes place in the lands occupied by the Ibo people, and involves two of the more forceful personalities from the entire era of

European over-rule on the African continent. Ja Ja of Opobo was an Ibo entrepreneur of wide-ranging vision with an acute interest in the palm products trade. Sir Harry H. Johnston, who finished as one of the most experienced and influential men in the British Colonial Service, was still relatively early in his administrative and literary careers.

Harry Johnston has left an account of the "Opobo matter" in his autobiography that portrays the essential facts of the case in the following manner. Ja Ja had risen from slavery to become an important Ibo leader, with headquarters on the bank of the Opobo river in eastern Nigeria. Another British diplomat, Charles Livingstone, David's brother, "made a treaty" with Ja Ja in 1873 that allegedly recognized him as an "independent chieftain."[37] The palm forests of the Nigerian interior had become more valuable, as demand for their products, oil and kernels, increased. Palm oil, for instance, was used to make soap; baths were becoming more popular in Europe and elsewhere.

Ja Ja, with a deep appreciation of the techniques and goals of concentrated economic power, tried to make himself both a monopsonist and a monopolist in the palm trade in his region. That is, he strove to be the only buyer (monopsonist) of palm products from the interior and the only seller (monopolist) of those commodities to foreign merchants who had set up operations in the coastal areas of eastern Nigeria. In fact, he came in time to designate one European firm, A. Miller Brothers of Glasgow, as the sole firm to which he would deliver palm oil and kernels. So emerged a classic example of a middleman with increasing economic clout. Ja Ja's power greatly irritated the British, who saw it through the lenses of their definition of "free trade." For Harry Johnston "Ja Ja represented the whole crisis of our Protectorate over southern Nigeria: our attempt to establish freedom of trade."[38]

As Johnston described it, Ja Ja "assented" to travel to Accra to have his dispute with the British government tried by a person appointed by the British government. Sir Walter Hunt-Grubbe, the Royal Navy's Commander-in-Chief on the Cape of Good Hope and west Africa station, "gave Jaja a very fair trial, spent, indeed, several days beforehand mastering all the written and printed evidence." He found "the old man" guilty of breaching three counts of that 1873 treaty; he dismissed the fourth count. Ja Ja was, therefore, "deposed" and "banished" for five years. Pardoned by Lord Salisbury after four years residence on St Vincent, in the Caribbean's Windward islands, Ja Ja decided to return home to Opobo, "but fell ill on the voyage and died at one of the Canary Islands."[39]

This account, by a central player on the winning side, understandably puts the actions of his government in the best possible light. But there remain major unanswered questions about the "Opobo matter." The self-styled "trial" is addressed in an incomplete and biased manner. Accepting as legal only "evidence" that was "written and printed," as seems the case, puts defendants who come from societies that prize oral tradition at a huge disadvantage. Whether Ja Ja was permitted a legal defense is not stated; Johnston's description makes the legal proceedings seem more like a one-way tribunal than a trial with adversarial interplay. This was, after all, a colonial environment laced with racism and cultural imperialism. Johnston's *en passant* remarks set this tone. Accra, where Ja Ja's "trial" was held, was the "first civilized town he had seen."[40] And while Johnston concluded that Ja Ja was "not harshly treated" because his wealth was "secured to him" and he allegedly received an allowance during his years in exile, the circumstances surrounding Ja Ja's death remain a mystery.[41]

Ja Ja was a threat to the British in more than one way. He was using his wealth to build political power and might have unified the Ibo peoples, if his career had not been shortened by colonial intervention. The British preferred to rule people who were as divided as possible, and the prospective unification of one of the major ethnic groups in Nigeria disquieted them. In any event, Harry Johnston stressed the economic dimensions of the "Opobo matter." The removal of Ja Ja was instrumental, he suggested, in "an enormous increase in Opobo trade, on the part of the natives as well as of the Europeans." And "the settlement of this test case … ended the tyranny of the 'middle-man' which had been the great obstacle to a wide development of trade in the vast Niger Delta for a hundred years."[42]

This case study is one of many that led scholars to coin the phrase "imperialism of free trade." It means that by imposing "free trade" on local citizens the way was cleared for superior British economic and military power to assert itself and push the penetration of Africa further inland. In many coastal environments the British had the economic and military numbers – of merchants and Royal Navy ships.

So fighting for "free trade" became part of the dynamic of economic imperialism. This dynamic can lead to establishment of formal administrative imperialism. The resolution of the "Opobo matter" contributed to this dynamic. The activities of the Royal Niger Company, a British chartered company, to the west and northwest of the Niger River delta also embodied economic imperialism (see Chapter 2). Nigeria was a case of economic imperialism begetting administrative imperialism. The Royal Niger Company, a "shadow government" with its own military force, created a situation, by its inability to "pacify" the people completely, that pushed the British government to formalize its colonial administration of what became Nigeria in 1914.

"Free trade: imperial preferences"

"Imperialism of free trade" has other meanings, besides its reference to a British strategy for penetrating the African interior in the nineteenth century. Another major example pertains to the British presence throughout the world and emerges in the twentieth century. It is important to remember that Great Britain was developing two global organizations from the nineteenth century on. The long-lived British Empire was joined by the British Commonwealth. Many members of the Commonwealth would in time be former British colonies that achieved their "flag independence" but chose to remain in close association with Great Britain.

Another instance of the "imperialism of free trade" can be found in a certain set of preferential trade agreements concerning both Empire and Commonwealth. These were negotiated at the Imperial Economic Conference in Ottawa, Canada, in 1932.[43] The agreements originated in how the British government initially reacted to the Great Depression. Along with other countries, including the United States, Great Britain responded to the global contraction of the early 1930s by protecting its home market. It imposed a 10 percent tariff on most imported goods. The Ottawa agreements then exempted other Commonwealth countries from this duty.

This was "free trade" with protectionist and imperialist thrusts. The barrier removed for insiders was one recently thrown up to hamper outsiders, and membership in the "insiders" hinged on imperial identity. So these trade preferences can be seen as another version of the "imperialism of free trade" for Great Britain.

These two versions of the "imperialism of free trade" were both techniques of imperial economic integration but they had different long-term consequences. In the short term, their effects were alike: the British gained. The removal of Ja Ja of Opobo facilitated penetration of the west African interior and supposedly boosted trade. The Ottawa agreements stimulated economic activity in Great Britain and its preferential trade partners. In the longer term, over the ensuing decades, the resolution of the "Opobo matter" contributed to the eventual establishment of official British rule over major portions of west Africa. From an imperial perspective, then, the defeat of coastal African intermediaries benefitted the empire in the short and long term.

The longer-term consequences of those preferential trade agreements are another matter. To outsiders, they signaled that empire and commonwealth were becoming more an economic fortress than major players in maintaining global stability. And by protecting domestic industries from the bracing winds of international competition they made the British economy too reliant on its old engines of growth – textiles, iron, and steel. Over the longer term the British economy would have been better off by shifting earlier to such newer sources of growth as electronics and automobiles.[44]

The distinctiveness of British imperial economic integration, illustrated here with reference to "single currencies" and two versions of "the imperialism of free trade," clearly derives from the ethos and culture of the British Empire. It developed an appropriate amount of decentralization in a measured, systematic manner. But decentralization also nurtured the official system numerous African political parties chose to stay within as they worked for the independence of their countries. Once "flag independent," most former British territories remained associated with Great Britain in the British Commonwealth, itself a decentralized organization.

The French Empire

With a longevity that rivals the British Empire and possessions in many parts of the world, the French colonial empire presents a contrasting case study of a global organization that favored centralization much more than decentralization. Every colonial empire reflects characteristics of the founding imperial state, and this is especially true in the French case. France itself has had a national government dedicated to the serious centralization of power at least since the 1600s, when absolute monarchy received its fullest expression during the times of Cardinal Richelieu and Louis XIV. In the early 1800s Napoleon Bonaparte reformed but further entrenched centralized political power in the life of the French national state. This is a comprehensive and long-lasting involvement in society and economy known as *étatisme.*

The French colonial empire came to be associated with four governing principles. The first is centralization. The inward centralizing thrust of the French state developed a companion outward push in relation to empire. But centralization, like decentralization, is neither a homogenous concept nor process: there are types and nuances of both concepts in theory and practice. As the British approach to decentralization merited refined consideration, so the French treatment of centralization deserves studied attention.

Centralization in the French colonial empire gave rise to a major kinship concept known as assimilation, the second governing principle. Assimilation had three varieties: administrative, political, and economic. Administrative assimilation meant that France viewed its overseas possessions as outward extensions of itself. The overseas territories became *France Outre-Mer* or France Overseas. Political assimilation operated on two levels. The first concerned the residents of *France Outre-Mer*. Some, with proper education and great difficulty, might qualify to become French citizens or *citoyens*. In practice, very few of vast numbers of subjects or *sujets* became *citoyens*. But the door was ajar, however slightly, for some of the colonized to become full-fledged French citizens.

The second level of political assimilation was based on the first. French citizens in France Overseas deserved political representation in the metropolis; that is, in France itself, in what is now the National Assembly in Paris, known as the Chamber of Deputies before 1946. In practice, this was not the equivalent of a "one-person, one-vote" system, and the representation of *France Outre-Mer* in Paris was always modest in relation to those elected from France itself. But the British approach accorded neither citizenship nor representation in the British Parliament to British colonial subjects.

Economic assimilation was facilitated by administrative assimilation but was rooted in long-standing notions of mercantilism. *France Outre-Mer* performed the two classic functions assigned to colonies by mercantilism: as sources of unprocessed materials for the home country and as markets for imports from France itself. Assimilation, especially its administrative and economic dimensions, had profound consequences for the economic integration of the French colonial empire. Administrative assimilation gave the French empire a centralization of great consistency. This coherence imparted a special closeness to economic relations between France itself and *France Outre-Mer*.

While dominant, administrative assimilation was not all embracing. A contrasting approach to French colonial administration, known as association, influenced ground-level organization for long periods during recent centuries. Association became the third governing principle.

Some have likened association to British indirect rule. This was an administrative philosophy in great vogue in parts of the British Empire, especially Africa and India, in the early decades of the twentieth century. Colonial administrators claimed to rule their subjects indirectly, through indigenous leaders. It was a striking manifestation of the decentralization that marked the British Empire. Association apparently was an endeavor by French colonial administrators to govern by using indigenous rulers as intermediaries. In that sense indirect rule and association are analogous.

But there were far-reaching differences between them that reflect British and French interpretations of their colonial mission. The British, as they tried to organize indigenous societies, strove for the same standardization of bureaucratic forms that characterized their empire on all levels. Hence, under indirect rule there appeared numerous native administrations or authorities that were supposedly based on pre-existing local structures, such as ethnic groups or "tribes." The British saw their mission mainly in political and constitutional terms, of bequeathing organizations and documents local peoples could use to express their own cultures.

The French, even when they used association, sought much greater cultural penetration of indigenous societies. While many British believed that British administration was good for the rest of the world, many French were convinced that French culture was good for the rest of the world. So the French colonial mission had an enveloping cultural dimension that British colonial administration lacked, even though British strengths in administration, politics, and constitutional matters are highlights of British national culture.

The French view their culture as a national patrimony worth sharing with the world. In the colonial era the sharing was often forced, which made France the leading cultural imperialist of all the European colonial powers. But imposition, the initial mode of presentation, cannot fully explain the extent of French cultural penetration of *France Outre-Mer*. There was willingness, especially among indigenous peoples who thought of themselves as the local elites, to accept, even embrace, French culture. This process led to a wrenching soul-searching among some as to how one could accept French culture without destroying one's original culture.

To the governing principles of centralization, assimilation, and association one must surely add cultural penetration. This was not just the diffusion of the French language in France's overseas possessions. This was also the propagation of a culture deemed worthy of study and appreciation by everyone, whatever their original background. The effectiveness of both diffusion and propagation created a deep and lasting cultural penetration.

Aspects of assimilation survived the formal decolonization of much of the French colonial empire in the 1960s and beyond. French territories, upon obtaining their formal independence, were no longer assimilated in an administrative or political sense. But economic assimilation remained for many and cultural bonding persisted for all.

France retains a significant number of possessions, which are placed in different categories. The overseas departments are French Guiana on the northwestern tip of South America, Guadeloupe and Martinique in the Caribbean Sea, and Reunion in the Indian Ocean. The overseas territories are French Polynesia in the South Pacific, Wallis-and-Futuna in the South Pacific, and the French Southern and Antarctic Territories. The "territorial collectivities" are Saint-Pierre-and-Miquelon, in the North Atlantic south of Newfoundland, and Mayotte, in the Mozambique Channel off South Africa. New Caledonia, in the South Pacific east of Australia, now has a special status in France, which gives it a degree of autonomy.

French culture also infused the structures of the empire and influenced the conduct of its administrators. One aspect of French culture deserves special mention as a fifth and final principle of imperial governance. Joining centralization, assimilation, association, and cultural penetration is Gallic logic. A distinctive perhaps unique feature of French culture, Gallic logic saturates the other four principles. Gallic logic partakes of the Aristotelian tradition, but aims to illuminate relations between the parts and the whole with an elegant exactitude.

The "whole" and "the parts" have numerous connotations. For example, a country is one "whole" that has different sets of "parts": geographical as in regions, provinces, or departments; human as in groups or classes of people; and corporate such as businesses, schools, and churches. A project or *grand travail* is another "whole" that has different types of "parts," such as the chronological phases of construction and the constituent elements of the finished work. Other examples abound, but the preceding analysis of centralization, assimilation, and association fits right in here: an "empire" is yet another "whole" that has administrative, political, and economic "parts." And "parts" can subdivide, as the administrative "part" of an empire reveals levels of bureaucracy. The organization of the French colonial empire is a classic illustration of Gallic logic, which informed imperial economic integration and influenced those doing business both within and across its borders.

"Single currencies"

As did the British, the French pursued a panorama of techniques of imperial economic integration. These included different kinds of taxes and regulations, with some taxes having a regulatory dimension as well. But as with the British, so also with the French the drive to diffuse and enforce official "single currencies" was central to imperial economic integration.

The French campaign for "single currencies" evolved through three major stages, involved variations of a "single currency," and embodied mixes of two governing principles – assimilation and association. Centralization characterized the overall evolution of "single currencies." But as assimilation sometimes coexisted with association in French colonial administration, so was monetary centralization counterpointed by a decentralization manifest in variations of the "single currency."

The "single currency" was the French or metropolitan franc. The French strove to impose their franc throughout their empire "as a common currency" that had "free convertibility."[45] The first major stage of monetary centralization for the French empire in the modern era, from the nineteenth century on, lasted until World War II. It divides into two periods. The first was diffusion and enforcement. By 1914 all French African colonies had only the metropolitan franc as legal tender. Tunisia and Morocco were French protectorates in Africa and as such kept their own currencies that were linked to the French franc. A second period lasted from 1914 until 1938. Its main theme was greater bonding: "colonial currency was identical" with the French franc and "automatically devalued" with it.[46]

The French franc was the legal standard-bearer of economic assimilation. But there was some freedom at the colonial level to determine how it would lead in the first major stage of modern monetary centralization. Local autonomy affected paper money, not coinage, which remained under metropolitan control. The main instrument of decentralization was the chartered bank. This was a financial institution set up and empowered by a document or charter from the French government. The chartered bank was given a monopoly of note-issue in a designated area that consisted of one or more French colonies.

The second major stage of modern monetary centralization for the French colonial empire began during World War II and lasted until 1958. This was the year Charles de Gaulle, as President of France, offered French colonies in west Africa the option of total independence or an independence that retained strong ties with France itself. This stage reveals both continuity and new directions. The continuum resided in uninterrupted control from the center in key respects. From 1939 until

1958 France itself directly managed two areas pivotal to centralization: all foreign currency exchange and all hard currency reserves within the empire.

The new directions resulted from a traumatic rupturing. World War II destroyed the unity of the French franc. The singularity with which the franc had expressed itself in both France and its empire unraveled under the duress of war and its impact: but it is crucial to remember that the French franc did not disappear. To the contrary, it persisted, although its presence within the empire would become pluralistic. An important manifestation of this pluralism was the creation of the CFA franc in 1945 for all French African territories. CFA first meant *Colonies françaises d'Afrique* (French African colonies), but later stood for *Communauté financière africaine* (African financial community).[47]

The CFA franc departed from the economic assimilation associated with the years from 1914 until World War II. But the CFA franc still represented a high degree of economic integration between colonies and metropolis. In its early years the exchange rate between the CFA franc and the metropolitan franc was much more favorable than it became. In 1945 the CFA franc bought 1.70 French francs; in 1948, it purchased two French francs.[48] But in 1949 the CFA franc underwent a dramatic depreciation in relation to the metropolitan franc: the exchange rate was fifty CFA francs for one French franc.[49] The ratio of 50 to 1 lasted until 1994. After 1958 this exchange rate governed all of France's former sub-Saharan African colonies, except one. Guinea, under the leadership of Sékou Touré, was the only sub-Sarahan French territory to take General de Gaulle's option of complete independence from France. All the other French territories in sub-Saharan Africa opted for an independence that kept close relations with France. The formal decolonization of much of France's African empire, which took place in the early 1960s, marked the emergence of a franc zone that existed apart from the trappings of formal colonial administration.

From a monetary standpoint, complete independence allowed Guinea to sever its links with the franc, and then set up its own currency and central bank. Guinea's currency, on its own, was subject to volatility, which could become intense. The countries that remained in the franc zone, tied to the French franc through its CFA version, were, some maintain, guaranteed more stability in monetary matters.[50] The backing of the French franc, one of the world's major currencies, supposedly imparted a protection that an independent monetary policy and the vagaries of international markets could never provide. But the stability of the CFA franc depended upon the stability of the French franc itself. This currency had its own ups and downs, including devaluations, some of which occurred in 1960, 1969, and 1974.

Stability entailed significant costs. Devaluations of the French franc affected the balance of payments, which includes foreign trade, of the countries that still embraced the CFA franc. While one French franc still bought fifty CFA francs, those francs were worth less in currencies other than the French franc. For the CFA countries, a devaluation of the French franc increased their external debts denominated in currencies other than the French franc. So stability may have been comforting, but it was illusory. Had devaluations of the French franc been accompanied by downward revisions of the exchange ratio between metropolitan and CFA francs, the stability argument would have some merit. To purchase a devalued French franc, in a world that preserved the real stability of the CFA franc, one should have paid fewer CFA francs. The fixed exchange rate, then, underpinned a version of monetary union that clearly benefitted the home country but produced increasingly more troubled results for the former colonies.

It was not the link between the French franc and the CFA franc that was in itself harmful. Mismanagement was the problem: the CFA franc had not been revalued on its own for decades. The fixed exchange rate at 50 to 1, in place since 1949, was one of the factors that contributed to a serious recession in francophone west Africa in the late 1980s. In particular, the Ivory Coast (*Cote d'Ivoire*), which had been a success story through much of the 1980s, lurched into major economic downturn later in that decade. Recovery was slow, but it began in 1989.

One long overdue change helped accelerate this process. In 1994 the CFA franc was finally devalued. The new exchange rate was: 100 CFA francs to one French franc. Devaluation boosted the exports of countries in the franc zone, but it also inflicted considerable local distress. Imported goods cost much more, and zooming prices for these commodities hurt many consumers in those countries, which led to social unrest.

The CFA franc zone still exists, though the French franc has disappeared. The new European currency, the euro, introduced on January 1, 1999, eliminated the French franc. Since the advent of the euro, one CFA franc has been worth 0.00152449 euro. One euro buys 655.957 CFA francs.

French imposition of "single currencies" had enormous implications on the local level. With respect to the personal actions of Africans, there are strong parallels between what happened in French and British colonial Africa. Our approach to the study of moneys in colonial Africa, summarized above in connection with British "single currencies," also applies to the French colonial experience.

Paper money was usually regarded as worthless for meeting personal transactions, precautionary, and speculative demands for money. There were exceptions to this statement for African business people dealing with foreigners who accepted paper money in business transactions. The individual African might, therefore, accept paper money for business purposes but not for his or her own money portfolio, as it were.

The issuance of paper money by those chartered banks mentioned above created opportunities for anyone, African or expatriate, enterprising enough to explore the possibilities of currency arbitrage. The Bank of Algeria, created in 1851 as a chartered bank, was reorganized and became the Bank of West Africa in 1901. It furnished paper money for all the French colonies in west Africa from that time.[51] The nominal value for each denomination of those notes was the same throughout all the areas in which they circulated. But their exchange value in French coinage, and other currencies that circulated illegally such as British colonial money and indigenous moneys, varied both with respect to location and time. The exchange value of French coinage in local moneys, such as manillas, cowries, gold, and cloth strips, fluctuated widely, sometimes within the same district. This situation parallels the British experience. These differentials are the stuff of currency arbitrage, as the arbitrageur moves money to where it gets the best return.

Money arbitrage was one way for individuals to benefit in a "single currency" environment that was relentlessly colonial. But arbitraging money is trading the medium in the moment, not building the future. Money arbitrage is sometimes depicted as "unproductive" in the long term. No long-lasting physical capital, like a house or highway, is the immediate goal of money arbitrage.

But under colonialism, where Africans faced all kinds of restrictions aimed at limiting their economic behavior, money arbitrage generated income for its practitioners and their dependents. The shackles of colonialism on indigenous business and economic conduct were extensive. They included legal restrictions on African access to bank credit, as well as fees and regulations designed to make it very difficult for an African to become a large-scale trader. With so many avenues to economic advancement blocked or narrowed, money arbitrage was a practical alternative for African entrepreneurs. And who can blame them? Money arbitrage was one way the Medicis, Rothschilds, and Függers started their family fortunes.

The French imposition of a "single currency" distorted local economic decisions by making them focus too much on the media of exchange. The medium truly became the message.[52] But France gained from its ability to maintain a powerful monetary influence over its former and present territories. The persistence of the CFA franc zone in Africa, to which fourteen countries belong, testifies to the lasting effectiveness of cultural penetration.

There were other techniques of economic integration, besides "single currencies." We next consider two: trade manipulation and investment penetration.

"Managed trade"

Unlike the British, who at least had a rhetorical commitment to "free trade" for their empire in its last century or so, the French government made no such pretense at any time. This stance is consistent with the long-standing tradition of centralized political power in France. The issue for the French was not whether trade between home country and colonies should be manipulated or managed, but how. The question was not whether tariff policy should promote closer economic integration, but whether that integration should become assimilation.

Much like assimilation and association co-existed in French colonial administration for decades, so after 1883 tariff policy reflected elements of both complete economic assimilation and integration without assimilation. The latter emphasized tariff preferences for French overseas territories in the French home market.

After 1928 integration without assimilation became the more used approach. French West Africa, from its beginnings as a corporate entity in 1905, had received preferential treatment, excepting Dahomey and the Ivory Coast. These two territories were not included in the tariff structure for French West Africa until 1936.[53] From the late 1920s and early 1930s, French and British approaches to tariff policy became more similar. Both countries used preferential tariffs or, in the language of the times, "imperial preferences" to foster a greater economic integration of their respective empires that benefitted the home country most of all.

Trade management has other techniques in its arsenal, in addition to preferential tariffs. The controlling country, as Fieldhouse notes, could deploy "quotas, bulk buying, control of shipping, and currency allocation."[54] France used all these methods to consolidate its economic position vis-à-vis its colonies. After World War II, a period of disruption, France regained its role as the "chief market" for its territories and furnished a major percentage of their imports.[55] French domination over the trade of its former colonies has lessened in recent decades. It is not so hegemonic anymore, but significant trade relations still exist between France and its former colonies.

Investment penetration

French private investment in all of French Africa amounted to about 1,224,000,000 British pounds during the period from 1945 to about 1960. This sum was considerably greater than British private investment in Africa at the same time, which came to about 280,000,000 British pounds.[56] French public investment affected education, other social spending, public works, and the machinery of colonial government itself. Colonial bureaucracies always received enough financial support to survive, but it was not until the later colonial years that French public investment in public works, education, and other social spending became substantial.[57]

In light of the French commitment to cultural penetration, it may seem surprising that African education, conducted in the French language and emphasizing French culture, did not receive more generous funding earlier on. The French were always more concerned with identifying and promoting the most academically gifted students than with the educational leavening of the majority.

Public investment enlarging the public sector created African versions of the *étatisme* that has dominated the French economy itself for centuries. Government built and ran the twin infrastructures of transport and communications. Transport encompassed roads, railroads, ports, harbors, and airports. Communications included the telegraph, telephone, and post offices. A public sector that is too large in relation to the private sector is a striking example of the effective reproduction in French Africa of a dominant feature of France itself in recent centuries.

Of all the European imperial powers, France today retains the strongest economic presence in its former colonies. This longevity rests on deep cultural foundations. French cultural penetration enveloped the techniques of imperial economic integration, such as monetary centralization, trade management, and investment penetration. French culture has a special ability to bridge other cultures and connect with them. Its pretensions to universality can, if carried too far, lead to cultural imperialism. But its richness and elegant logic, communicated through an alluring language, make French culture one of the world's most unifying cultures.

2 Merchant associations

Merchant associations are important in the history of international economic integration for two reasons. First, they reflected certain kinds of economic integration in their own structures and procedures. Second, their activities created types of economic integration and disintegration in their working environments.

This chapter considers two types of merchant associations. The first is the *chartered company*. This organization receives a written document or charter, usually from a government, head of government or state, or government agency. The charter empowers the company to engage in specified activities, sometimes in a designated geographical area.

The chartered company has taken four different forms throughout history. These do not represent stages of evolution, since some later companies embodied earlier designs. They are listed here in order of appearance. The first was the regulated company; it was a partnership of individuals given royal letters patent that bestowed a monopoly of a specific trade. "Royal letters patent" constituted, in effect, the charter of a regulated company. The second form was the semi-joint-stock, an awkward name that reflects the transitional nature of this company. This enterprise did not issue permanent stock in itself, but rather sold it for particular activities it was promoting. The third type was the joint-stock company, which became the most used and influential plan of organization. This enterprise did sell shares of stock in itself. The fourth and final type embraces what were, in effect, quasi-chartered companies. These were the voluntary associations and partnerships that lacked the legal standing of a chartered company but whose members invested their resources in joint stock and traded as if they were chartered companies.[1]

A second type of merchant association is the *merchant league*. A league can be a covenant or compact among people or groups with similar interests. It can also refer to an association created by that covenant or compact, or it may stand for an organization that arises from ongoing activities. Some merchant leagues, especially in the European Middle Ages, have also been called confederations.

We now turn to an historical overview of chartered companies in the overseas expansion of Europe and select companies from the French, Dutch, British, and German colonial experiences. After that, we introduce the Hanseatic League as the classic case study of a merchant league.

Chartered companies: an historical overview

The chartered company has historically been associated with the overseas expansion of Europe, which unfolded over more than 400 years. Most start this era in the 1490s (AD or CE), when Christopher Columbus began the first of four expeditions to the "New World." This phrase, which refers to the western hemisphere, reflects a European viewpoint. For the many Native American groups already living in North, Central, and South America, as well as on numerous islands in the Caribbean Sea, the "New World" was their world and not so new to them when the Europeans arrived, uninvited.

European overseas expansion, which others trace back to European activities on islands off the shores of north and west Africa from the thirteenth century on, evolved through four stages. These phases, which overlap in practice, are demarcated by both chronology and geography. Each location experienced its own rates of exploration, economic penetration, physical subjugation, and human settlement. European settlement in Africa, for instance, was largely coastal until the mid-1800s, except for southern Africa, into whose interior Afrikaners began trekking in a major way in the late 1700s and early 1800s.

Chartered companies played roles in all four stages – exploration, economic penetration, physical subjugation, and human settlement – not only in Africa, but also in the Americas, Asia, and its subcontinent. But the exact role that a chartered company had in one or more of those stages depended, in large part, on whose empire it represented and when and where. Each colonial empire had its own objectives, as readers will soon see, and a chartered company was supposed to promote those interests. Differing imperial approaches produced, therefore, contrasting behaviors among chartered companies associated with various colonial empires.

A colonial empire did not necessarily have a uniform approach to all its territories at the same time. And it could also change its policies and their implementation. These facts render elusive a complete historical overview of all chartered companies in these pages, but one can consider a number of colonial empires and propose tentative generalizations about the activities of some of their associated chartered companies. These generalizations may occasionally be empire-wide, but more often they will pertain to a particular area during a certain time period.

With these caveats in mind, let us consider, in turn, European expansion into North America, Africa, and Asia; and draw examples from the French, Dutch, British, and German colonial experiences. For North America we consider companies from France, the Netherlands, and Great

Britain. For Africa, we highlight British companies, with references to the other three national experiences. For Asia we counterpoint Dutch and British companies.

North America

One common generalization about the empires established by the European powers in North America in the 1500s and 1600s features a sharp contrast. It places the British Empire on one side and all others on the other side. The key difference is that the British were supposedly more interested in long-term human settlement than the other empires. They, to the contrary, were allegedly more focused on short-term profits from trading. This generalization may be, in part, the result of reading history backwards: Britain had more settlements that lasted longer, some became the North American colonies in the British Empire, and some of these in turn the cradles of the United States Revolution.

In fact, other empires were also interested in human settlement in North America. But French and Dutch approaches were unbalanced and too short-term. British techniques were more balanced and long-term. So it is not the interest in human settlement per se but rather its implementation that is central. And it is important to remember that the above generalization was never intended to be an exclusive dichotomy, but rather to convey different emphases. All empires pursued a mix of objectives, including short-term material gain and long-term human settlement. But the British had a better mix that was based, at least until 1763, on a political decentralization that accorded the British North American colonies a substantial amount of local decision-making autonomy. This was the crucial safety valve that preserved imperial longevity for so long.

The different emphases of imperial policy appear in the activities of various chartered companies from France, the Netherlands, and Great Britain.

North America: France

For France, chartered companies were critical; they "created" the French empire in continental North America (and the Caribbean). Between 1599 and 1789 seventy-five French chartered companies emerged, a majority came into being in the 1600s.[2] While the French state was undergoing greater centralization during much of this time, the chartered companies themselves reflected both public and private elements.

Indeed, the launch and management of these chartered companies counsel caution in saturating all aspects of the French imperial experience with the notion of *étatisme*. Private initiative drove French chartered companies in North America and the Caribbean; and it was private initiative for the most part, not government, stimulating a private response. Without the distinctive opportunities for cooperation between the public and private sectors that the chartered company provides, the foundations for the French empire in North America and the Caribbean would never have been laid. The structures and relations of these companies show how they bridged public and private domains. The French monarchy, acting as the public sector in this drama, claimed ultimate control over its chartered companies, but in practice each could make many decisions on its own. The monarchy gave some royal support by encouraging emigration to the colonies, but emphasized that the chartered company existed at the pleasure of the state, to which company rights would revert at some future date.[3]

French chartered companies in North America and the Caribbean had powers and responsibilities that changed over time. Before 1660 companies were "given ownership of the land they occupied, a monopoly of trade, and varying degrees of administrative autonomy."[4] In a gesture so typical of the imperialist's arrogation of power, the French monarchy assumed it had the legal right to delegate land ownership in foreign environments to its chartered companies. A monopoly of local trade came within the context of a wider imperial monopoly: exports had to go to France itself. The phrase "varying degrees of administrative autonomy" is significant: all chartered companies at this time were not identical in their structures and procedures.

The activities of John Law cast special light on the fate of French chartered companies in the 1700s. John Law was a writer, a creative financial thinker, and an entrepreneur with perhaps an excessive capacity for risk-taking. At the outset he used one company as his base: the Company of the West, which in 1717 acquired the monopoly trading concession for all of French Louisiana. This territory was then extensive. It embraced all the lands that now make up the US states of Arkansas, Illinois, Iowa, Louisiana, Minnesota, Mississippi, Missouri, and Wisconsin.

Law's vision was panoramic and he moved fast. By 1720 he had created a massive holding company, reminiscent of a distended conglomerate, which became known as the Mississippi Company. This company encompassed all the French trading companies, including the Company of the West, such other agencies as the French mint, and such other items as the French national debt.[5] The Mississippi Company gave rise to one of history's greatest financial scandals, the Mississippi Bubble, which eventually burst and took down the Mississippi Company with it.[6]

In sum, French chartered companies dealing with North America have a checkered history. Most had their primary impact in laying the groundwork for empire, but then disappeared by the 1660s. The burden of initial construction proved too much. Financial distress mounted, as returns were inadequate to finance the tasks at hand and debts became crushing. In truth, the chartered company came up against its own limitations and could not surmount them. Never created to be a government, the chartered company was forced by circumstances on the spot, such as uprisings, to act like one. Ironically, the French chartered company, which stood for a time as a counterpoint to the tradition of *étatisme* that was developing in France itself, crumbled under burdens of government it could not escape.

As French chartered companies vanished, their legacy became clear: they had paved the way for the establishment of formal colonial administration. The decentralization represented by those companies yielded to the centralizing thrust of the French empire. The disappearance of most chartered companies meant that the international economic integration of the French empire would feature a growing public sector promoting even more administrative centralization.

North America: the Netherlands

Unlike the French experience in North America, which featured many chartered companies, the story of the Dutch Empire in North America and the Caribbean is that of far fewer companies. Two successive companies, both with the name of the West India Company, usually get the most attention. The first West India Company started in 1621 but went bankrupt by 1674 and dissolved. This company initiated Dutch colonization in the western hemisphere. At its zenith in the mid-seventeenth century, it controlled possessions in North and South America, as well as trading bases in the Caribbean and along the west coast of Africa. In North America the company by 1648 claimed to control Delaware and two territories in what is now New York state: New Amsterdam and Long Island.

The first Dutch West India Company encountered insoluble problems after 1650. It suffered from poor leadership, the loss of political allies, and not enough resources to defend its possessions in the predatory world of internecine colonial rivalries. There were too few Dutch settlers, insufficient military protection, and the lack of political will. But the original West India Company experienced a fate that awaited few other chartered companies: from its own ashes emerged its successor, which very much resembled its parent.[7]

The powers and structures of both companies reflect Dutch conceptions of empire and indeed of their own home government. The United Provinces, the technically correct name at this time for the Netherlands, were politically decentralized. Decentralization marked both West India Companies. In fact, the decentralization of the second West India Company was so pronounced that perhaps diffusion is a better way to characterize its structures. The second West India Company was at best a holding company with few powers and functions of its own. Real power rested with its participants back home – local political and administrative units known as Chambers, and other shareholders. The shell company gave at least nominal coherence to the activities in which its members engaged, such as the slave trade, and the administration of "New World" possessions. In fact, different Chambers individually managed some of these possessions.

Of all the European powers that colonized the western hemisphere, the Dutch came closest to the crude formulation of that aforementioned generalization which began the section on North America. At least in their initial forays, they construed colonization "in terms of war or commerce rather than of emigration and settlement. . ."[8]

And when they did try to encourage population growth in their colonies, their actions went awry. In 1629, for instance, the Dutch government announced a new initiative: anyone who brought fifty people to a colonial settlement and paid their travel expenses would get a large land grant located along the coast or on a navigable river. The people receiving the land were known as *patroons*; they got title to the land and feudal rights over the people they transported.[9] "Feudal rights" meant that a person was subordinated to a *patroon*. Unlike indentured servitude, which lasted for a fixed period, the feudal rights conferred by the *patroon* system do not appear to have had a fixed expiration date. A promise of indefinite subservience was not a great incentive for anyone wanting to settle in the "New World." The Dutch cherished their liberties, which the *patroon* system greatly reduced.

This ill-conceived attempt to stimulate emigration, therefore, had the opposite effect. Too few Dutch colonists, a factor that contributed to the demise of the first Dutch West India Company, would remain as a great constraint limiting the longevity of most Dutch settlements in the western hemisphere. Left today are the three Dutch islands in the southern Caribbean known as the Netherlands Antilles: Aruba, Bonaire, and Curaçao.

Both the French and the Dutch were intensely interested in the fur trade in North America, profits on the quick for traders on the make. Preoccupation with this trade produced an unbalanced approach to colonization for both countries. Permanent settlements require lasting populations with the freedom to develop enduring attachments to their land. Sedentary agriculture is one way to achieve this bonding; farmers who live on and preferably own the land they cultivate are a mighty source of stability. Both French and Dutch decisions worked against the emergence of this group but from different angles. In the French case, the monarchy was so devoted to the fur trade that it enacted regulations to preserve wilderness habitat, which had the effect of discouraging an expansion of farming. The Dutch, most concerned with short-term profits from the fur trade, did not think through all the implications of the *patroon* system for human settlement. The French discouraged the occupation – farming – while the Dutch scared away the people who might have done it – the farmers.

The essentials of chartered company activity in French and Dutch approaches to human settlement are well established in scholarship. But these actions have not been sufficiently analyzed with respect to economic integration and disintegration. There is a striking contrast between how French and Dutch chartered companies embodied the kind of imperial economic integration their national governments were seeking. Dutch companies were direct manifestations of the decentralization that marked institutions in their home country. Most French companies, with important degrees of autonomy, did not reflect the centralizing ethos of their parent government, although their eventual disappearance strengthened, as noted, government domination of business activity within the French empire.

Chartered companies operating in the western hemisphere have major legacies of international economic integration and disintegration. These arose in connection with their trans-Atlantic trading activities. The most harmful domain was the slave trade, which would forever link the destinies of Africa and the Americas. These international legacies will be analyzed at the beginning of the section on Africa.

North America: Great Britain

The British record in North America shows how chartered companies helped human settlement, even when they ultimately failed. The joint-stock company, in which shares were sold, made a number of appearances in the British settlement of North America.

Joint-stock companies played checkered roles in the very first permanent British settlement in North America. This was Jamestown, founded in 1607, by the London Company. The London and Plymouth Companies received a charter from King James I in 1606. These companies were to search for gold, seek a route to India, and develop trade. They were given rights to land but not self-government and thus remained closely tied to the monarchy.

Founding Jamestown brought the London Company daunting problems its inadequate capitalization could not surmount. The London Company, as many other chartered companies in other venues, had started with more hope than finance. It was restructured in 1609 to make owning shares in it more financially attractive. This was an intelligent attempt to build on its nature as a joint-stock company.

But the endeavor never reached fruition. In fact, the capitalist thought perished in a socialist solution. Proceeds from company land sales were deposited in a "common storehouse" and "no distribution of profits occurred."[10] The London Company never realized its full potential as a vehicle for promoting lasting settlement, because it was never properly treated as the capitalist agency it was. No wonder it failed. In 1624 King James I dissolved the charter and designated Virginia a royal colony.

The joint-stock company made a fateful appearance in the Pilgrim experience. Driven by religious persecution in England, the Pilgrims sought a new home in the "New World" and eventually found it in Plymouth Colony. Central to the early stages of their dream was a creative agreement they made with the Virginia Company, a joint-stock company. Hard pressed for cash, the Pilgrims offered to invest their labor in the company. They agreed to work a portion of the company's large acreage in Virginia. But the Pilgrims landed in Plymouth instead. The original agreement with the Virginia Company was never fulfilled, because it did not apply to New England. Still, that agreement may be viewed as one key to sustaining the Pilgrim vision when it was under grave assault in Europe.

Africa: French, British, and Dutch participation in the slave trade

Chartered companies helped establish some of the most important connections between Africa and the western hemisphere by their participation in the trans-Atlantic slave trade. This "illegitimate commerce" began in the 1440s and lasted into the twentieth century. It harshly transported millions of Africans from their home continent to the "New World," which held no promise of liberty for them.

Chartered companies were most active in the Atlantic slave trade in the 1600s and in the early decades of the 1700s, but even then their participation did not bring them financial success. When the slave trade expanded in the 1700s, they found it harder, though not impossible, to compete with private traders, who had lower overhead costs and more operational freedom. Private traders were not obligated to governments or shareholders, more personally involved, and thus better able to adapt to rapidly changing market conditions: they "could trade when, where and on what terms they chose."[11] Chartered companies cannot, therefore, be held primarily accountable for sustaining the Atlantic slave trade throughout the eighteenth and nineteenth centuries. Private traders must shoulder most of the blame in those centuries. In the 1700s, for example, private English ships carried across the Atlantic about two-thirds of the slaves coming from west Africa; private French vessels brought another one-fifth of the total.[12] Still, chartered companies are among the primary agencies for getting the trade up and going on the massive geographical scale the later centuries of the trade would reinforce and amplify.

The slave trade evolved within the wider context of an emerging Atlantic economy, which linked Europe, Africa, and the Americas. The nascent Atlantic economy in the earlier centuries of European expansion, roughly from the late fifteenth into the nineteenth centuries, was more a designation than a reality. "Triangular trade" used to explain a developing Atlantic economy.

The following is an over-simplified version of "triangular trade." A ship left England with trade goods, none too up-scale, sailed to Africa, traded these commodities for enslaved Africans, and transported them to the

"New World." Here slaves were exchanged for other commodities, like sugar that could be used to make rum, and our ship returned these goods to England. The "triangular trade" construct correctly identified the three pillars of the embryonic Atlantic economy – Europe, Africa, and the Americas – but misrepresented its internal trade dynamics.

These were more bilateral than trilateral. Ties between Europe and Africa, between Africa and the Americas, and between the Americas and Europe were more integrated than the overall Atlantic economy itself. And, of course, the same ships did not necessarily service all three geographical areas and their subdivisions. For example, the Atlantic slave trade featured two main sets of oceanic routes. The first connected west and southwest Africa with North America and the Caribbean. The second tied southwest Africa, especially in the environs of what is now Angola, with South America, particularly Brazil.

Two main factors thus complicate an evaluation of the impact of chartered companies on international economic integration and disintegration. The first is the fact that slave trade unfolded within an emerging Atlantic economy. The second is the fact that chartered companies had their greatest influence in the earlier, not the later, centuries of the trade. As to the first, the Atlantic economy featured trading in numerous commodities, including sugar, tobacco, fish, lumber products, and naval stores, besides the unholy transport of human cargo. Whether some of these other lines of trade would have arisen on the geographical scale they did without the slave trade and its profits can only be known in a counter-factual world to which this author does not have access. In short, it is impossible to remove the threads of the slave trade and assume that the tapestry of an emerging Atlantic economy would still have had the preliminary cohesion it exhibited. As to the second factor, the same caveat applies. Chartered companies pioneered the principal Atlantic slave trade routes and destinations. It is, likewise, impossible to assume that without their participation the slave trade would have emerged in the same way, with the same timing, and with the same patterns.

One fact we know for sure. Chartered companies engaged in the slave trade share responsibility for a perverse kind of international economic integration that was based on creating or sustaining economic disintegration in Africa itself.

The Atlantic slave trade fed on African wars and other destructive indigenous rivalries. These produced prisoners and other outcasts, the people most vulnerable to enslavement either by capture or by sale. While the slave trade did not directly cause many of these local conflicts, it was surely an accessory during and after the fact. The activities of slavers or those who would deal with them destabilized many areas in west, south central, and southwest Africa over a period of more than four centuries. This destabilization promoted local economic disintegration by retarding or destroying economic groups of different sizes. These included regional polities, groups based on contacts between villages, and families and extended families with different geographical reaches.

Households and extended families are sometimes neglected in this roster of harm. But in discussing the harmful impact of the slave trade on local economic organization, one must emphasize the destruction wrought on African kinship structures. Indeed, one of Africa's greatest contributions to human living is the sophistication of its kinship structures. These operate over extended distances and provide comprehensive support to their members, without the supervision of government bureaucracies.

The root of "economy" is the Greek word, *oikos*, which means household. It is altogether appropriate that the household, in whatever anthropological form, should feature prominently in any accounting of local economic disintegration.

Chartered companies from France, the Netherlands, and Great Britain were involved in the transport and distribution of slaves to North America and the Caribbean. Major French chartered companies conducting the slave trade were, in the order of their founding, the *Compagnie des Indes Occidentales* (1664), the *Compagnie du Sénégal* (1673), and the *Compagnie du Guinée* (1684). After 1713 the *Compagnie du Sénégal* and the *Compagnie du Guinée* encountered increasing financial difficulties, but still managed to transport slaves. Their problems made them ripe for absorption, which the company established first, the *Compagnie des Indes Occidentales* or the French West Indian Company, accomplished in 1721.

Thereafter the only French chartered company remaining in the slave trade tried several different approaches. The first was a short-lived attempt to work out a modus vivendi with the one group that would come to dominate the slave trade later in the 1700s: private traders. The company licensed private traders to do the actual trading through 1722. But from the start of 1723 through April 1725, the company re-asserted its monopoly over the French slave trade and insisted on conducting the trade on its own.[13] After this period, the company apparently reverted to a series of practical arrangements with private traders.

The story of British chartered involvement in the Atlantic slave trade is writ largely in the activities of the Royal African Company. This joint-stock company was founded in 1672 and succeeded the Royal Adventurers into Africa, established in 1660.[14] The Royal African Company was headquartered in London, which was the main British slave port in the 1600s.

As went the hegemony of London in the slave trade, so would go the fate of the Royal African Company. The company enjoyed its greatest dominance in the English slave trade between 1673 and 1689, in spite of the presence of numerous illegal competitors.[15] By the early 1700s London was losing its primacy as a slave port. Two other British ports, Bristol and Liverpool, were emerging as leaders in the Atlantic slave trade. The decline of the Royal African Company further weakened London's grip on the English slave trade. But even a rejuvenated company would have found it difficult to compete with private traders, whose energy sustained the rise of Bristol and Liverpool. The role of Liverpool was especially important: by 1750, it was the leading port for the slave trade in Europe. It kept this status until 1807, when the British Parliament made it illegal for British nationals to participate in the slave trade.[16]

Dutch chartered involvement in the Atlantic slave trade featured companies introduced earlier in this chapter, the two Dutch West India companies.[17] Some chartered companies in the slave trade engaged in other lines of commerce, the "non-slave exports." The Royal African Company, for example, exported gold from the Gold Coast and many other products from elsewhere in west Africa, including wax, hides, and gold dust.[18] But the second Dutch West India Company concentrated on the slave trade. Indeed, "its main collective activity was the slave trade between Africa and the Caribbean…"[19]

Africa: other British chartered companies

Many chartered companies in Africa played no part in the gruesome international business that was the Atlantic slave trade, but their presence in Africa came from other aspects of the interventionist dynamic that drove Europe to dominate much of that continent by the end of the nineteenth century. Three British chartered companies, each operating in a different part of the continent, illustrate other kinds of business activities that would all contribute to the establishment of British colonial administration in their respective regions. We highlight as our west African example the Royal Niger Company in order to complement the story of Ja Ja of Opobo told in the previous chapter. We then offer cameos of two other companies: from east Africa, the Imperial British East African Company; and from southern Africa, the British South African Company.

The Royal Niger Company

The Royal Niger Company established a pivotal beachhead in what would become Nigeria, by 1914 a unified British colony. In response to a petition from Sir George Goldie, this company received a royal charter from Queen Victoria in 1886 that detailed its pursuits, powers, and obligations.

Selected excerpts from this document reveal how careful British law officers were to present colonial penetration as a legally correct process. The company was "to carry on business" in the United Kingdom, Africa, or "elsewhere."[20] This "business" covered a wide range of activities. Among these were the rights "to form or acquire" trading stations, factories, and stores "in Africa and elsewhere";[21] and "to purchase, or otherwise acquire, open and work mines, forests, quarries, fisheries, and manufactories…"[22] This chartered company, a creation of the 1880s, had another mission that clearly distinguished it from some chartered companies of an earlier era. The Royal Niger Company was to work against slavery within its African territories: "The Company shall ... abolish by degrees any system of domestic servitude existing among the native inhabitants..."[23]

The charter accepts the contention in the petition concerning the legal status of indigenous lands. Petitioners maintained that the "Kings, Chiefs, and peoples" living in the Niger River basin had "ceded the whole of their respective territories to the Company by various Acts of Cession" listed in an attachment to the petition.[24] These land transfers were often based on misunderstanding and fear. To describe them as "acts of cession," which implies voluntary agreement, is misleading.

Representatives of the Royal Niger Company "negotiating" with African leaders had themselves little or no knowledge of local land laws. While these laws were not identical from one group to another, many did acknowledge the local chief as the primary "trustee" and even ultimate owner of community lands. Many also distinguished rights to what the land produced – usufructuary rights – and what was built on the land from the land itself, and treated these products and appurtenant structures as private property. The individual person could own the products and structures, but not the land itself, which remained community property.

These laws usually did not empower chiefs and other African leaders to dispose of community lands, usufructuary rights, and other private properties unilaterally to outsiders. So the leader possessed the land as the representative of a community, as a trustee, not as one person with private property rights in it.[25] Therefore, there was no basis in most indigenous land law for a leader unilaterally "ceding" land that was community property *de jure* to a company that was claiming private property rights *de facto* to the African land itself. But this is colonialism, not an impartial court of cross-cultural law, and even western academics at that time had imperfect knowledge of indigenous land law. These points are, nonetheless, important for understanding in retrospect the kinds of local economic integration and disintegration the Royal Niger Company was creating.

The most important kind of economic integration the company greatly influenced was the creation of Nigeria itself. This process unfolded from three major bases. The first was Lagos in the west, which became a protectorate over most of the Yoruba people. The second was in the east, in the Niger River delta, where Great Britain worked to destroy the power of African middlemen, such as Ja Ja of Opobo. The third was to the north, in the environs of Nupe and southern Hausaland, where the Royal Niger Company was trying to establish its own administration.

Efforts in the third base brought some success. Sir George Goldie entered into tranquil relations with much of Hausaland by fashioning a treaty of friendship with the sultan of Sokoto in 1885. But the Royal Niger Company encountered stiff resistance in Nupe and the emirate of Ilorin, and its own army, the West African Frontier Force, had to subdue these populations. The company was also coming into military conflict with French forces, which were using the Niger River to move towards Dahomey in the west. The Royal Niger Company, a private enterprise, was forced by indigenous unrest and Anglo-French rivalry to act more and more as a government. Even with its own army, it could not successfully function this way, and the British government withdrew its charter in 1898.[26]

As had so many other chartered companies in other situations, the Royal Niger Company pioneered the way for official colonial administration. The creation of Nigeria continued apace. In 1900 Great Britain took direct control of northern Nigeria. Southern Nigeria was emerging in the early twentieth century as a separate administrative entity. The British then merged the two regions into a unified Nigeria, which came into existence on January 1, 1914. The administrative unification of Nigeria, partly based on the work of the Royal Niger Company, established the territorial framework for two related types of economy, neither of which was primarily designed to serve the needs of indigenous Africans.

The first was a colonial or export economy. This was the creation of foreign and indigenous business interests working together. It sought to guide Nigerian output towards export markets. A major goal was to integrate local activities with external demand. This integration sometimes required diverting labor away from production for local consumption and towards crops or other items destined for export.

The second was a bureaucratic economy. It was the creation of British administrators and their territorial bureaucracy. The bureaucratic economy manipulated indigenous activities to maximize revenue from taxes and preserve a colonial version of law and order.

These two types of economy overlapped, but the intersection was not always harmonious. There were areas of agreement and disagreement. Bureaucrats, for instance, often favored greater exports, because these commodities generated more revenue, by way of export taxes and other fees imposed on the movement of commerce within the country.

Disagreements between the two versions of economy arose from several sources. Contentious areas were taxation and fees government charged for certain services. The level of rates imposed by government railroads, for example, was a frequent source of complaints from private businesses that regarded them as too high and a restraint on the growth of commodity exports.

The "colonial economy" and the "bureaucratic economy" are useful constructs across the colonial experience in Africa. Their particular configurations and relations vary from colony to colony. But one generalization is valid: these two economies were designed mainly to use and sometimes abuse Africans. This exploitation rested on a strategy that employed local economic disintegration as one of its principal features. Indigenous economic structures had to adapt, assume a disguise, go underground, or die.

In Nigeria this disintegration affected local life comprehensively. Most troubling from the perspective of capitalism was colonial treatment of the land itself. The two most fundamental rights of private property reside in the land and in one's own person. Slavery negated the latter and colonialism, in many cases, snatched away the former. Overriding indigenous land law, and its recognition of private property rights in usufruct and buildings, relied on a technique of British colonialism which this author has introduced elsewhere.[27] British administrators manipulated their own language to serve their colonial objectives. This technique is known technically as language manipulation at the semantic level: it abuses the content of words. As applied to African lands, word abuse was profound.

The most manipulated word in connection with land was "public." Many colonizers, including the British, assumed that the community character of much African land meant that these lands were public in a western sense; that is, public property as distinct from private property. But this is a western dichotomy, not an indigenous reality. Local land laws, as noted, commingled elements of private property with community possession. The British, perhaps unknowingly, manipulated African versions of "public." The British, knowingly, manipulated their own conceptions of "public" to justify their alienating indigenous rights in land.

Some telling illustrations of manipulation in northern Nigeria come very early in the twentieth century, before it was merged with southern Nigeria in 1914. Robert Shenton has provided revealing evidence on this matter in his careful analysis of the writings of principal British administrators on the spot, including the words of Lord Lugard, then the British Governor of Northern Nigeria.[28]

Lugard proposed several types of alien land tenure: ways in which the British occupiers held Nigerian land. The first was Crown lands: for Lugard these were the private property of the British government. Crown lands included properties that the British government had acquired from the Royal Niger Company after the revocation of its charter in 1898. Also in this category were the sites of administrative officers and military encampments.

A second type of land tenure consisted of "public lands." These were far more extensive than Crown lands. But they were government property as well, though not in exactly the same fashion as Crown lands. While Crown lands were immediately the private property of government, public lands were those to which government held the "ultimate title" by right of conquest or "peaceful submission." Lugard justifies his analysis by referring to statutes that British colonial administration had already enacted. This is the argument for present correctness based on past validity: "I am correct now, because we were right in the past."

In any event, the word "public" now means private property, not owned by indigenous people or communities but by the colonial power itself. This is a most blatant form of language manipulation: forcing a word to function as its opposite. Colonialism was a universe of contradictions, as British manipulation of the word "public" in relation to Nigerian land testifies.

The British version of northern Nigerian land law, which would characterize the unified colony from 1914, abolished private property for Africans. This policy wrought a local economic disintegration that touched the legal bases of many African relationships. While the Royal Niger Company was long gone before the final abolition occurred, it did play an important role in the kinds of extra-legal land transfers that created the backdrop for the eventual suppression of indigenous rights in land.

The Imperial British East Africa Company

Both the Royal Niger Company and the Imperial British East Africa Company had relatively short lives as chartered companies. But both had an important impact on the subsequent course of colonization, and economic integration and disintegration, in their respective regions. As the fate of the Royal Niger Company was partly influenced by Anglo–French rivalry in west Africa, so the origins and development of the Imperial British East Africa Company were affected by growing Anglo–German competition in east Africa. These European rivalries drove the so-called "scramble for Africa," which partitioned much of Africa among European countries from the 1880s into the twentieth century.

William Mackinnon, the Scottish shipping magnate, was trying to create his own trading empire in east Africa in the 1880s. He envisioned an organization that would reach from the ocean to the lakes: from the Indian Ocean port of Mombasa in the east to Lake Victoria, the largest of the African great lakes, in the west, a distance of almost six hundred miles. His efforts received recognition with a royal charter that transformed his business into the Imperial British East Africa Company. The British government granted charter status in order to help Mackinnon and his associates compete more effectively with the formidable German East Africa Company (*Deutsch Öst-Afrika Gesellschaft*).

This organization, sanctioned by the German government and led by Carl Peters, had aggressively penetrated the interior of what is now Tanzania in the early 1880s and claimed to have secured the signatures of numerous African chiefs on papers ceding their land to the company. The conditions in which these "treaties" were signed, and even who signed them, are murky issues. The signatures are a series of Xs, and the company asserted that African acceptance was given voluntarily and with full knowledge of the consequences.

While the "treaties" lacked legal credibility, they constituted a compelling geopolitical warning to the British government. The German government was establishing a major sphere of influence in east Africa, which reached Lake Victoria, the major source of the Nile River upon which depended the economy of Egypt. The British had a huge stake in Egypt, because of the Suez Canal. From its opening in 1869 this waterway was a great strategic flashpoint. It provided a shorter route between Great Britain and India, the "jewel in the crown" of the British Empire, than the old sea route around the Cape of Good Hope in southern Africa. The British knew they had to accelerate the process by which they would eventually absorb Kenya and Uganda into their empire.

As in west and south Africa, the chartered company was to play a pioneering role in extra-legal land acquisition in the northern region of east Africa. Enter the Imperial British East Africa Company, which through "negotiations" and "consultations" would claim to have acquired rights to vast amounts of land in what were to become Kenya and Uganda. The Royal Niger Company created, as noted, only one of the three beachheads from which Nigeria emerged. The Imperial British East Africa Company was the central advance agent in the creation of Kenya colony, and exerted significant influence in lands to the west that became part of British Uganda. It thus laid the foundations for the emergence of two British territories and the kinds of economic integration and disintegration both would formally amplify.

The company lost its charter in 1893, five years before the Royal Niger Company experienced a similar fate. But by then the Imperial British East Africa Company had assembled the territory that the British government itself took over in 1894–95. And by then the forces of economic integration and disintegration that colonial administration would strengthen had long been unleashed.

The British South Africa Company

Like the Royal Niger and Imperial British East Africa companies, the British South Africa Company embodied the entrepreneurial drive of one man, Cecil John Rhodes. While the influence of both George Goldie and William Mackinnon on European penetration was largely expressed through their respective chartered companies, Cecil Rhodes had an impact on southern Africa that included but went far beyond the record of the British South Africa Company. The longest-lived of these three British companies, the British South Africa Company received its royal charter in 1889 and gave it up in 1923.

All three companies employed methods of land acquisition that were extra-legal, but the British South Africa Company also specialized in physical intimidation and violence. This company sought lands both above and below the Zambezi River and secured control over them in a manner not noted for diplomacy. The company's claim to Mashonaland, in what was to become southern Rhodesia and now Zimbabwe, was based on concessions "extracted" from the African leader Lobengula.[29] And the company fought the Matabele in 1893.[30]

The British South Africa Company neither originated nor culminated the ethos of violence that clouded the lands of southern Africa for centuries. But it greatly exacerbated relations between Africans and Europeans by its swashbuckling behavior. Its actions further associated European land acquisition with force and entrenched the tradition that land obtained through violence could only be kept through violence.

Capitalism has many faces. Its least attractive is that of the "robber baron": the capitalist of greed, not just profit. In the annals of colonial infamy, the British South Africa Company ranks right behind what Leopold II did to the Congo and how the German East Africa Company behaved in its sphere of operations. In attacking African rights in land so fiercely, all greatly undermined the legal foundations of indigenous economies and fostered their disintegration. In its land acquisitions, which covered major parts of southern Africa, the British South Africa Company laid the basis for the emergence of another imposed form of economic integration: the "settler economy." This is a creation of outsiders who penetrate an area and "settle" on land they seize. The "settlers" then exploit the local residents and other resources.

The classic beginnings of a "settler economy" in one region of southern Africa occurred in the aftermath of those concessions "extracted" from Lobengula. With these concessions as their justification, groups of farming and mining settlers entered Mashonaland in 1890, where they founded Fort Salisbury, the capital of southern Rhodesia.[31] The British South Africa Company provided the administrative infrastructure for the development of this "settler economy," as it governed the colony of southern Rhodesia until it surrendered its charter in 1923.

This was a rare case of a chartered company succeeding as a colonial government for several decades. It is also a strong example of the direct involvement of a chartered company in creating a territorial framework for economic integration that was predicated on ongoing local economic disintegration. In southern Rhodesia there was considerable overlap between the "settler economy" and the "bureaucratic economy." The chartered company, representing the settlers, was the government and so strove to minimize any friction between those two versions of economy.

Indeed, the "settler economy" seeks to plant itself in decomposing indigenous economies or close to other local resources it can manipulate. It organizes what is left of indigenous economies after the alienation of their land has harmed local farming patterns and destabilized traditional business relationships. It thrives on taxes and regulations imposed by colonial administrations that endeavor to destroy indigenous economic choices and force Africans to work in the "settler economy." This is what happened in southern Rhodesia and other colonial situations in Africa that featured an important "settler economy," such as southwest Africa (now Namibia), Kenya, and South Africa itself.[32]

"Settler economies" can involve agriculture or mining. Cecil Rhodes developed two major mining companies that would exert enormous influence in southern Africa and on the global metals industry. Rhodes set up Consolidated Goldfields in an attempt to organize the gold industry in South Africa and give it some global clout. He also founded DeBeers to control the South African diamond industry and hoped to make this company a major world player. In DeBeers he created a company that today, in the words of the *Financial Times*, still "dominates the world's diamond business."[33]

To sum up, European chartered companies in Africa have a long history that divides into two major phases. The first was earlier, largely before 1750, and associated with but not limited to the trans-Atlantic slave trade. These operations, insofar as they concerned Africa, were usually confined to the coasts and worked through intermediaries with up-country connections. The second phase was later, mainly after 1880, and focused on the European penetration of the African interior. Chartered companies were asked to perform more functions in their second African period. To trading and coastal reconnoitering were added a series of chores concerned with the interior: its exploration, subjugation, and governance. The companies in the later period were able to explore the interior, but once there all encountered major difficulties in "winning the hearts and minds of the people." They all ended up using physical force that had to be backed eventually by military forces from their own national governments. Only the British South Africa Company, because of the distinctive way it embodied both "settler" and "bureaucratic" economies, was able to govern a colony for several decades.

East Asia and the Indian Ocean littoral: the Dutch and English East India Companies

Our last geographical theater offers two chartered companies with wide-ranging connections: the two East India Companies, one from the Netherlands, the other from England. Their formal names are the Dutch United East India Company (*Vereenigde Oost-Indische Compagnie* or VOC)[34] and English East India Company (or EIC). They exhibit similarities, but also display striking contrasts.

Both companies share a common historical background. Both advanced the expansion of Europe into the Indian Ocean and beyond after AD 1500. European thrusts into the Indian Ocean and its surrounding lands came in three pounding waves of imperialism. The Portuguese were first, the Dutch second, and the English third. To grasp better what the Dutch and English companies did in their time, one should have the following sketch of earlier Portuguese activity.

The Portuguese, as they had in Africa, led European intervention – this time across the Indian Ocean into Asia. Two major motives powered this vanguard. One was evangelical: Roman Catholic missionaries had burning desires to preach their message in yet farther reaches of a world still little known to Europeans. The other driving force was economic, commercial really, and often had one meaning: fine Asian spices, such as peppers. These were in increasing demand for the many cuisines in Europe and elsewhere.

The Portuguese strategy of domination was simple and effective. It is important in its own right, but also as a benchmark for comparing and contrasting the approaches of Portugal's successors, the Dutch and then the English. The Portuguese analyzed the existing Muslim trading network that transported Asian spices to Europe and then sought to take over its key entrepots or transshipment points. Their strategy was, in short, to control the chokepoints of commerce.

This approach had a geopolitical and geoeconomic simplicity. It was also efficient: one did not have to control every part of the network, only its major centers, of which there were three. In 1510 the Portuguese seized Goa, on the west coast of India, in 1511 Malacca on the Malay peninsula, and in 1515 Hormuz, at the mouth of the Persian Gulf. Three chokepoints, three pillars of control: Malacca to the east, Hormuz to the west, and Goa in between.

From the perspective of international economic integration, the Portuguese forcibly grafted their version on one already existing. In so doing, they retained the nerve centers of the original framework, but thrust out its creators and maintainers from positions of power. The imposition of Portugal's will, then, perpetrated an economic disintegration not of design, but of personnel. The indigenous Muslim traders were either eliminated or reduced to subordinate roles in the new Portuguese commercial empire.

That it was, because in Asia, unlike in Brazil, the Portuguese were principally interested in a commercial, not a territorial, empire. And the strategy of chokepoints was designed to monopolize trade between Asia and Europe. That goal proved elusive: the Portuguese lacked the resources to control the alternative land routes between Asia and the Mediterranean. Nor could they establish naval supremacy everywhere in the Indian Ocean littoral. Turkish naval power proved too daunting, for instance, in the Red Sea. But their chokepoint strategy enabled them to develop powerful administrative enclaves, which anchored the framework of a commercial empire well into the 1600s.

Malacca had the greatest strategic value. The straits of Malacca, then as now, are among the most vital sea lanes in the world. They are narrow, which makes them easier to dominate from Malacca itself. Portugal controlled Malacca from 1511 into 1641 and was able to compel most passing sea traffic to stop at the port of Malacca. While they did not succeed in monopolizing all trade between Asia and Europe, the Portuguese established control over major parts of it.

Portugal's major agency of commercial penetration contrasts with an approach the Dutch and English shared in common. Portugal used an organization that was a direct extension of the state itself: the *Estado da India.* This technique reflected the administrative centralization of the Portuguese state, which was greater than that of either the Netherlands or Great Britain. Both the Dutch and British extended the decentralization that marked their national states into their overseas organizations. Thus, while Portugal dispatched an organization that remained under strict controls from the center, both the Dutch and the British chartered trading companies that were autonomous both on paper and in practice.

The similarities between the VOC and EIC appear to go beyond historical background and administrative decentralization. Their charters gave them both considerable powers. Each commanded substantial resources, had powerful friends in politics, and pursued, at least initially, the same strategy.

These similarities are general and, on closer inspection, reveal important contrasts. The chartering process, the rate at which each company acquired resources, and the combined influence of these two on company structures all show significant differences between the two companies. Consider first the VOC. The Dutch government founded the VOC in 1602 with a strong charter that conferred wide-ranging powers. The VOC was empowered to enter into treaties and alliances, wage war, levy and collect taxes, raise troops, and appoint governors and judicial officers. Its charter was subject to periodic renewals, but these did not expose the VOC to the kind of turbulence which charter renewal brought the EIC. Under its founding charter, granted in 1600, the EIC received capital for only one voyage at a time. This arrangement apparently made the company a semi-joint stock arrangement. A new charter granted in 1657 enabled the EIC to seek capital on a permanent basis. This power transformed the organization into the traditional joint-stock company. The EIC, unlike the VOC, faced uncertainties and irregularities in its charter renewal. Until 1773 renewal was irregular. After that, the process occurred every twenty years, which provided opportunities for inquiries by the British Parliament and major changes in the company.[35] The VOC did not have to deal with the intense governmental oversight that took place in England. The States General in the Netherlands examined the accounts of the VOC and renewed its charter, "but made no attempt to influence policy" nor revise its structures.[36] So while the capital of the EIC became permanent from 1657, an attribute that the VOC had from its inception, the structures of the EIC were open to substantive revision by Parliament.

The VOC had, therefore, a huge head start in the areas of financial continuity and organizational coherence. These two types of stability greatly facilitated the economic integration of the company itself. The VOC had substantial operating capital from its earlier years and deployed it to good advantage. It showed a profit for most of the century and a half after 1623.[37] In fact, pressure to show success by maintaining high dividends contributed to the company's bankruptcy in 1795. The company should have reduced its dividend, which was always over 10 percent per year, as its debt burden increased in the latter decades of the 1700s, but it did not. Its unhappy demise should not obscure the fact that the VOC was an outstanding investment for a very long term.

It would take longer for the EIC, in its own life, to achieve levels of administrative strength and financial power comparable to those of the VOC. The EIC encountered major hurdles that slowed its own economic integration. The EIC faced rockier political and financial times at home and a changing mission abroad. While the VOC and EIC both had powerful friends in politics and finance, the EIC had more enemies. The VOC had the backing and involvement of key government leaders on both national and local levels. Some of these sat on its national board of directors, the College of Seventeen that set general policy. Others were directors of the six local chambers, one for each major commercial area; in these chambers reposed "real power."[38] The VOC was thus better integrated with its own national and local centers of power.

The EIC, to the contrary, ran into intermittent but fierce opposition at home from political and business interests. These attacks were most troublesome during its period of greatest institutional and financial vulnerability, before 1709. In the 1690s it confronted the hostility of Whig politicians, who claimed it was too Tory, and independent merchants, who chafed at their exclusion from the Asian trade.[39] Then in 1709 the EIC merged with a rival, received a monopoly and more supportive charter from the British Parliament, and emerged much stronger than before in terms of its own economic integration. It would need this greater strength as the immensity of work in its primary venue, India, became clearer to government leaders back home in England.

In general terms, the VOC and EIC pursued similar strategies of commercial penetration at the outset. These were based, in part, on the Portuguese approach of controlling the chokepoints of commerce in the Indian Ocean littoral. Like the Portuguese, the Dutch and then the British would build on the original Muslim framework but in different ways. The Dutch were initially attracted to the Portuguese chokepoint strategy more as blueprint for military conquest than a lasting commercial strategy.

But they would soon graft their own approach on it. The Dutch succeeded in capturing Malacca in 1641, but much earlier had made a key decision that would govern their long-term strategy in the Indian Ocean littoral. In 1609, seven years after receiving its charter from the States General, the VOC decided to concentrate more on controlling the supply of commodities than on their transshipment points.[40]

These turned out, in fact, not to be mutually exclusive targets, as efforts to control supply naturally had to concentrate on entrepots. And without some control over the transshipment points, it would be difficult to monopolize supply. These efforts might prove unavailing if a hostile power controlled the entrepots. So the Dutch supply strategy really rested on a continuation of the Portuguese approach. But the Dutch painted it differently and added elements of control designed to radiate out into the territories surrounding an entrepot. They could attempt this, because in contrast to the Portuguese, the Dutch saw their bases not as enclaves but as stepping stones for dominating the interior.

A case in point is Malacca. From this port and entrepot the Dutch moved into the interior of Malaysia, which the Portuguese had never tried on a large scale, and forced "contracts" on the Malay states, which were weak militarily. These "agreements" required the Malay states to trade only with the VOC. The Dutch meant business, in a military as well as a commercial sense. The VOC often resorted to war as it tried to control the supply of commodities. The Dutch also at times blockaded the straits of Malacca in order to control tin exports, as they were interested in more than just fine spices.

The British, like the Dutch, possessed an unusually potent combination of financial and seafaring skills. They were able to defeat and displace the Dutch in the Indian Ocean for two main reasons. The first was their greater economic and military strength. Great Britain, for centuries a major sea power, grew more dominating as its Industrial Revolution strengthened its national economy. The second major reason was strategic. The British took the chokepoint strategy and refined it. Malacca was again a major flashpoint, this time for an accelerating Anglo–Dutch rivalry in the eastern region of the Indian Ocean littoral. The British, as so often was the case in their empire, preferred indirect and long-term approaches.

They did not attack Malacca directly, but used pincer tactics that unfolded over decades. In 1786 the EIC established a trading station on Penang, an island off the west coast of the Malay peninsula.

The pincer to the left of Malacca was in place, but the British did not view Penang only in geopolitical terms. It would have geoeconomic meaning in their struggles with the Dutch. The latter, as noted, were using Malacca to monopolize trade as much as they could; this effort upset many merchants, settlers, and other business people. The British showcased Penang as an entrepot with fewer restrictions. This business-friendly strategy worked. Much business migrated from Malacca or was attracted to Penang in the first place. This is geoeconomics in practice: Penang was used to erode the commercial hegemony of Malacca. And Penang was doing double-duty, as the potential left pincer for an eventual takeover of Malacca itself.

Penang never became the left pincer in a military sense, until there was a right pincer in place. This happened when the British founded Singapore, at the southern end of the Malay peninsula, in 1819, thirty-six years after the EIC built the trading station on Penang. The establishment of Singapore sealed the fate of Malacca as the center of international commerce in the region. The British officially acquired Malacca from the Dutch in 1824, but that act only formalized its long-term commercial decline. Malacca retained its great strategic value as a military chokepoint, but other locations, Penang and especially Singapore, had emerged as centers of vibrant business activity in the region.

The essentials of a chokepoint strategy remained intact: control a region by dominating its key areas. But the British made that strategy more flexible and creative by challenging its literalness. Why accept only existing chokepoints as the basis for action? Why not develop new centers, with combined geoeconomic and geopolitical functions, that could in time tip the balance of commercial and military power in your favor?

The VOC and the EIC both played major roles in the implementation of the particular chokepoint strategy pursued by their home countries. And each found the pace of its own economic integration greatly affected by factors special to its own national milieu. The EIC, as mentioned, took longer to achieve the level of economic integration that blessed the VOC from its earliest days.

Both companies share one final feature: each caused economic disintegration in its overseas environments. As far as Malacca itself was concerned, the VOC reinforced the disintegration of the entrepot's original character the Portuguese had started. Malacca had been for centuries, before the arrival of the Europeans, an emporium in the indigenous Malay tradition. Founded in 1400 by King Parameswara at the mouth of the Malacca River, Malacca became a thriving center of international commerce, under indigenous control, during the fifteenth century. Malacca also became the seat of an empire, which tried to monopolize commerce in the region.

So from a local perspective, the Portuguese conquest of Malacca in 1511 meant that one monopolizing power replaced another. From another viewpoint, Portugal's imposition of its own version of international economic integration on Malacca retained a central feature of the Malaccan empire – its tendency towards commercial monopoly – but eliminated Malacca as its headquarters and thereby undermined the economic integration of the Malaccan empire.

The Dutch, through the agency of the VOC, took this process of economic disintegration more forcefully into the interior. The monopolistic trading agreements which the VOC forced on the states of the Malay peninsula further weakened them by disrupting traditional trading patterns. This was indigenous economic disintegration on a large scale.

The British intensified the local economic disintegration of the Malay peninsula. But sustained imposition of a British version of territorial economic integration would come later, in the nineteenth and early twentieth centuries. The EIC was not involved in that process, but did serve in the vanguard of British penetration with its acquisition of Penang and other activities on the Malay peninsula. The EIC, therefore, played an important part in reinforcing the disintegration of indigenous economic structures in the eastern region of the Indian Ocean littoral.

The EIC's greatest impact on local economic structures came not in Malaysia but in the northern region of the littoral, in India itself. The company started the British occupation of India and would function as its first colonial government.

Chartered companies in retrospect

The experiences of the VOC and EIC, like those of the chartered companies considered in previous sections, sound the themes of international economic integration and disintegration in several keys. All endeavored to impose some version of international economic integration on their overseas environments. These efforts often caused various sorts of local economic disintegration, which harmed indigenous peoples. Besides exterior imposition, there is internal development. Each company analyzed here underwent its own internal economic integration and eventually its own economic disintegration. The latter may not have been a gradual unraveling, but rather a dissolution of a company caused by charter surrender or revocation.

Chartered companies have rightly received attention from scholars under many valuable rubrics. They were important vehicles for expanding world trade and establishing intercontinental business ties. To the extent that they amassed large numbers of transactions, chartered companies realized economies of scale and could thereby lower transactions costs, which in turn might stimulate commerce. Some chartered companies served as historical antecedents to the multinational corporations that would emerge in the nineteenth and twentieth centuries.[41] Chartered companies were thus among the pioneers of modern international business. How they developed their own managerial hierarchies, developed cost controls and information flows, and operated on the spot are also important topics, but chartered companies deserve another look from the perspectives of economic integration and disintegration.

Merchant Associations: the Hanseatic League

Another type of merchant association is the merchant league. In the later European Middle Ages, after about AD 1000, merchant leagues found conditions ripe for their growth. Trade was quickening in Europe, but this acceleration was occurring in an environment marked by considerable political fragmentation. There were numerous small polities and only a few emerging nation-states, like England and France. The barriers to continental trade were thus formidable: many local moneys, many local tariffs, many local laws, many idiosyncratic judges, and many local thieves. These obstacles, in a climate of otherwise stellar economic opportunities, compelled merchants to band together for self-help. They sought to develop cross-border organizations that could substitute, in key respects, for the absence of national political organization on a large-scale. The merchant league was one such solution. These could cross political borders, involve people from many backgrounds, furnish a forum for standardizing exchange, develop international commercial law, and provide protection and at times diplomatic representation for members. The one merchant league in late medieval Europe that fulfilled all these functions and lasted the longest was the Hanseatic League.[42] This association originated in increasing cooperation among German merchants going back to the 1200s if not before. It received some formal organization in 1367, peaked during the 1400s, but ran into increasing difficulties later in that century.

Hanseatic comes from hansa, whose Gothic root means "company." Hansa can also refer to a guild of merchants. These companies or guilds of merchants became deeply involved in the development and administration of many towns, whose locations ranged all over the northern half of Europe, from England, across Germany, and into the Baltic states and beyond. The towns, sometimes called Hansatowns, were the formal members of the Hanseatic League. But the hansas that fostered the emergence of these towns as commercial centers were the real rocks upon which the Hanseatic League rested.

The Hanseatic League vividly shows how economic integration is both an economic and a political process. The Hanseatic League is a classic case study in political economy, which combines political science and economics. Politics infuses all organizations, not just governments. The merchants who created and sustained the local hansas took their politics beyond those organizations and into the realm of governments, with their participation in the development of the Hansatowns. Hansas and Hansatowns originated in local politics, but they served as stepping stones in the creation of an international organization, the Hanseatic League. All the while, politics promoted commercial interests on a progressively larger stage. Indeed, the Hanseatic League is one of the most important historical antecedents to the continental economic integration that now occupies Europe, as its sphere of influence embraced the northern half of that continent.

The Hanseatic League embodied economic integration on several levels. On the continental level, the league was an alliance of those who pursued common goals in the business arena. Two widely shared objectives were the standardization of exchange forms and the protection of commercial privileges member groups obtained. The league was not a federation. It had no powerful executive, no secretariat, and no court of last resort in Lübeck in northern Germany, which functioned as its headquarters city.

The Hanseatic League exhibited elements of a confederation. It had a governing body, the "Hansetage," which was an assembly of town representatives. The "Hansetage," according to conventional wisdom, did not have regular formal meetings and when it did convene, gatherings were supposedly not well attended. The conventional interpretation is vague. What constitutes regular meetings, especially formal ones, and significant attendance? Whatever the case, the existence of a governing body furnished a framework for ongoing, informal consultations among members. Confederations are governed loosely from their centers; the Hanseatic League certainly fits that description.

To complicate discussion, some scholars consider the term "Hanseatic League" incorrect and insist on referring to the association that may have embraced almost 200 cities and towns as "The Hansa."[43] While perhaps technically more pure, the designation "The Hansa" may be more confusing. There were numerous hansas (small h) of merchants in the Hansatowns, and another Hansa (capital H) presiding over all the towns. The Hansetage, the governing body in Lübeck, was less a close-knit company or guild as the hansas on the local level were and more an overarching assembly. The problem, then, is that the word "hansa" used on different levels of organization has the same general meaning – company or association – but different practical manifestations. So we prefer the term Hanseatic League when discussing the organization as a whole.

Whatever the Hanseatic League was, an organization with such flexible, at times latent structures at the top left many opportunities for local hansas and Hansatowns to pursue their own strategies of economic integration. Some also sought economic disintegration, among their rivals and enemies, their businesses as well as towns. Members of the Hanseatic League did encounter tough competition from other groups and alliances, including the Milan League, Venetian traders, and the Staple.[44]

In this competitive context one should remember the kind of overall economic integration the Hanseatic League itself was seeking. It was not economic integration for everybody, nor for all of northern Europe, but for the hansatowns, their surrounding areas, and the hansa merchants and their allies. The Hansatowns would dot the landscape of northern Europe like so many staging areas of selective economic integration.

Economic integration was selective, because the two goals of standardization and protection can conflict with each other. Standardizing the forms of business transactions can help one's own business, but also that of one's competitors. The late European Middle Ages were a proto-mercantilist world. Trade was sometimes viewed as an adversarial process in which one can only gain at the expense of another: the zero sum game, in more contemporary language. The protection of one's privileges can lead to commercial and then military war. These two types of war are the engines of economic disintegration, not integration.

Let us first consider local strategies of economic integration, then those of disintegration. These all depended on local conditions. The kind of town in which a merchant community found itself was crucial. There were two major types of towns: those formally recognized as Hansatowns; and others, not Hansatowns, but with connections to the League.

The following lists of both kinds of towns are substantial but not necessarily complete. Hansatowns were located in what are now Germany, Norway, Poland, Latvia, and Estonia. German Hansatowns included Lübeck, the headquarters; Hamburg, with Lübeck the League's other founding force; Bremen; Cologne; and Magdeburg. Bergen in Norway was the most northerly Hansatown. Polish Hansatowns featured Danzig, Stettin, Cracow, and Torun. Riga in Latvia and Tallenin in Estonia were more easterly Hansatowns.

Important towns, not recognized as Hansatowns but with ties to the League, fall into two distinct geographic groups. First were those close to what became the League's core in Germany. And second were those situated on the outer perimeters of the League's sphere of influence. Closer to the League's German core were towns in western continental Europe: Amsterdam, Bruges, and Ghent, as well as towns in more northerly locations, Copenhagen in Denmark and Göteberg in Sweden. On the outer perimeters of the League's sphere of influence were, in the west, London, England, and, in the east, Novgorod, Pskov, and Vilna. There were sometimes significant numbers of both kinds of towns in the same region, as in the League's eastern zone, which contained both the Baltic States and far western Russia.

In Hansatowns merchants usually found municipal structures and business cultures that helped them.[45] This was not always the case in towns that had ties to the League but were not official Hansatowns. Every town, whatever its type, has its own story, which deserves to be told. Here we offer a sketch of the London hansa, its own economic integration, and the role it played in the international economic integration that was emerging within the League's sphere of influence.

The London hansa was situated in a town that had links to the League but was not an official Hansatown. This fact greatly influenced the conduct of the London hansa, which was headed by Bruges, itself a non-Hansatown in Belgium. The London hansa was thus a foreign creation with continuing leadership from across the English Channel. The London hansa was a commercial enclave; it became known as the Steelyard, the area along the Thames River where its members lived.[46]

The London hansa, as outsiders, struggled against many obstacles and achieved some victories. By 1350 members had obtained royal protection for themselves. The Steelyard itself received a kind of extra-territoriality, which made the commercial enclave a diplomatic sanctuary as well. Members were able to trade legally wherever they pleased in England, so long as they paid taxes.[47]

The evolution of the London hansa reinforces the proposition that economic integration melds politics and economics. Constructive relations between the London hansa and the English monarchy greatly contributed to the economic integration of the London hansa itself. They also enabled the London hansa to participate more effectively in the international economic integration that was occurring under the League's umbrella.

This cross-border economic integration was propelled by a specialization that foreshadowed a central insight of Adam Smith. In 1776 the founding father of classical political economy wrote that the division of labor is limited by the extent of the market.[48] This axiom means the following. The wider or deeper any market is, the greater is the incentive to subdivide tasks and have people specialize in these separate tasks. A wider market is one that covers more territory; a deeper market is one that is more densely populated in the same location.

The dynamic underlying the axiom is simple. Specialization increases output over a situation in which the same person does everything connected with making a certain product. A wider or deeper market can produce greater demand for a product or service; hence, the need to specialize in order to increase output to meet that rising demand. Adam Smith told the story on the microeconomic level – that of the individual household or factory. But the axiom holds on various macroeconomic levels as well.

Review the experience of the Hanseatic League in the 1200s and beyond. Its cross-border trade, especially in the thirteenth and fourteenth centuries, pivoted on four locations; these "factories" were the initial pillars in an ongoing process of international specialization that added other dimensions later on. The four "factories" were London, Bruges, Bergen, and Novgorod. Each "factory" played a special role in the expansion of Hanseatic commerce. All four were entrepots; they shared the same service specialization.

But within this framework there was developing a product specialization in at least two locations. London concentrated on wool, while Bergen supplied fish. The other two "factories" were less specialized in product transshipment. Bruges was a general entrepot for the Low Countries and Novgorod collected Russian produce. This was a creative pattern of product specialization emerging at different rates in different locations. It also shows that League members were using a mix of transport modes on both land and water, although over time members would specialize more in sea transport.

The forces of economic disintegration surged both outside and inside the Hanseatic League. Members of the League engaged in numerous conflicts with outsiders during its history. The London hansa was no exception. Relations between the Hanseatic League and England soured in the mid-1400s. The British monarchy was weak and unable to continue its protection of the London hansa. English merchants lobbied to have its privileges revoked.

Commercial disputes, as noted, can easily escalate into military conflict in an adversarial trading environment. This scenario proved true: there were detainments of Hanseatic merchants and naval battles on the high seas.[49] The military phase of the Anglo–Hanse war lasted from 1468 into 1474, but political relations still experienced periods of turbulence after the cessation of physical hostilities.

The potential for economic disintegration was always present within the Hanseatic League itself. Its structures and membership created fertile ground for internal conflicts. Remember that this was an association in which most power resided on the municipal level. The League had originated in merchant hansas that were based in towns; many of these hansas became so involved in their towns that these acquired the status of Hansatowns. The towns cherished their municipal liberties and the merchants valued their economic freedoms. And many of these were strong-willed entrepreneurs with a great capacity for taking risks and a commensurate determination to preserve what they had achieved.

The history of the League over its centuries is thus replete with internal squabbles. Some of these were the normal disputes that arise in the everyday conduct of business. But others threatened the coherence of the organization as a continental force. Some of the most dangerous quarrels exposed the deep rifts between the London hansa and the hansas in Germany.[50]

The slow unraveling of the Hanseatic League resulted from a combination of external and internal factors. External forces included shifting trade preferences and patterns, the rise of nation-states, and the emergence of other business forms, like chartered companies. From within, the League faced more destabilization from conflicts among towns. These disputes often featured greater assertions of municipal independence from any kind of central supervision.

The fate of its twin goals – standardization and protection – yields other insights into the eclipse of the Hanseatic League. In its earlier years the League furnished members an efficient way to seek both objectives simultaneously, but the emergence of nation-states created other agencies of international protection. Depending on the effectiveness of its diplomatic service and the strength of its military reach, a nation-state might provide more efficient protection for its nationals or allies than a merchant league could.

One of the League's greatest accomplishments was to promote a standardization of exchange forms. These efforts also nurtured an international commercial law that was in its infancy. But again, as the years went by, other agents and agencies also began to promote standardization and seek uniform commercial laws. Nation-states, to be sure, were more concerned with these matters within their own borders. But other agencies of international business besides the League, like the chartered companies and their predecessors, imparted a thrust to standardization in their cross-border activities.

This writer believes that the League, even in its later years that extended into the early 1600s, remained a potential arbiter of cross-border trade disputes and the most promising European cradle for international commercial law. But by 1600 Europe, especially in England and France, had entered the era of full-blown commercial mercantilism. Nation-states, not leagues, became the dominant players and trade relations were politicized and sometimes militarized to great lengths. The realities of national power politics and, under mercantilism, national power economics would postpone efforts to advance international economic cooperation to a much later day.

3 Religious empires

The next two chapters analyze organizations that are seemingly at the opposite poles of human behavior: religious and criminal empires. An empire results from the activities of a core group that wants to extend its power and influence over other people (see Chapter 1). Many associate empires with evil, but builders of religious empires consider their motives sacrosanct.

In this spirit we spotlight the Roman Catholic Church. There are other religious empires worthy of scrutiny in the context of international economic integration.[1] But the Roman Catholic Church was the first international religion to evolve into a cross-border business that resembles a modern multinational corporation (MNC).

To appreciate the analogies between the Church and the modern multinational corporation one should consider the following definition. A MNC is an international business that has certain structures and procedures. As to structures, it has at least one headquarters that oversees downstream subsidiaries or affiliates, some of which are based in foreign locations. The center directs its subsidiaries through an administrative hierarchy of managers that reaches from the very top to the most local level. These hierarchies, sometimes called managerial hierarchies, are crucial to the articulation of a business over longer distances, particularly overseas.

As to procedures, a MNC tries to ensure that both headquarters and subsidiaries are pursuing coordinated policies. The Roman Catholic Church, as it evolved during the Roman Empire but especially from the European Middle Ages to the present, has acquired and refined those primary characteristics of the modern multinational corporation.

The emergence of the Church as a major international business is, in crucial respects, the story of how it pioneered certain techniques of international economic integration. To tell this tale one must begin with the essentials of the Church's own developing bureaucracy. This bureaucratization integrated the organization or, in the language of our theme, contributed to its internal economic integration. Economic integration within was central to the Church's emergence as a multinational corporation. The following section distills the ABCs of church organization.

The Roman Catholic Church as international business: the ABCs of organization

The headquarters of the Church are located in Vatican City, which is an enclave within the larger city of Rome, Italy, sometimes called *Roma Aeterna*, the Eternal City. Vatican City, from the Lateran accords of 1929 with Italy, received recognition as a national state and thus has diplomatic extra-territoriality.

Here develops the central government of the Roman Catholic Church, which features the Roman Curia, *Curia Romana*, as its secretariat or administrative center. The central government also includes a judiciary, which has two main courts: the Sacred Roman Rota; and the Supreme Court of the Apostolic Signatura. The Sacred Roman Rota is an appeals court; many of its cases deal with applications to have a marriage nullified. The Supreme Court of the Apostolic Signatura has wider duties: the supervision of lower courts within the Church to "ensure the *fair administration of justice*."[2] And in Vatican City resides the Pope, who is the president, the chairman, and chief executive officer of the Roman Catholic Church.

The Curia is a major organization in itself. It contains an array of agencies that assist the Pope in managing the global Church. Today these agencies include the Secretariat of State, congregations, tribunals, Pontifical Councils, Pontifical Commissions, and the Synod of Bishops.[3] There are, for example, the Congregation for the Evangelization of Peoples and the Congregation for the Sacred Doctrine of the Faith. For routine business the Church may have one or more senior operating officers. These are usually cardinals, who are the most senior managers within the ecclesiastical bureaucracy beneath the Pope, who was usually a cardinal before his elevation. On a crucial matter, whatever its purview, the Pope himself would be both chief executive as well as chief operating officer.

The Papacy is, narrowly, the office of the Pope, the Pope himself, and his immediate household and staff. Technically, the Papacy presides over the Curia. But in practice the institutions of Papacy and Curia are so intertwined that it is sometimes difficult to separate them. And that is why together the Papacy, Curia, and other parts of the Vatican state are frequently called the Holy See.

This central bureaucracy has developed a detailed table of organization for the Church as a whole. Key to its operation is an elaborate administrative hierarchy that is managerial, symbolic, ritualistic, and salvific. There is a hierarchy of titles that does not necessarily correspond to levels of territorial responsibility for two reasons. The same person can have several titles. And a higher title does not always mean responsibility for a larger territorial unit within the Church. The hierarchy of titles goes from the Pope at the apex, down through the cardinals, archbishops, bishops, monsignori, and priests without special titles.

There are some indisputable facts about the occupants of this hierarchy. All are male. All are ordained priests in the Church. Archbishops oversee archdioceses, which are larger and more populated than dioceses, over which preside bishops. The parish, in the care of one or more priests, is the key local unit of church organization. And the Pope, while bishop of Rome, is also the head of the universal Church.

But there straightforwardness ceases. A cardinal may also be an archbishop, actually directing an archdiocese. A cardinal, however, may also be a very senior manager in the Roman Curia, but not an operating archbishop, although cardinals in such high executive posts often have titular ties to some archdiocese, diocese, or parish. In fact, parish, diocese, and archdiocese constitute an ascending hierarchy of administrative units, each constituting a larger congregation. There are as well national organizations of bishops, archbishops, and cardinals from their respective home countries. Sometimes these national organizations are said to preside over national churches, like the French church and the church in the United States.

Within the Roman Catholic Church there are numerous other organizations, called religious orders and religious congregations. A religious congregation in this context is not the same as the congregations within the Curia cited above, nor the congregation of the pastor of a parish, although the root meaning – an assemblage of people with a common purpose – is identical. Religious orders and congregations often come into existence because one person, with incredible spiritual energy, decides that a special group is needed to pursue some aspect of the Church's mission in a distinctive way.

An order is more centralized than a congregation. An order has a chain of command that runs upward through the levels of hierarchy: from individual houses, through provinces, to the head or general. A congregation is more decentralized. The local units of that organization possess considerable autonomy, and the head of the entire group may have powers more honorific than substantive.

As with most things in the Church, what is easy to define in theory is more complicated in practice. Consider the Society of Jesus and the Benedictines. Founded by St Ignatius Loyola in 1539, the Society of Jesus (Jesuits) is a religious order.[4] Technically, among religious institutes in the Church, the Society is a mendicant order of clerks regular; that is, a body of priests organized for apostolic work, following a religious rule, and living on alms.[5]

The Jesuits are a religious order in the conventional sense. They have a defined managerial hierarchy, with significant power residing in the person at the top of the order. The Society is divided into provinces throughout the world. Each province may contain secondary schools, colleges, universities, churches, parishes, and other organizations for which Jesuits have responsibility. Each local unit has a superior. Provincials head provinces. A Father General, the person at the top, supervises the entire order.

The Benedictines are a religious order, but not in the conventional sense. St Benedict of Nursia did establish a monastery at Monte Cassino, Italy, about 530, which became the cradle of the Benedictine order. This order is in practice an assemblage of congregations, with no head at the top of the order, and with each congregation exercising almost complete decision-making power. But the Benedictines derive great coherence from the Rule of St Benedict, which is their rock.

It would be wrong to write that each Benedictine congregation is autonomous with respect to the center, because there is no center. The Pope, though, is said to be the ultimate head of the Benedictines, but then he has that role with regard to the Jesuits and every other religious order and congregation in the Church.

These ABCs show how refined the bureaucracy of the Roman Catholic Church has become. This bureaucracy greatly promoted the internal economic integration of the Church. There is a crucial interplay between internal and international economic integration in the history of the Roman Catholic Church. The internal economic integration of the Church increasingly had an international dimension as the Church became more global. Its techniques of international economic integration thus have strong connections with the internationalization of its own bureaucracy.

The Roman Catholic Church and international economic integration: the Roman and medieval years

These techniques of international economic integration reach back to the early centuries of the Church, which was founded in the early AD 30s by Jesus Christ with Peter as the first Pope and bishop of Rome (*Tu es Petrus, et super hanc petram aedificabo ecclesiam meam*). To appreciate the head start the Church had in developing techniques of international economic integration one must recall its relationships with the Roman Empire.

The Church took root in the soil of that empire. It was fiercely persecuted by that organization and remained an underground organization in the catacombs until the Emperor Constantine "converted" to Christianity in the early AD 300s and made it the official religion of the Roman Empire.

The Roman Empire faced a mounting array of problems in its later years. These included over-extension, penetrating incursions from hostile military forces, a decline of civic spirit and public participation among many of its more able citizens, a crumbling infrastructure of roads and aqueducts, and a great weakening of the will to have an empire. The disintegration of the Roman Empire in the west, which acquired momentum in the 300s and accelerated during the 400s, left the Roman Catholic Church as the only major international organization standing in many parts of Europe.

The boost the Emperor Constantine gave the Church as an evangelical organization is well known, even though he manipulated its structures for his own imperial purposes. Not so appreciated is how the Roman Empire, in its unraveling in the west, contributed to the emergence of the Church as an international business that would develop expertise in the techniques of international economic integration. The Empire in the west never vanished completely. It broke up into its parts, many of which were towns that had served as administrative and military centers and so had given the Empire an organizational coherence. Many of these towns also became ecclesiastical posts, as the Church was able to develop more freely its own organization above ground after Constantine stopped its persecution. The Church, in other words, piggybacked its own expanding cross-border presence on the urban infrastructure created and for so long maintained by the Empire. This ecclesiastical infrastructure, for the most part, survived the collapse of the Roman Empire in the west and provided the foundation for the further penetration of the Church throughout Europe. It also gave the Church sufficient if embryonic strength as an international organization to develop some techniques of cross-border economic integration.

From the Church's perspective, the "Dark Ages" were not so gloomy after all. This term designates the times after the Roman Empire in the west disintegrated. They begin about AD 476, the official date for the fall of the western empire, and sometimes extend to about AD 1000, when Europe underwent a major economic revitalization. The "Dark Ages" refer to the breakdown of central civil authority, with the capacity to enforce law and order, and a concomitant decline in personal security, caused by an increase in lawless behavior. The "darkest times," from this perspective, were the latter fifth, all of the sixth and seventh, and much of the eighth centuries.

The days become "less dark" in both political and economic senses as one gets closer to the second millennium AD. The organizing work of Charlemagne in politics, which bridged the eighth and ninth centuries, did cast a vast light. And the gathering agricultural revolution of the 900s and beyond was laying the foundation for a significant increase in the food supply. There was also a surge in intra-European trade after AD 1000, which contributed to the emergence of new cities and the rejuvenation of some that were older. This urbanization, the trade-based expansion in Europe from about AD 1000 into the centuries beyond, captures the greatest attention in conventional accounts of economic developments in medieval Europe.

The other major urban story for international economic history has been insufficiently reported. It concerns the strengthening by the Roman Catholic Church throughout the "darkest ages" of an urban infrastructure that would serve as a springboard for its own ventures into international economic integration. The towns in this network were also "patches of light in a vast gloom" in ways not adequately acknowledged. Besides their roles in evangelism and in preserving the urban lineaments of western civilization, they constituted a framework that gave the Church a head start in developing and deploying its own techniques of international economic integration.

These techniques started with what all organizations need most: money. It was in the movement and management of money across international frontiers that the Roman Catholic Church gained its first major area of expertise in international economic integration. The Church relied upon its own developing international organization, including the dioceses that were headquartered in those towns and cities, and the monasteries that also contributed to the preservation of writing during those "darker times." The Church did not act alone in these matters. It formed relationships with people and institutions, such as the Medici Bank, that could help it.

The needs for the Church to develop its own expertise in money, and to establish connections with outside specialists in this area, were most pressing in medieval times. There were many political entities to cultivate, many international borders to cross, and many local moneys to fathom. Some have remarked that, throughout history, four of the most difficult subjects to learn have been Egyptian land law, the Internal Revenue Code of the United States government, medieval European weights and measures, and medieval European moneys.

It was not only the multiplicity of those moneys, but also the lack of standardization among them that proved so daunting. The members of the Hanseatic League were driven to cooperate across international borders by the lack of standardization in commercial transactions. The Roman Catholic Church was compelled to develop expertise in medieval European moneys, because these would constitute its operating capital. This "cash" had to "flow" through a maze of numerous coins from throughout Europe whose extrinsic and intrinsic values varied greatly.

The Church, like any organization with great plans for expansion, needed a lot of money. It could get this money from a number of sources and in different ways. The most cost-efficient way is to get it from one's members; they do not charge interest or assess other transactions costs. For religious organizations the most dedicated contributors are their faithful, the actual or prospective members of their own churches. Fund-raising today has become more enveloping, as technology makes the process more persuasive, in a visual sense, and more continuous, in a relentless manner.

But the Church in those earlier times had its own forms of persuasion. As far as contributions from the faithful were concerned, the Church took no chances. It imposed levies or taxes on the faithful and some of their own organizations, like the monasteries. Indeed, the spiritualization of taxation is one of the Church's most important innovations in ecclesiastical finance. So besides the donor's gift, there was the faithful's tax: both were cost-efficient ways to get revenue.

The Roman Catholic Church early on developed a sophisticated strategy of fund-raising that reflected its international nature, was tailored to both the means and spiritual predilections of its followers, and was refined to meet changing financial demands. The Church pioneered both regular and special collections. Regular collections, often at weekly Mass, go for local needs, such as maintenance of parish buildings and personnel. Special collections may involve a construction project or an overseas mission. They may be connected with a parish religious exercise that extends over days, like a triduum (three days of special prayers) or a novena (nine days of special prayers).

The revenue profile of the medieval Church contained many categories. These included donations, land rents, moneys obtained from the monastic production and marketing of agricultural produce, fees charged for judicial services, and proceeds from the sale of indulgences.[6] Let us reflect briefly on each category in turn. Two important types of donations were bequests and tithes. A bequest was a transfer of assets to the Church, usually upon one's death. A tithe was a regular donation of a portion of one's income to the Church while one was still living. The Church was a major landowner: the Pope ruled the Papal States in Italy; bishops were often large landowners themselves; and the monasteries controlled vast tracts of land. Landowning, with a significant amount devoted to agriculture, explains the importance of the categories of land rents and moneys received from the monastic production and marketing of agricultural produce.

The Church was developing a court structure that matched its international reach. These ecclesiastical courts enforced agreements within the Church that sometimes required the payment of fees to the Vatican. But they also performed functions sometimes associated with secular courts, especially during the earlier Middle Ages, when civil authority on a large scale was in disarray. Hence, fees charged for judicial services played an important role in the finances of the medieval Church.

Last but not least in the revenue profile of the medieval Church is the portentous category of proceeds from the sale of indulgences. An indulgence forgives part of the time one would otherwise have to spend in Purgatory. In Roman Catholic theology Purgatory is a spiritual halfway house, where one must undergo purification before one can enter heaven. One obtains an indulgence for some constructive act, like reciting a prayer, attending a religious service, or performing the corporal works of mercy, which includes visiting the sick. Selling indulgences destroys their spiritual underpinnings.

This category of indulgence revenue was a slow-release poison into the bloodstream of the Church itself. The sale of indulgences would become so rampant and corrupt in late medieval and early modern times that these practices would contribute to the Reformation in the 1500s, which tore apart the Roman Catholic Church. So the sophisticated fund-raising strategy the Church developed contained one technique that got out of hand.

But for the less turbulent medieval moment, the revenue the Church obtained from all these sources was substantial. There is no doubt the

Church had healthy cash flow, and some even believe that the Church "controlled most of the liquid capital in the West."[7] The zealous pursuit of money so disturbed some critics of the Church that the following Latin acronym found increasing favor among them. *Radix Omnium Malorum Avaritia* forms the acronym *Roma* or Rome. Its English translation is the root (*radix*) of all evil (*malorum*) is greed (*avaritia*).

One special collection in medieval times that deserves mention was called Peter's pence. It began as a tax of one penny (pence) levied on every Christian. Ingeniously named, with an alliterative crispness and simplicity that might even find favor in contemporary advertising circles, Peter's pence was a special collection to benefit the Papacy (Peter's). This collection was part of the Church's comprehensive approach to fund-raising. It also promoted international economic integration.

This revenue strategy did not omit any of the Church's key parts. The combination of regular and special collections was targeted at a mix of local, national, and international needs. Peter's pence served the international component of that strategy: to support the central symbol of the universal nature of the Church, which is the Papacy.

Peter's pence was a standardized collection that yielded diverse coins, in large amounts, from all over Christendom. The exact amount derived from this collection over the years, as well as from other sources of church revenue, is not quantifiable, because the Church did not fully disclose its wealth and income, a practice that is now a tradition. It was in the movement and management of all the money coming to the Vatican that the Church discovered how a time-honored financial technique could be linked to its international fund-raising.

That technique is arbitrage. Its essence is to take advantage of price differentials for the same asset in different markets. The asset may be money, a commodity, stocks, bonds, or other financial instruments. A simple example is the traveler abroad who seeks the best exchange rate for currency. That person may have to learn the hard way that a better deal is available from a downtown bank than from a branch of that same bank in an airport or train station. The medieval Church did not invent arbitrage. But the Church, in consort with its bankers, internationalized this principle as it applied to money in a manner never accomplished before.

Such an elaborate configuration of revenue and so creative a vision for its maximization required a bureaucracy with structures and skills proportionate to the tasks at hand. For the latter Middle Ages, beginning in the late 1100s, the nerve center of revenue collection for the Papacy was the apostolic *camera* (from the Latin meaning "vault" or "vaulted room"). The *camera* was a bank, a treasury, and a court of law. It became a triple bureaucracy in itself, with growing numbers of civil and religious servants in such fields as tax collection, record keeping, and litigation. As a court it had two ways of enforcing its decisions: excommunication from the Church and imprisonment.[8]

The apostolic *camera* deployed its own chain of command. This featured some people already in the ecclesiastical hierarchy but also integrated some outsiders and their activities. Downstream from the *camera* were its regional and local fiscal agents; these were the papal nuncios and legates.[9]

The terms nuncio and legate today refer to posts in the Vatican diplomatic corps, but in medieval times nuncios and legates also played major roles in tax collection. Usually ordained priests who often had a higher ecclesiastical rank, they transferred revenues to the Papacy through an associated network composed of cameral merchants or bankers. These merchants and bankers were the outsiders the Church involved in its finances in strategic ways; hence, the term *cameral* merchant or banker, which signifies the closeness of the relationship. The Medici, through their bank, were foremost among the cameral or papal bankers in the late medieval era.[10] The Medici Bank, which lasted from 1397 to 1494, extended credit to the *camera* by granting it overdraft privileges. The Medici Bank, and the other cameral banks, also performed crucial arbitrage functions for the Papacy that supported the Church's role in international economic integration.

The transfer of revenue to the Vatican was not necessarily a delivery of the original moneys as collected in some foreign location. These transfers were "often in specie."[11] But specie is generic: it refers to minted coins with gold and silver metallic content (or intrinsic value). With the multiplicity of medieval moneys, there were numerous coins that qualified as specie, though their intrinsic values differed greatly. No wonder that perhaps the greatest growth industry for enterprising financiers in the medieval and early modern eras was currency arbitrage.

There was no unified market for money standing on its own in medieval Europe. The political fragmentation of that time was matched by excessive monetary localism. There were many local markets for money, with different exchange rates for the same coin. These conditions provided many opportunities for sophisticated currency arbitrage both in transit and once in Vatican City itself.

In an environment of market fragmentation there is an even greater premium placed on detailed local knowledge. But it required a cross-border organization helped by monetary specialists to transform disarray into benefit. The Roman Catholic Church and its cameral bankers accomplished this feat and, in so doing, may be said to have created their own European money market: a significant feat of international economic integration for its time.

Cross-border money management anchored in its own expanding urban infrastructure created this market. This stewardship employed arbitrage to increase the already considerable revenue coming to the Vatican. Just as the Church had used the urban infrastructure of the Roman Empire as its springboard, so also the Medici Bank built on its connections with the Church to become a major European financial force.

Relations between Church and Bank were mutually productive. The Medici Bank, headquartered in Florence, established branches in other major European cities, including Rome, Venice, Naples, Milan, Pisa, Geneva, Lyons, Basel, Avignon, Bruges, and London.[12] These urban branches enabled the Medici to function more efficiently as papal *arbitrageurs*, because their network contained more fixed locations wherein one could capitalize on differences in exchange rates.

The creation of a money market by the Papacy and its bankers, which was primarily for their own benefit, produced destabilizing side effects for others, which exemplify international economic disintegration. These monetary movements removed considerable amounts of specie from many locations in Europe. This drain caused a perceived shortage of specie. Many people concluded that their own national balance of payments was hemorrhaging as much needed specie left their country. Scholars still debate how serious, in actuality, the specie shortage was in different parts of Europe during the late medieval era, a controversy this author acknowledges but cannot resolve.[13]

There are certain monetary facts about the times that are, however, indisputable. Emerging national governments were not strong enough to impart total credibility to the extrinsic value of their currencies. This meant that the intrinsic value of a currency was still more crucial than its extrinsic value. Declining bullion (gold bars) and specie reserves in a country could, therefore, swiftly imperil the integrity and stability of its own money supply, control over which was then viewed as central to national sovereignty. The "specie shortage" controversy is not, then, a matter just for economics or history, but for political economy, because specie was in that era both a political and an economic commodity in an inseparable fashion.

There were widespread shortages of money in Europe even without all that money going to the Papacy. But those transfers certainly aggravated existing problems, caused new strains, and contributed to a huge problem in public relations for the Papacy. The monetary extractions were very unpopular. Indeed, they are analogous to an excessive expatriation of profits by a multinational corporation from a foreign country it was treating like an economic colony. Unrestrained papal siphoning of local moneys can thus be viewed as evidence of an economic imperialism, this time practiced by a spiritual power that was also pursuing its own secular agenda. Hostile reactions to papal monetary movements surged both in England and on the European continent. In 1366, King Edward III of England prohibited the collection of Peter's pence and forbade the transfer overseas of revenues obtained in this manner. In 1381, it was suggested at a monetary conference in London that papal revenues be transferred abroad in the form of English products, not specie, in order to save English specie. Other concerns about papal transfers of money from England recur in 1376, 1384, 1399, 1409, and 1433.[14]

In France, there was also considerable anger directed at the Papacy for its vigorous pursuit of French money. This frustration remained at a high level during the Church's "times of trouble," which had two phases. The first was the Babylonian captivity, from 1309–77, when the Papacy was resident in France itself, in Avignon. The second was the great western schism, from 1377–1409, when there were two rival popes, one in Avignon, the other in Rome, each pontificating over part of the Church.

French displeasure intensified after the schism within the Church was resolved and the Papacy returned to Rome. "Where we have records," Harry Miskimin observes, "it would seem that such concern [in England and France] was justified." Combining his research with that of Jean Favier on the Avignon papacy, Miskimin concludes that the annual amount of specie in gold that went to the Avignon papacy represented "more than one-third the total annual gold coinage of France during the same period."[15]

The specie drain associated with the papal or cameral money market harmed national money supplies. Money became even scarcer in many locations, as the repatriation of specie and sometimes bullion reduced the supply of intrinsic value that was then so crucial to developing the credibility of a national money supply and the popular confidence that monetary integrity inspires.

The Roman Catholic Church launched a frontal attack on exchange by promulgating its famous usury doctrine. Usury concerns the charging of interest on loans. Today usury usually refers to excessive interest, but for the Church usury meant any interest. The Church prohibited lenders from assessing any interest at all on their loans. The origins and evolution of the usury proscription have been ably tracked elsewhere.[16]

The consequences of this doctrine, however, deserve reconsideration here in the context of economic integration. Though its complete enforcement was never practicable, the usury doctrine constituted a kind of moral suasion that had the central consequence of deflecting and channeling entrepreneurial energies in creative directions. These new avenues produced innovations and refinements in financial technique and organization that had an enormous positive impact on economic integration, both nationally and cross-border.

A principal area of dynamic change involved credit and its mechanisms. The usury doctrine, as a product of canon or church law, emphasized formal interest, the costs of borrowing explicitly stated. To bypass the usury doctrine, financiers had to deal with those costs in informal or implicit ways. One result was a new credit instrument: the bill of exchange, sometimes called the letter of credit. The bill of exchange dealt with interest so informally, in fact, that the entire loan, including the costs of borrowing, was embedded in an exchange transaction. Interest was concealed, though its presence was well known.

The design of this medieval version of "creative financing" was necessary to win the approval of most theologians. Canon law distinguished an exchange transaction (*cambium per litteras*) from a loan (*cambium non est mutuum*). It further stipulated that an exchange transaction might be either the commutation (exchange or substitution) of moneys (*permutatio*) or the buying and selling of foreign currency (*emptio venditio*).[17] An exchange transaction accomplished through a bill of exchange was canonically permissible. So if a loan were embedded in a *cambium per litteras* and not standing by itself, it would be legitimized. The argument and the instrument both worked. The nature of the solution had a great impact on the development of European financial institutions, especially banks. "The practical consequence," Raymond de Roover observed, "was to tie banking to exchange, be it manual exchange or exchange by bills."[18]

The bill of exchange was an early instrument of international economic integration *par excellence*. It facilitated cross-border exchange. Indeed, its workings take advantage of floating exchange rates for different currencies. These fluctuations give participants in a bill of exchange the opportunity to disguise the interest on a loan that is wrapped inside a foreign currency transaction. A bill of exchange required the holder, who became the debtor, to pay back the bill at some future time in another location in a foreign currency. In practice, bills of exchange could become complicated, as the following example illustrates.

[on the front of the bill] 20 July in Venice
[Ducats] 500
Pay at usuance to G. Canigiani 500 ducats in sterling
47 per ducats by Medici & Company.
Signed Bartolomew Zorzi & I. Michiel
[on the back of the bill] F. Giorgio and Petro Morozino

Professor Gilchrist explains this bill of exchange as follows.

> In Venice the Medici Company lend Zorzi & Michiel 500 ducats. This sum must be repaid in London in sterling at the rate of 47 pence per ducat, i. e. 97 pounds, 18 shillings, and 4 pence at usuance. Usuance (the period allowed for movement of bills between cities) was three months for Venice to London. Therefore repayment will be 20 October. Giorgio and Morozino will repay the money to Canigiani. In practice, the bill is protested and therefore sent back to the place of issuance to be repaid by the borrower. Canigiani rewrites the bill for 97 pounds, 18 shillings, and 4 pence plus his fee of 4 shillings. On 20 October the rate of exchange is 44 pence to the ducat. The return bill is 535 ducats again payable at usuance of three months. Therefore on 20 January the Medici Company can collect 535 ducats from Zorzi & Michiel. This gives a per annum rate of interest of 14 per cent.[19]

Let us analyze Professor Gilchrist's description. Between 20 July and 20 October the pound sterling had strengthened against the ducat; fewer pence were needed to purchase one ducat. Rewriting the bill in sterling, as Canigiani did, gave him, as a representative of the Medici Company, the opportunity to capitalize on an appreciating pound in relation to the ducat. Exchanging back from pounds to ducats meant more ducats. In this case the debtor had to pay back more than the original sum of 500 ducats, 535 in fact.

This example is presented in detail to show exactly how interest could be "concealed" in an exchange transaction. A favorable movement of exchange rates for the creditor allowed positive interest to be realized. A movement of exchange rates in the other direction, if sufficient, could have produced zero and even negative interest on the transaction. Wrapping a loan in a bill of exchange, then, did not guarantee that a positive rate of interest would be realized, but only created the opportunity that this might happen. Embedding loans in bills of exchange made even more valuable the services of specialists with knowledge of local currency markets. They might have a better chance of structuring bills of exchange based on their hunches as to possible favorable movements in exchange rates for foreign currencies.

The bill of exchange was a crucial innovation in finance that deserves appreciation as a pivotal instrument of international economic integration. It spread as a counter-response to the Roman Catholic Church's efforts to influence exchange by outlawing formal interest. In the area of credit, then, the Church had a positive impact by stimulating the appearance of a major cross-border credit instrument. This effect was unintentional, of course. Two great consequences for the European money supply are thus associated with the Roman Catholic Church in the Middle Ages – the bill of exchange and specie drains.

But they had strikingly opposite effects. Papal revenue movements reduced the specie component of national money supplies. The bill of exchange, by making credit more available, increased the broader money supply: one that included credit instruments in addition to the "harder" components of specie and bullion. The bill of exchange, in addition, provided a way for banks to recover their costs of borrowing and so contributed to the solvency and growth of those institutions. The Church, in sum, was responsible for a drain and a boost. It "took" from money supplies with papal revenues but "gave" by its role in stimulating new credit instruments. Raymond de Roover's earlier analysis of the impact of wrapping loans in exchange transactions can be related to our central theme. "The practical consequence was to tie banking to exchange..." with these further implications for intentional economic integration. The new credit instruments, such as the bill of exchange, promoted the development of a cross-border financial infrastructure, which featured banks in directing roles.

The "drain" and the "boost" in relation to the European money supply by no means constitute the totality of ecclesiastical involvement in medieval economic and business life. The Church promulgated other doctrines, such as that of the just price, which influenced economic thinking.[20] It engaged in other activities, such as the Crusades, that had a major economic impact.[21] We have concentrated on monetary matters, because money is one of our sub themes, and we can clearly connect the monetary "drain" and "boost" to our central theme of economic integration.

Scholarly consideration of the impact of the Roman Catholic Church on economy and business in the Middle Ages has moved through at least two major phases.[22] The first is associated with Max Weber, the noted scholar of bureaucracy, who opined that the Church had a negative impact on such activity. The Weberian approach was followed by the Schumpeterian view, after the influential analyst of economic development, economic thought, and business cycles. Joseph Schumpeter argued that the Church had a positive impact on medieval economy and business. The Schumpeterian position acknowledges the analysis of medieval economic change outlined earlier, which features significant economic growth accelerating after AD 1000.

The jury is still out on the question of ecclesiastical impact in the Middle Ages. The portrait of Church involvement, while more life-like than it was decades ago, needs even more refined and complex strokes. As far as monetary matters are concerned, the "drain" (Weberian) and the "boost" (Schumpeterian) may largely cancel each other out and the net effect of Church activity in this domain may prove neutral.

The Church and modern economic integration: the Vatican Bank

The Church's relations with outside bankers during the medieval era, like the Medicis, were among its strongest pillars of financial strength. Brought inside as cameral bankers, they furnished the expertise in cross-border money management that greatly assisted the developing church bureaucracy. Their adeptness at arbitrage increased church revenues. And their creativity in pioneering new financial instruments, like the bill of exchange, facilitated international exchange, helped themselves and supported the Church. A stronger financial infrastructure of banks benefitted the Church, because the Church still relied on their financial acumen and influence.

Through the years the Roman Catholic Church continued to exhibit a common characteristic of corporate evolution. As corporations develop, many seek an integration of structures. This integration can be either vertical or horizontal and is part of the internal economic integration of the business itself. A corporation pursues vertical integration, when it tries to bring in-house all major functions associated with its operations. A corporation engaged in vertical integration tries to own and control, for instance, its own sources of supply and networks of distribution. The more complete the ownership and control over its entire economic process, the more vertically integrated the corporation is. A corporation involved in horizontal integration attempts to acquire or merge with outside businesses pursuing one of its activities. Horizontal integration can also occur when separate businesses performing the same part of an economic process, like manufacturing a common product, come together.

The analogues between structural integration in the secular and sacred worlds of business abound. Roman Catholicism is an evangelical religion that actively seeks converts. Conversion is a horizontal integration of outsiders following another religion or none at all into the body of the Roman Catholic faithful. Vertical integration marks the growth and development of the church bureaucracy, as it seeks direct control over all matters deemed pertinent to its mission.

A classic case of vertical integration, with implications for economic integration, occurred in relations between the Church, banks, and bankers. From the days of the apostolic *camera* in the Middle Ages, the Church has always had some banking activities in-house. The *camera* itself, readers will recall, was a bank, a treasury, and a court. And the *camera* had its own cameral bankers, outside banks given a special in-house role.

Besides structural integration, the history of corporate evolution reveals a second major theme that characterizes the Church. This is specialization of function. Division of labor, a companion concept, permits this specialization. Division of labor and specialization are well-known principles from classical political economy, but they also apply to the study of bureaucracy. Adam Smith, the father of classical political economy, wrote in his *Wealth of Nations* that "division of labour is limited by the extent of the market."[23] Transposing this axiom into organizations, one observes that the greater the extent of a bureaucracy's "market," the more division of function is possible, which means more specialization.

The key phrase here is bureaucracy's "market." This market can be internal or external: the organization itself or the outside consumers it services. The expansion of bureaucracy creates a larger internal bureaucratic "market," which facilitates a greater division of labor with its concomitant specialization of function.

This expansion can result from a widening (in a horizontal sense) or deepening (in a vertical sense) of the bureaucracy's external market. A market widening is geographical; it occurs when a market covers more territory. A market deepening is demographic; it results from greater consumer penetration of the same geographical area. The expansion of bureaucracy need not only be linked to its external market. Bureaucrats themselves, for many reasons, can decide to increase the size of their organizations. Whatever the triggering forces, the outcome is identical: functions divide, titles multiply, and jobs and their descriptions proliferate.

This is the dreary dynamic of bureaucracy, a process that may stop only when resources run out or the bureaucracy hits its own version of the immovable force, like a reformist leader with great personal strength and political support.

Vertical integration and the bureaucratic versions of those economic principles greatly illuminate the evolution of ecclesiastical bureaucracy. The entire history of church administration could be recast in this framework, but our concern here focuses on the Church's relations with banks and bankers, because these pertain to economic integration. Vertical integration is allied with centralization, and the decentralization which characterized the Church's ties with banks and bankers in the medieval and early modern eras yielded to a vertical integration that centralized more banking functions in-house. The culmination of this process was the founding in 1887 of the *Instituto per le Opere di Religione*, the Institute for the Works of Religion, sometimes called IOR from its Italian acronym. The IOR is also known as the Vatican Bank. Let us first discuss the circumstances surrounding its establishment, from perspectives both remote and proximate.

An organization sometimes resorts to vertical integration for defensive reasons. The Church had long ago lost the primacy in people's lives it enjoyed in the Middle Ages. The Reformation (1500s) shattered its unity and reduced its influence. The Counter-Reformation, which followed the Reformation, energized the remaining faithful but did not reclaim many of those who had departed to the multiplying Protestant sects. Both the yield and efficiency of the revenue network the Church deployed during the late medieval period, which included tax and rent collectors all over Europe, declined substantially during the 1500s and 1600s. The indulgence scandals that were among the causes of the Reformation reduced church revenue. Rising hostility to the Church in many European locations destroyed key parts of that collecting network and so greatly impaired revenue efficiency.

The status of the Church as a temporal or secular power, which some say began to decline after the Papacy of Innocent III (1198–1216), remained intact, albeit at diminished levels, as long as the Pope retained control of the Papal States in Italy. These were areas that comprised a large district in central Italy, which the popes ruled as a temporal domain beginning in AD 755; but they were lost in the early 1860s, in connection with the struggles that resulted in the unification of Italy, which took place in the 1860s and early 1870s. The loss of the Papal States effectively ended the status of the Church as a credible temporal power, which was not really essential for its evangelical mission anyway. A far more ominous consequence for the Church was losing the revenue from the Papal States. The Church could flourish without being a temporal power, but it could not long survive without enough money.

The latter half of the nineteenth century was not a benign time for the Roman Catholic Church. Besides losing the Papal States and suffering an irrecoverable blow to its temporal power, the Church confronted increasing attacks on its teachings. The forces of rampant secularism, in whose vanguard was ethical relativism, were assaulting the immutability of Catholic values and so endeavoring to weaken the Church as a spiritual power.

Facing fierce onslaughts both temporal and spiritual, the Church pursued a strategy that contained both offensive and defensive elements. Offensive components featured an initiative to reinforce the position of the Pope as the Church's prime teacher. The doctrine of papal infallibility, which emerged from the First Vatican Council in the early 1870s, explicitly states that primacy.

Defensive aspects of that strategy included the further centralization of banking activities in-house with the founding of the Vatican Bank. Its establishment in 1887 was a response to the need for an organization to manage the Church's finances after the fall of the Papal States.[24] But the nature of the bank, as an in-house organization that seemed to be a "full service" bank in terms of it times, is related to the long-term process of vertical integration of ecclesiastical banking activities. The hostile forces besieging the Church in the latter nineteenth century accelerated this trend.

There is a timeless lesson here for all organizations. When in crisis, bring inside what is essential: the better to protect and control what you need to survive. The founding of the Vatican Bank is a classic illustration of vertical integration implemented for defensive purposes. And this was a vertical integration that embodied the highest centralization, because the Vatican Bank is really the Pope's bank: he, in effect, owns and controls it.

A defensive element in any strategy can lay the foundation for an offensive thrust. No longer a credible temporal power after losing the Papal States, the Church still remained an important organization with a global reach. But it needed permanent financial power in-house to strengthen its institutional independence from foreign powers and external financial interests. The Vatican Bank enabled the Church to go on the offensive, as it were, and strive to maintain and increase that independence. This self-reliance was especially important to the Church during the Fascist era in Italy, which lasted from the early 1920s through most of World War II.

The Vatican Bank has not had an altogether exemplary history. Its special status as the Pope's bank could be used for good or ill. The Vatican Bank always provided financial services to people and groups with direct institutional links to the Vatican, such as religious orders, dioceses, Vatican agencies, Catholic charities, and other church organizations. But its constituencies became too extensive over the years, as "numerous lay Italians friendly with the church also used its facilities."[25] Therein lay the source of dangerous problems that would become more publicized in the 1980s. The Bank was acting appropriately in furnishing financial assistance to its institutional constituents. It comported itself recklessly when it got involved with outsiders, even when their connections to the Church were based on the intangible attributes of "friendship" and "good will." Though perhaps innocent and tangential at the outset, these extra-institutional relations were the pathways to financial imprudence and tarnished reputations.

The murkiness of these ties provided the shady, wet soil in which damaging rumors easily germinated. The Bank, it was alleged, helped wealthy Italians avoid taxes and pay bribes; it also supposedly laundered money for the Mafia. The evidence supporting these charges is largely anecdotal. It is even cinematic, as the third and last movie about the Corleone crime family, *Godfather III*, took note of the Vatican Bank and the diverse clients it served. Stories linking the bank to organized crime, even when false, are impossible to refute in the court of public opinion. No matter what the facts are, the mystique of the Mafia guarantees that the allegations will have an eternal life in conspiracy lore.

The single most damaging episode to the reputation of the Vatican Bank came from its tangled involvement with the Banco Ambrosiano, a major Italian bank that collapsed in 1982. This fiasco revealed yet another case in which the Vatican Bank had over-extended its mission. Continuing poor financial judgment compounded the perils of over-extension. Two key actors in this financial morality play were Archbishop Paul Marcinkus and Roberto Calvi. Marcinkus headed the Vatican Bank; Calvi, the Banco Ambrosiano. The crucial snare was set when Marcinkus supposedly gave Calvi so-called letters of patronage; these proclaimed that the Vatican Bank supported Calvi's activities in regard to the Banco Ambrosiano. Marcinkus apparently believed that he had protected the Bank, because Calvi was allegedly required to give Marcinkus a letter "freeing the IOR [Vatican Bank] of any responsibility."[26] Letters, those of patronage and one of absolution, were thus central documents in this drama.

The letters of patronage had, it seems, a wider circulation. Calvi's creditors, it has been asserted, never received a copy of the letter that arguably freed the Vatican Bank of any responsibility. An outside observer might rightly ask, what exactly does "backing" mean without the "backer" accepting any "responsibility" for extending support or accepting its consequences? Backing without any assumption of responsibility satirizes proper financial methods, but this may have been standard operating procedure in Italian banking, some of whose practices at the time have been described as "shady."[27]

This imbroglio has another source, and it resides in the background of Archbishop Marcinkus. He had no training in banking or international finance. This incredible omission may astonish some readers. But there is a long history, in both sacred and secular domains, of elevating bureaucrats to posts for which they are unsuited. They may lack knowledge, experience, judgment, sometimes all of these, or just prove straightaway incompetent.

The Ambrosiano matter was both an embarrassment and a wake-up call. In 1984 the Vatican, while denying any wrongdoing, paid out $244 million to the creditors of the Banco Ambrosiano in return for their dropping any future claims against it. And, clearly, the Vatican Bank had run aground, not financially, because it even made money during the long tenure of Marcinkus (1971–89). But the Bank had crashed procedurally, and this was painful for a Church bureaucracy that was supposedly expert in proper administrative procedures. What lessons, then, did the Church learn from the Ambrosiano matter? And are there any lessons that the Church overlooked?

The Church recognized the need for major changes in the Vatican Bank. A series of reforms initiated in 1989 included the establishment of a supervisory council of five financial experts to oversee the Bank and appoint its first lay director general.[28] The director general supposedly runs the bank, with light to moderate oversight from the supervisory council.

These two reforms – the supervisory council and the lay director general – deserve further comment. Appointing a full-time head that is not "in holy orders" and has extensive banking experience is a major improvement. Archbishop Marcinkus was not only financially unsophisticated; he was also overworked. He held two other "full-time" jobs as head of Vatican City and organizer of Pope John Paul II's foreign trips.

While the full-time lay director general is a sound move, one is not so confident about this particular supervisory council, its mandate, and procedures. Here is why. A commission of five cardinals designated by the Pope appoints the members of the supervisory council. The council is empowered to supervise the activities of the bank, but the commission is responsible for ensuring that the bank obeys its statutes.[29]

This is a version of dual control, which historically has been a recipe for problems. In this case, the mandates of the commission and council overlap. Ensuring compliance with bank statutes – the task of the commission – is a type of supervision. And it is hard to imagine how the council could supervise without cognizance of bank statutes. Where does dual control leave the lay director general? Unfortunately, with two managerial masters, arranged hierarchically above him or her but with overlapping, direct responsibilities on the operational level.

This arrangement violates the managerial commandments of streamlined missions and procedures. The Church started down the right path with the establishment of a supervisory council and appointment of an expert director, but then relapsed into the fallacy that more hierarchy and dual control would mean better management. A commission of cardinals could still appoint the members of the supervisory council, but the functions of direct supervision should be consolidated in that council.

To its credit, the Church is still trying, according to its best lights, to strengthen the Vatican Bank. In 1994 the bank underwent its first outside audit, conducted by Price Waterhouse. One knows neither the results of this exercise nor whether it will become an annual practice, which it should. The bank is striving to introduce, in today's parlance, more "transparency" in its operations. It is sharing its records, for example, with authorities investigating allegations of illegal activities associated with the bank.

The Vatican Bank, then, has played a central role in the modern economic integration – both internal and international – sought by the Roman Catholic Church. It represents a greater vertical integration of ecclesiastical banking activities in-house and so strengthens the internal economic integration of the Church. As an active agency it promotes the kinds of international economic integration the Church desires. The mission of the Church can conflict with the foreign policies of secular powers, and here the ability of the Vatican Bank to coordinate and direct global flows of liquid capital is relevant. These worldwide channels are themselves types of international economic integration that sometimes transcend or circumvent national laws. A most pointed example of an ecclesiastical override concerns the economic embargo the United States has maintained for over four decades against Cuba. The Vatican opposes this embargo on religious and ethical grounds, and so the Vatican Bank serves as a conduit for funds from the United States destined for Cuba. This procedure effectively circumvents US law.

While the Vatican Bank deals with international flows of capital, there are other forms of global exchange that present major opportunities for the Church to develop new types of economic integration both internally and internationally. As was the bill of exchange in late medieval and early modern times, so is the Internet an instrument of economic integration *par excellence* now and for the foreseeable future.

The Internet is an entry ramp to the World Wide Web, but it contains countless other inter-connected networks that are not part of the Web. Both Internet and Web are vast inter-related galaxies that are growing very rapidly. All networks and galaxies have great implications for economic integration. As markets of information, with interactive potential, they create bonds between producers and consumers that drive market integration. These technologies can affect everyone on planet Earth. So the economic integration that results from their diffusion should concern every organization.

The next chapter considers criminal empires and the major techniques of economic integration and disintegration they have developed and deployed.

4 Criminal empires

Just as the Roman Catholic Church was the first international religion to resemble a multinational corporation, so also was the Mafia the first major transoceanic crime syndicate to develop techniques of organization associated with the modern multinational. The special historical role of the Mafia makes it the main case study of this chapter. To assess the Mafia's major contributions to economic integration and disintegration, one must appreciate how this organization originated and developed.

The Mafia started on Sicily, an island southwest of mainland Italy, sometime during the European Middle Ages. The American version of the Mafia is also known as *La Cosa Nostra*, which means "our thing."[1] Exactly who founded the original Mafia and precisely when are shrouded in mystery, as befits an organization that strives to remain clandestine

The word "Mafia," however, supposedly comes from an incident that took place on Sicily in 1282, when Sicilians rebelled against French rule.[2] The patriotic slogan became "*Morte alla Francia Italia anela.*" Translated into English, this means, "Death to the French is Italy's cry." In Italian the slogan produces the acronym M-A-F-I-A.

The main job of the Mafia in its early years was to protect the estates of owners who were away. There was a continuing need for this service, as law enforcement never penetrated rural areas in an effective way. This state of affairs held even after the unification of the Italian nation-state in the 1860s supposedly gave the country some administrative coherence. But the protection the Mafia offered extra-legally for so long became entangled with illegal activities over the years. During the 1800s the Mafia became more of a criminal organization.

The origins of this organization provide insight into its enduring mystique. The Mafia emerged to provide a service that government could not deliver: protection of property and, by extension, the owners of that property. This response was rational and the service was legitimate. The owners of those estates were invoking their right of self-defense when they hired the Mafia. The right to private property originates in one's right to possess one's own person. So in summoning extra-legal guardianship for one's property in land and dwellings when no legal protection was available, one was invoking self-defense.

The Sicilian Mafia, more criminalized by 1900, became an important international organization during the 1920s and 1930s and would have an impact far beyond Sicily. Its initial internationalization largely resulted from one criminal trying to eliminate others. Benito Mussolini, the Fascist leader who ruled Italy as premier from 1922 into 1943, tried to suppress the Sicilian Mafia. While "*Il Duce*" did not succeed, his campaign generated considerable pressure on local Mafia leaders and many traveled to the United States. This immigration provided important leaders who would found the offshoots of the Sicilian Mafia in the United States.

The development of the Sicilian Mafia in the United States continued the criminalization of the protection it offered, reinforced its hierarchical organization, and broadened its range of services. How the Mafia has transformed the concept of protection furnishes one of the most powerful keys to its mystique. The legal status of its protection changed radically over time. It began as extra-legal, but then traversed the boundaries between extra-legal and illegal so many times that the distinction became blurred.

The Mafia has legitimate origins and, even in its modern criminal version, still performs community services that are entirely legal. Indeed, for some people who have no links to the organization, the Mafia constitutes the last "social safety net." These facts clash with the characterization of it by contemporary law enforcement as entirely criminal. A long menu of illegal activities does not per se make an organization criminal in every respect.

The Mafia is, on balance, much more sinner than saint. But its origins, as an extra-legal provider of needed protection, and its ongoing record, in furnishing efficiently services that government can not or will not provide, both underpin the ethos of a necessary rogue. Here is an organization that has shown great skill in exploiting the seams in the defenses of the legal economy and in diversifying the choices available to consumers in the "underground economy." Even though some of its top leaders in the United States have been successfully prosecuted, the Mafia as anti-government, rogue, and underdog still appeals greatly to similar instincts in many people. This attraction holds, even though the business itself partakes of bureaucracy and has some gruesome procedures.

The Mafia as international business: the bonds of internal economic integration

The bonds of internal economic integration feature the managerial hierarchy and its kinship concept of chain of command. The Mafia has developed a streamlined managerial hierarchy that economizes on levels of middle management. The conventional chain of command, which all sources acknowledge, features, from top to bottom, a Boss or Don who is the Head, an Underboss who is second in command, the *Caporegima* (Capos) or captains who are the sole level of middle management, and the soldiers, on the street or in the field, who enforce daily discipline on both insiders and outsiders.

Other positions connect to this managerial hierarchy. The Consigliore or counselor advises the Don or, if the latter is absent, incapacitated, or deceased, the Underboss. Some speak and write about a group loosely known as associates. These are nonmembers who may be on the payroll or just in acquiescence, such as corrupt judges, police, and journalists.

This managerial hierarchy applies to individual crime "families," not to the organization as a whole. There is no formal, ongoing bureaucracy that connects every crime "family" to an overseeing edifice of administration. The "families" compete with each other; sometimes one will try to establish domination over the others, with various outcomes. The pretender may lose and recede in influence. It may win by eliminating opposing leadership and assimilating some surviving members of the defeated "families." It can also win but elect to remain *primus inter pares*: as the dominant but collegial leader assigning market shares and maintaining the "peace" among all the crime "families" in a city or region. The leader of this type of family is sometimes known, in popular parlance, as the "Boss of Bosses."

While individual "families" function as businesses with managerial hierarchies and chains of command, the Mafia as a whole derives coherence more from ethnicity and culture. Its ethnic base consists of Sicilians, although the Mafia has never been exclusively the domain of Italians, from Sicily or anywhere else in Italy. Just as the Mafia does not exhibit ethnic exclusiveness in its membership or associates, so also must one remember that the vast majority of Sicilians, both past and present, have never belonged to that organization. If ever the injustice of stereotyping has found fertile soil, it is in Sicily and the United States in connection with "Da Mob."

The cultural heritage of the Mafia did accumulate on Sicily during the centuries it was based primarily there. On that island developed the customs and rituals that are so central to the tradition that is the backbone of any culture.[3] *Omertà*, the blood oath of secrecy, bonds members, many of whom already shared a common ethnicity and aspects of broader island cultures. *Omertà* bonds with finality, because breaking the oath is a self-imposed death sentence.

A vivid description of a Mafia induction came during a federal trial in US district court in Cleveland, Ohio, in 1999. Lenine Strollo, once allegedly "head of the Youngstown [Ohio] mob," was a cooperating witness in a trial of three men who were once supposedly part of his "organized crime family." On March 3, 1999, Strollo was asked on the witness stand about the ceremony that marked his induction into the

Mafia in Pittsburgh. He said, "you get together with the other members, you took an oath, draw blood from a finger and burn a religious card to take an oath of silence."[4]

Clearly, the Mafia is a secretive organization that neither forgives nor forgets. Revenge for perceived injustices is inter-generational: the retribution may not be delivered for years or decades. Contrary to some stereotypes, the Mafia does not impose the death penalty for every offense against it or those it protects. There is, at least in some of its quarters, a semblance of the principle of proportionality: the "punishment" should fit the "crime."

While Sicily remains its cultural cradle, the US Mafia is experiencing an ongoing Americanization. This process produces cultural hybrids that blend basic traditions and values with the distinctive characteristics of particular crime "families" in the United States. There is more diversity within the culture of the Mafia than much contemporary writing on crime matters has acknowledged.[5]

The cohesion of the Mafia as a whole thus comes much more from ethnicity and culture than from structure. Individual crime "families" do share common customs, rituals, and other procedures. They do exhibit similar structures, as previously sketched. But the Mafia is not a unitary organization in administrative terms. There is no centralizing bureaucracy "upstream" from the "families." In that sense, the Mafia truly never existed, and repeated denials of its existential reality by its alleged members are not entirely wrong.

To be sure, there have been, from time to time, special gatherings of leaders from various crime "families" to discuss urgent matters of common interest. The most infamous convocation of such notables that has so far come to light occurred in November, 1957, on an estate outside the community of Appalachin in up-state New York. And there have been commissions, or leadership groups of Mafia dons, that have operated for certain periods both in Italy and the United States.[6] These commissions supposedly try to "coordinate" the business activities of crime "families" and regulate the use of violence.

In the United States some commissions have been more organized and lasted longer than others. That 1957 meeting was supposedly the work of a commission and suggested to some that the Mafia had a "national structure."[7] But what that "national structure" entails is another matter and has apparently changed over time. Charles "Lucky" Luciano, one of the best organizers in the history of crime, set up the first national commission for the American Mafia in the 1930s. The Luciano commission apparently had more coherence and clout than some that followed. The analysis of Joe Bonanno, another Mafia godfather, offered several decades ago still seems accurate today. In the United States, the commission has influence but no executive power; it functions above all as a forum.[8]

The Mafia as pioneer in economic integration: the Prohibition Era (1920–33)

Earlier in the twentieth century the Mafia foreshadowed what it could do in economic integration during the Prohibition Era in the United States, which lasted from 1920 through 1933. Prohibition was an attempt by the federal government to repress "intoxicating liquors for beverage purposes." This is a classic era in the history of criminality, which has not yet received sufficient attention in the context of economic integration.

Amendments to the US Constitution both began and ended the Prohibition Era. The Eighteenth Amendment forbade the "manufacture, sale or transportation of intoxicating liquors, for beverage purposes." This amendment went into "full force and effect" on January 16, 1920. Almost fourteen years later, the Twenty-First Amendment repealed the Eighteenth Amendment, when it was officially ratified on December 5, 1933.

This experiment in government regulation of personal conduct failed miserably. But its abject outcome is only part of the legacy of Prohibition. Government's attempt to suppress the "manufacture, sale or transportation of intoxicating liquors for beverage purposes" created the environment in which "organized crime" emerged.

Prohibition opened up great opportunities for the Mafia in manufacturing, sales, and transport that lasted almost fourteen years. The challenges of the Prohibition Era compelled the Mafia to organize itself as a big business with professional procedures. So in trying to eradicate "demon liquor" the government conjured up a much more dangerous genie, "organized crime," with the organizational capacity to outmatch law enforcement, especially on the local level.[9]

Alphonse Capone played a major role in the emergence of "organized crime" in the Chicago region during Prohibition. He and Jake Guzik, his top accountant or "money man," organized the Chicago syndicate and so gave it internal economic integration, as its structures and procedures gained coherence. Some of their business activities also exemplify pioneering patterns of international economic integration.

While the Chicago Mafia continued its criminal involvement in prostitution and gambling during the Prohibition era, it devoted considerable energy to those three activities mentioned in the Eighteenth Amendment. It focused on the manufacture, transport, and sales of intoxicating beverages but in different ways. The syndicate developed substantial manufacturing capacity, especially for beer, in the Chicago region, but also relied on foreign sources for imports of spirits that benefit from a longer maturation period. Frank Nitti, Capone's chief enforcer and an excellent businessman in his own right, created a classic instance of international economic integration, when he supervised the importation of major quantities of whiskey from Canada. In this commerce the Chicago Mafia outsourced manufacturing, strove for complete control of transport, and then distributed those prized bottles of Canadian whiskey to the speakeasies, or clubs, where alcoholic beverages were illegally sold. Many, perhaps all, of the speakeasies belonged to the mob's own distribution network.

The Canadian connection was expensive. The costs of longer transport and associated protection, like more officials to bribe, all added up. But it was worth the effort. It was very difficult to produce whiskey of Canadian quality in the mob's Chicago facilities. Manufacturing on-site in the Chicago area economized on these costs. But the risks of these operations became much greater with the appearance on the scene of Eliot Ness and his band of federal agents called "The Untouchables."

It was the Internal Revenue Service, not "The Untouchables," that eventually derailed Capone, because he had evaded federal income taxes. But Ness and his crew did inflict major damage on many of the mob's manufacturing sites in the Chicago area and so provided graphic material for one gritty television series and one somewhat fictionalized movie, both named *The Untouchables.*

The Mafia: contemporary strategies of national and international economic integration

Today the Mafia is refining its strategies of national and international economic integration. Three stand out: concealment, integration with the legal, and diversification.

Concealment

Concealment as a strategy befits a clandestine organization that values secrecy. Let us consider concealment in the area of structures.

Structure has both internal and external dimensions. The internal structure of the Mafia has become less mysterious as the result of continuing disclosures by insiders. The first highly publicized revelations were the Valachi papers in the late 1960s.[10] A more recent contribution to the genre is *Underboss: Sammy the Bull Gravano's Story of Life in the Mafia.*[11] While the Mafia has experienced a partial unmasking of its internal structures, it has had better luck in disguising its external structures and their exact connections to inside operations.

These external structures consist of the various businesses that the Mafia runs directly or indirectly. The direct businesses have involved, over time, gambling, prostitution, narcotics, and the enterprise overarching all of these – protection. Nowadays gambling is known as "gaming," and prostitution and narcotics come under the rubrics of "personal services" or "personal enhancement." The direct businesses also include the legitimate businesses that "front" or disguise the illegal ones. The list of these legal businesses is diverse, but many of them have centered on real estate, especially hotels and casinos.

The businesses or organizations that the Mafia runs indirectly are those that are nominally under the control of others but substantively under its influence. Historically, the indirect businesses have also covered a wide spectrum. The Mafia, for example, ran the docks of the port of New York City for years back in the 1940s and into the 1950s, because it controlled the International Longshoreman's Union. This situation inspired the classic film *On the Waterfront*. The Mafia also infiltrated the business of professional boxing in the 1950s and was able to "fix" a number of fights to benefit bettors. Perhaps the most famous fight that was deliberately lost involved "The Raging Bull," Jake LaMotta.

In the early 1950s, criminal elements, some with presumed Mafia ties, corrupted a number of college basketball players and paid them to "shave points." That is, the players did not have to lose a game, but they had to win by fewer points than the "spread" dictated; the "spread" is the winning margin predicted by gamblers. The resulting scandal that doomed college basketball at the City College of New York and harmed programs at Long Island and Bradley Universities is hauntingly portrayed in the excellent Home Box Office sports documentary called *City Dump*.

More recently, the Mafia dominated trash collection in New York City, especially Manhattan, which enabled it to reap substantial income. It intimidated existing operators and then charged for protecting them from itself. Those businesses passed the cost of protection onto consumers through much higher prices than legitimate costs of doing business would have warranted.

The Mafia has excelled in developing business structures that remind one of the shell game played so adeptly on the sidewalks of New York. The entertainer, who must also be a magician, claims that there is a ball under one of the several shells that he quickly moves around: which shell conceals the ball? But the viewer has to wonder whether there really has been a ball under one of the shells during the entire game.

The shells in the game are analogous to Mafia corporate structures, when these feature "shell" businesses or corporations. In the business world there are four different kinds of "shells." The first, like the one in the game with the ball under it, is a legal corporation that exists only on paper but disguises illegal activities. Another shell may be a legal corporation, with minimal business operations, that is not a "front" at all, but was created to divert or confuse outside investigators probing "the structures of organized crime." This kind of shell raises concealment to the level of disinformation, which is the deliberate dissemination of incorrect or confusing information. A third type of business shell is the legal corporation, with substantial legitimate activities, that also contains illegal operations. There is yet a fourth type of corporate "shell": a successful business whose assets have been so plundered that it exists only as an empty legal "shell." The key questions, then, for outside observers are: what kind of "shell" is it? If it is empty, is it always empty? And if it is full, does it always stay that way? The providers of vice are creative architects of magical business structures, as they try to disguise some and make others disappear.

Concealment, the Mafia's first strategy for national and international economic integration overlaps with the second. Simply put, this strategy is integration with the legal. It involves building bridges between legal and illegal economies.

Integration with the legal

This strategy has classically employed legitimate real estate as bases or staging points for illegal operations, to use military terms. The real estate is legal as purchased and operated, although techniques of extraordinary persuasion may be used to entice an unwilling seller to part with a coveted property. Hotels with casinos, in states that permit gambling, are favored bases.

The ironies are inescapable. Driven by needs for revenue, state governments have entered a business that has traditionally been a source of illegal income for the Mafia. By legalizing operations in an area where the Mafia has great historical expertise, they are helping it immensely in its endeavors to integrate with the legal.

The hotels and riverboats are now legal bases that can be used as staging points for unleashing the forces of corruption. Even if real estate serves only as a legal meeting place where agents of the sinister can "rub shoulders" with susceptible citizens, it promotes integration with the legal on a personal basis. As legal locations for planning and launching criminal penetration of gambling or some other business, legitimate real estate exemplifies the strategy of building bridges between legal and "underground" economies.

Besides revenue, governments offer another justification for legalized gambling. It is "economic development."[12] They seek to reawaken an economically depressed area by locating a magnet industry – gambling – in it. This revitalization presumably leads to greater economic integration of the unemployed, now working, with their local economies, and of a deprived region with its more prosperous neighbors.

These legal modes of economic integration present opportunities for those pursuing less beneficent varieties. The Mafia can piggyback its own types of economic integration on efforts to create legitimate versions of the same force. Such an approach elevates integration to a higher level: the integration of two genres of economic integration. This theme holds in domains other than legalized gambling, such as financial markets, which will be discussed later in this chapter.

Preying on legal economic integration to promote illegal versions is part of the bridge building between legal and illegal economies that is central to the strategy of integration with the legal.

This strategy fosters some of the most effective types of concealment available to organized crime. Mixing legal and illegal elements in new combinations blurs and may practically dissolve distinctions between the two; it certainly makes it harder to identify which is which. Concealment and integration with the legal thus apply to Mafia structures. But they also characterize Mafia procedures, strikingly in the areas of income and wealth. The process that best illustrates concealment and integration with the legal at work protecting the income and wealth of the Mafia is money laundering.

Case study: money laundering

This term covers an expanding array of procedures that all alter money in some way.[13] In this area modern technology has elevated the strategy of integration with the legal to its highest level, which is assimilation with the legal. Assimilation is the most intense form of integration. Computers and other electronic devices make assimilation with the legal a feasible goal for money laundering. Tainted money, by electronic manipulation, becomes legal money; integration is now assimilation.

Money laundering is not an innovation of the twentieth century.[14] Coinage debasement, in which governments and rulers have engaged from time immemorial, is a type of money laundering. Those debasing a coinage are altering it in one of two ways. They either remove or reduce its content of precious metals, or they increase the extrinsic value of a coin whose precious metallic content remains the same. These actions both fall under the rubric of money laundering.

In colonial situations, like those we analyzed in Chapter 1, coinage issued by the imperial power became the object of money laundering in several senses. Colonial subjects, suspicious of their rulers and doubting the extrinsic value of official coinage, sometimes melted the coins down in order to remove precious metallic content, which could include gold, silver, and copper. This process extracted the intrinsic value of the coinage, which was universal. Imperial rulers also laundered their own monies, as they sometimes debased them.

In another context, the Papacy, as we described in Chapter 3, laundered national money supplies. Its taxes and other fund-raising activities removed coins with substantial intrinsic value from countries like England and France.

But laundering a national money supply was not an innovation of the Roman Catholic Church. The history of warfare going back millennia shows conquerors laundering the money supplies of the vanquished. Removing precious metals, whether as bullion, coinage, or *objets d'art*, was money laundering on a grand scale. *Objets d'art*, with precious metallic content, may not be directly part of a money supply, but they are wealth and certainly convertible into bullion or coinage. Moreover, economic anthropology reminds us that *objets d'art*, with precious metallic content, may function as money in a particular area, if residents there see it that way.

Money laundering thus has a long history, which has not received enough attention because the modern criminalization of the process, especially in high-tech fashion, concerns most analysts. The Mafia did not invent money laundering, but it has a special historical role in diffusing money laundering as a set of techniques for transforming ill-gotten gains into legal income and wealth.[15] And the Mafia, ever a crime pioneer, is pushing the process onto the frontiers of global economic integration, particularly into international financial markets. Let us concentrate on the Mafia as a crime pioneer in refining money laundering in the context of global financial integration. To appreciate the Mafia's role one must first have in mind some essentials of money laundering in its current criminal manifestations.[16]

US Customs and Border Protection, Department of Homeland Security, defines money laundering as "the legitimization of proceeds from any illegal activity." Money laundering, according to Customs and Border Protection, has three stages: "the initial *placement* of illegal funds into the banking system; *layering* funds through a series of mechanisms, such as wire transfers, designed to complicate the paper trail; and finally, *integrating* the laundered funds back into the legitimate economy through the purchase of properties, businesses and other investments" (emphasis added). Through money laundering "the criminal transforms the monetary proceeds from criminal activity into funds with an apparently legal source."[17] This three-stage definition of money laundering is most useful, but it does not go deep enough into the process of *integrating*.

When Customs and Border Protection observes that the transformation produces "funds with an apparently legal source," it misses a crucial feature of money laundering as it has evolved during the late 1990s and into the third millennium. The key word here is "apparently." Transformation today can give "dirty money" not only an "apparent" legal source, but also a real legal source.

The distinction between appearance and reality is the difference between "integrating the laundered funds back into the legitimate economy" and *assimilating* them into that economy. Integration begets an appearance, assimilation a reality. This is assimilation with the legal, the level above integration, and the ultimate alchemy of money laundering. To be sure, money launderers may not in every situation have assimilation with the legal as their goal; integration may be sufficient for some activities. But a complete definition of money laundering must acknowledge the strategy of integrating with the legal as it ascends to the level of assimilation.

In fact, money laundering as total transformation, not just partial alteration, is the central theme of the process in the late twentieth and early twenty-first centuries. Criminal money laundering has always attempted to disguise the origins, destination, and ownership of money obtained from illegal activities. And money laundering, in its illegitimate versions, has always stressed the importance of controlling the funds as much as possible to avoid detection. But in recent decades more sophisticated attempts have been made to transform the money in some way as it is cycled into the legal economy. Let us discuss the concept of monetary transformation in more detail.

This transformation can alter the appearance of money or its functions or both. Appearance means in what vehicle the money exists. The most straightforward example of appearance concerns currency exchange: one currency can be exchanged for another. But appearance also covers an expanding range of other financial instruments, besides cash or coin.

These other instruments can involve either debt or equity or both. They include credit cards, stock, bonds, commercial paper, and a sub-set of financial instruments called derivatives. These are assets whose notional or face value comes from some underlying asset.[18] Some derivatives are arcane and require detailed technical knowledge for their construction and appreciation.

As the menu of financial instruments lengthens and includes devices of increasing complexity, the opportunities to develop more creative types of money laundering become richer. And the more chances money has to change appearances, the greater the likelihood that money laundering can result in assimilation with the legal. Put in strategic terms, there are today a growing number of "alternative routes" money laundering can follow in the pursuit of legal assimilation.[19]

"Alternative routes" make it easier to deceive law enforcement. As Sun Tzu wrote in *The Art of War*, "warfare is the Tao of deception."[20] This military proposition has profound criminal corollaries: successful money laundering is based on some sort of deception.

Money laundering is closely associated with the international traffic in illegal drugs. The Mafia and an increasing number of other crime organizations are deeply involved in this trade.[21] Indeed, the democratization of the international drug trade has reached many parts of the world. This illicit cross-border commerce now includes gangs from Jamaica and elsewhere in the Caribbean, as well as rising "mafias" in Russia and other former Soviet republics. These new entrants join such long-established participants as "families" from the US Mafia and the famous Cali and Medellin cartels from Colombia. Different groups have tried to work out informal divisions of labor and spheres of influence in this global commerce.[22] These arrangements can change so rapidly that one will not speculate on their details.[23]

The Colombian drug cartels introduced a major innovation in money laundering decades ago. Black Market Peso Exchange (BMPE) is a complex system that involves a third party known as a peso broker. It launders billions of drug money each year.[24]

One version of BMPE has nine steps:

Step 1: The Colombian cartels receive huge sums of money from cocaine sales in the United States.
Step 2: The cartels then sell these US dollars to Colombian money brokers.
Step 3: In return, the cartels receive "clean" pesos in Colombia.
Step 4: The money or peso brokers, in turn, put the drug dollars into the US banking system through various methods.
Step 5: The peso brokers then offer the drug dollars for sale to Colombian importers.
Step 6: The peso brokers receive pesos from the Colombian importers.
Step 7: The peso brokers route the drug dollars to US firms to pay for goods ordered by the Colombian importers.
Step 8: The US firms receive their payments in drug dollars.
Step 9: The US firms then ship the ordered goods to Colombian importers.

This is Black Market Peso Exchange as described in official records of the US government.[25] Organized crime has probably introduced variations in BMPE to stay ahead of law enforcement. The US government believes it has struck a major blow against BMPE. On 15 January 2002, agents from the US Customs Service in New York, in *Operation Wire Cutter*, "dismantled a major network of Colombian drug launderers." They arrested twenty-nine people in the United States, while their counterparts in Colombia arrested eight senior money brokers in Bogotá.[26] It is not clear from the present evidence what the precise role of this "major network" was in the overall constellation of all drug-related money laundering, whether related to BMPE or not.

Money laundering is becoming more complex as the integration of financial markets accelerates. The Mafia has already achieved a selective penetration of some US financial markets, like the "small-cap" market. With these bases established, the Mafia continues its endeavors to integrate traditional schemes for rigging the market with money laundering.

Evidence of Mafia penetration of US financial markets is mounting. Credible investigations published in the financial press raise serious questions. *Business Week*, for example, reported on 15 December 1997, the results of a six-month inquiry into chop stocks. "Chop" is slang for spread, the difference between what brokerages pay for stocks and the prices at which they are sold to the general public. Chop stocks offer huge opportunities for profit, and the Mafia has established a major presence here: "chop stocks constitute a vast underworld of the securities markets – a \$10 billion-a-year business that regulators and law enforcement have barely dented in their recent prosecutions."[27] Gary Weiss, the principal author for the *Business Week* story on chop stocks, also has an accompanying essay that addresses the question: how prevalent is the mob on Wall Street? The title of his essay embodies its major conclusion: "The mob is busier than the Feds think."[28] The Mafia is developing its own national network of securities dealers. Many people working in these firms have no idea who the major power behind the scenes is.

Besides chop stocks, the Mafia uses the "pump and dump" to realize great gains. The "pump and dump" is classic securities fraud. You drive the price of a stock up (the "pump") and then promptly sell it (the "dump").

Two kinds of integration are unfolding. On the level of technique, the Mafia is combining money laundering with long-standing devices for rigging the market, like the "pump and dump." On the level of structure, the Mafia is establishing substantial influence over major elements in some financial markets and interweaving its own operations with their procedures.

In late 1997 law enforcement thrust some intriguing activities into the public spotlight. On Tuesday, 25 November 1997, a federal grand jury in Manhattan indicted nineteen people, including five suspected of having ties to organized crime. They were charged in connection with an alleged scheme to manipulate the stock of HealthTech International, Inc.[29] Individuals with connections to the Mafia came from the Genovese and Bonanno "families," two organizations with long-standing bases in the New York City area.

The Mafia colluded with Mr. Gordon Hall, the chief executive officer of HealthTech, "to inflate the price of its securities in exchange for the company's stock and warrants."[30] The inclusion of warrants is significant, because they suggest the expectations of the participants in this scheme. A warrant is a way to wager on future stock prices: for a small fee, an investor gets the right to buy stock at a fixed price during a specific time period. If you think the price of a stock is going up, its warrant might be a good thing to own.[31] The company also overstated its assets by at least $10 million, according to a complaint filed by the Securities and Exchange Commission on 25 November 1997, in federal court in Manhattan.[32]

The scheme became even seamier. The Mafia pressured six brokers at Meyers Pollock Robbins, Inc., a small New York brokerage firm. By mixing bribes and threats organized crime came to "control" these brokers, who were also charged with criminal activities – applying high-pressure sales tactics and issuing false statements to get investors to buy company stock.

The course of this litigation became clouded in February, 1998, as a crucial witness list was improperly handled. But Gordon Hall, the CEO of HealthTech, was eventually found guilty in May, 1999, of "using mob ties"[33] and sentenced to eighty-seven months. Sixteen other defendants were also convicted, including one broker and some members of the Genovese and Bonnano organizations.

The "pump and dump" part of the HealthTech scheme was apparently small-time. The illicit gains allegedly came to about $1.3 million. This is petty cash by contrast with other exposed schemes that show no documented presence of Mafia involvement. For instance, the Sterling Foster firm allegedly reaped between $51 million and $75 million from its purported market-rigging activities.[34]

Nonetheless, other criminal episodes reinforce the ominous warning the HealthTech International case sounded about the enormous potential that exists in the financial markets for the Mafia. The Federal Bureau of Investigation ran "Operation Uptick," which led to the arrest of 120 people in June, 2000, in the Southern District of New York. This investigation "centered on organized crime's involvement in a series of schemes to artificially inflate the market prices of 19 public companies and then sell, to the unsuspecting public, stock in those companies which was held by an investment firm known as DMN Capital, Inc."[35] As of February, 2002, ninety-two people have been convicted on charges arising from "Operation Uptick," according to the US Attorney's Office.[36]

The FBI and the New York Police Department were also conducting an investigation that resulted in the indictments on March 1, 2000, of nineteen people in the Eastern District of New York on RICO charges. RICO stands for Racketeer Influenced and Corrupt Organizations Act, passed in 1970. The charges relate to the alleged fraudulent manipulation of securities by members and associates of the Gambino and Genovese "crime families" working with a Russian organized crime group.[37] Another investigation in the Eastern District of New York focused on yet more cooperation between the Mafia and Russian organized crime groups and their alleged participation in "large-scale stock fraud" and money laundering.[38]

While the FBI and local law enforcement are fully alert to increasing criminal penetration of the financial services industry, the Mafia strives to outrun them by making its strategy of diversification more sophisticated.

Diversification

The Mafia pursues diversification in many ways: in product, service, location, market, technique, and strategy.

The organization's involvement in gaming or gambling is a strong case in point. Over the years the Mafia has diversified the number of products and services its gaming operations offer. The organization has come a long way from its "numbers" days. It has diversified its markets geographically and enhanced the locations where gambling occurs. Casino gambling, which is advancing by both land and water inside and outside the United States, is the crucial hotbed of technological innovation in the gaming industry. Casino gambling is one of the "innovative and profitable technologies" the Mafia is penetrating, according to Sammy "The Bull" Gravano. His testimony against his former boss John Gotti was instrumental in putting the latter in a federal penitentiary for life, where he died on 10 June 2002.[39]

The Mafia's penetration of financial services is a second strong case in point. The Mafia has long been involved in "loan sharking," lending money at exorbitant rates of interest, and money laundering. The Mafia is diversifying its approaches to money laundering in the context of a strategy we call integration, then assimilation with the legal.

If casino gambling is a "profitable and innovative" technology, all the more so is the Internet, where the potential for criminal fraud is great. Some of the most intriguing possibilities for diversification within financial services are in cyberspace, where technology facilitates all modes of concealment.

Cyberspace is an enticing criminal environment, as already demonstrated by the thriving businesses dedicated to pornography on the Internet. Supposedly the top revenue producer in cyberspace, these operations have shown how anyone with access to a suitably equipped computer, an Internet provider, and a web master or mistress if one is needed, can start up a lucrative enterprise. This is an ideal market situation for clandestine operators: reasonable start-up costs, no insurmountable entry barriers, a proliferation of small-businesses that lends itself to setting up "fronts" that disguise criminal involvement.

The market is similar but not identical for those contemplating "financial services" fraud. While everyone can become expert in pornography and erotica, not everyone has sufficient financial knowledge and skills to perpetrate successful financial fraud on the Internet. So the start-up and maintenance costs of financial fraud in cyberspace must include personnel with knowledge, advice, service, and a flair for deception. And suspicious activities in financial cyberspace face a determined army of cyber-sleuths, with whom cyber-crooks will have to deal. A growing number of cyber-investors are reporting suspicious matters on the Internet to the Securities and Exchange Commission; sometimes these reports are exaggerated or misguided, but some are useful in identifying sources of real or potential fraud.[40]

With all the attention paid to the frontiers of criminality and the search for "profitable and innovative technologies," one should not forget the opportunities for diversification that conventional illegal activities present. Government, in its action and inaction, has historically provided major openings for crime done the "old-fashioned way." Criminals are exploiting weaknesses in the payment procedures for both Medicare and Medicaid, two health programs of the US government. The Mafia, in a well-documented case, exploited a federal program for assisting public housing in New York City. By rigging bids on contracts to install windows in those buildings, crime families illegally expropriated millions of dollars of federal funds for their own purposes. This scheme, which lasted for years during the 1980s, was highlighted in the trial of Vincent Gigante, supposedly the Don of the Genovese crime "family" in New York City. "Vinny the Chin" is an eccentric person who some say acts as if he is "insane," but what does that mean in New York City? He was adjudged competent to stand trial and was eventually convicted of murder-conspiracy and racketeering charges in 1997. A murder-conspiracy charge involved Peter Savino, who turned state's evidence and testified against Gigante. Savino was an "associate" who never became a full member of the Mafia or, to use Mafia language, he was never "made."[41] Racketeering is an organized criminal activity; in this trial, racketeering was the bid-rigging scheme. Salvatore "Sammy the Bull" Gravano also provided important testimony in the trail of Vincent Gigante.[42]

Indeed, Salvatore Gravano, in his inimitable way, may have just fingered one of the most crucial keys to the longevity of the Mafia as a world-class criminal organization: innovation. Innovations can be refinements or new items and they are essential to the health of every organization. They need not occur in every facet of a business all the time, but dynamic improvements, whether in product, service, structure, procedure, strategy, or personnel, are essential on a continuing basis if an organization is to survive.

Over the years, as we have shown, the Mafia has drawn strength from many innovations. Let us summarize innovations featured in this chapter. The Mafia's original industry, and still one of its main moneymakers, is protection, which is both a product and a service. The Mafia has always been customer-oriented, though not in every way the modern use of that phrase envisions. Over the years the organization has endeavored to improve protection as a product, by taking advantage of technology to make it more sophisticated. And the Mafia has remained focused on servicing its protection on an ongoing basis.

Innovations in structure have characterized the Mafia's internal organization as well as its external businesses. Al Capone and Jake Guzik organized the Chicago syndicate on a more corporate and business-like basis. The more intelligent use of concealment in relation to business "shells," and the development of gaming, from "numbers" in urban shadows to casino gambling in palatial surroundings, illustrate the dynamism of innovation with reference to the Mafia's external businesses. Innovations in procedure are strikingly captured in the refinement of money laundering. Strategies, both grand and specific, are another area in which significant innovation has occurred. Frank Nitti innovated the specific strategy of importing Canadian whiskey into the United States during Prohibition. This strategy was also a stunning early instance of North American economic integration. Illegal to be sure but creative it was, and it addressed the needs of the times. Where government did not provide economic integration, in this case endeavored to wreck trade in high-demand products, the Mafia was ready, able, and willing to create economic integration that got the goods and delivered them.

Indeed, this is the entrepreneurial spirit of the Mafia at its illegal best. Where government does not meet a human want or need, the Mafia will respond.

The two previous chapters have spotlighted economic integration as developed by private organizations, the Roman Catholic Church and the Mafia. The last three chapters return our attention to economic integration as fostered by governments.

We consider free trade areas in Chapter 5, customs unions in Chapter 6, and common markets in Chapter 7.

5 Free trade areas

This chapter presents an historical panorama of free trade areas. Some see the free trade area as the first step on the ladder of economic integration. The customs union and the common market are the second and third steps, respectively. But for some communities, the free trade area may be the most appropriate choice for their circumstances, and the ladder metaphor may not be the correct way to view matters.

Let us begin in Europe, visit Africa, survey the western hemisphere, and finish in Asia and the western Pacific.

Europe

In Europe today the largest economic community is the European Union (EU), which has taken great strides towards becoming a common market and is featured in Chapter 7. The EU began as the European Economic Community (EEC), which was created by the Treaty of Rome (1957) and came into existence on January 1, 1958.

There is another significant grouping in Europe today, which began in 1960 as an alternative to the EEC. This is the European Free Trade Association (EFTA). In the memorable title of a book published in 1961, Europe was at that time "at sixes and sevens."[1] The "sixes" were the inner six countries of France, Germany, Italy, Belgium, the Netherlands, and Luxembourg: these made up the EEC. The "sevens" were the outer seven of Great Britain, Denmark, Norway, Sweden, Switzerland, Austria, and Portugal: these formed the EFTA. Finland became an associate member of the EFTA in 1961 and a full member in 1986.

The inner six sought a closer form of economic integration – a common market – while the outer seven pursued a free trade area and that in limited terms. The EFTA treaty called for the elimination of tariffs only on industrial commodities traded among participating countries. It did not cover agricultural products, and a member could withdraw at any time.

The EFTA is thus an economic community with more modest goals than the EEC and its successor the EU. It is technically correct to describe the EFTA as "a much weaker union" than the EEC and EU.[2] But this judgment must be supplemented. It is based on the ladder of economic integration, discussed in the Introduction, which implies that a closer form of economic integration is altogether superior to a looser version. Though technically lower on the ladder of economic integration, the kind of bonding represented by the EFTA was and is perhaps the best its participants could hope for, given the political constraints each faced at home.

Both the EC and the EFTA underwent significant changes in the 1990s. The EC became more cohesive and extensive. On 1 January 1993, the EC became in practice a single market for goods and services. And in 1994 the EC officially became the European Union; this was a name change with substance. The "community" was evolving into a more coherent "union." It was formulating community-wide laws and regulations on such matters as banking, intellectual property, beer, and pasta. Arriving at standard definitions of the latter two proved especially controversial. The EU gained new members. Three came from the EFTA. Austria, Finland, and Sweden joined in 1995. This continued a trend of the EFTA members migrating to the EC and EU. Denmark and Great Britain entered the EC in 1973 and Portugal joined in 1986. Today only two of the EFTA's original members remain, Norway and Switzerland. But the EFTA has gained two new members, Iceland, from the north Atlantic, and Liechtenstein, which is a small principality in central Europe between Austria and Switzerland. Iceland joined the EFTA in 1970 and Liechtenstein entered in 1991.

Relations between the EU and the EFTA expanded considerably during the 1990s. These changes built on a history of substantive cooperation between the two communities going back to the 1950s. In 1972, for instance, the EFTA countries signed free trade agreements with the EC that eventually abolished import duties on industrial products in 1977. The EFTA members would continue to develop their preferential relations with the EC. These endeavors produced in the early 1990s the most striking example of cooperation to date: the European Economic Area (EEA), which came into existence on 1 January 1994.

The core concept underlying the EEA is internal market. Indeed, the EEA was originally named the European Economic Space (EES). But decision-makers wisely changed "space" to "area," because while "area" is somewhat vague, "space" was altogether surrealistic. A truer name for the EEA would be the European Single Market (ESM), because that is exactly what the EEA creates.

The EEA links three of the four EFTA members – Iceland, Liechtenstein, and Norway – to the EU in a single market. Switzerland, the fourth, signed the original agreement on the EEA on 2 May 1992, but backed out, after its citizens rejected participation in a referendum held on 6 December of that year.

Switzerland remains a special case in relation to the European Union. To minimize the adverse impact of the rejection of the EEA, Switzerland and the EU negotiated agreements in seven sectors. These are Free

Movement of Persons, Trade in Agricultural Products, Public Procurement, Conformity Assessments, Air Transport, Transport by Road and Rail, and Swiss Participation in the 5th Framework Program for Research. These negotiations, which began in 1994, concluded in 1999; agreements were signed on 21 June 1999. A referendum was held on 6 May 2000, and Swiss voters approved the agreements. EU member states ratified these seven agreements, and they came into force on 1 June 2002. Negotiations are under way in ten other areas. These include liberalization of trade in processed agricultural products and liberalization of services.[3]

Whatever the Swiss decide, the EEA remains an ingeniously crafted grouping that builds on the strengths of its members. What exactly is the EEA? It is easy to state what the EEA is not. It is not a customs union, because it lacks a common external tariff. It is not a common market, because it lacks the federalism of that grouping.

The EEA is a single market, not a common market. But it is much more than a conventional free trade area, in which members work to reduce internal barriers to exchange. The EEA actively promotes the same conditions of competition throughout the single market; the bureaucratic word here is "homogeneity." A joint committee overseeing the EEA endeavors to ensure that "relevant" EU legislation concerning the single market is extended to the EFTA states that belong to the EEA.

The EEA respects the sensitivities of its EFTA members. The citizens of Norway, for instance, rejected participation in the European Union in 1994. One reason was they did not want regulation of their fisheries industries coming from Brussels, the administrative capital of the EU. So the EEA does not have a common fisheries policy. Nor does the EEA have a common security policy. It would be hard to have one policy covering EFTA countries in such different geographical and strategic situations as Iceland and Liechtenstein.

With its bridge to the European Union in the EEA, the European Free Trade Association continues strong as a home for countries that need more political and psychological space than the EU provides. Today three institutions serve the European Free Trade Association: the EFTA Secretariat, the EFTA Surveillance Authority, and the EFTA Court. Each has its own web page.

The EFTA Secretariat has its headquarters in Geneva, with offices in Brussels and Luxembourg. The Secretariat manages the EFTA free trade area, the EFTA participation in the European Economic Area (EEA), and EFTA's network of free trade agreements.[4]

The EFTA Surveillance Authority, located in Brussels, "ensures that Iceland, Liechtenstein, and Norway respect their obligations under the EEA Agreement." The EFTA Surveillance Authority and the European Commission of the EU co-operate closely with each other.[5]

The EFTA Court, located in Luxembourg, has jurisdiction over the EEA EFTA states. It interprets the EEA agreement with regard to those countries.[6] The Court is "mainly competent to deal with infringement actions brought by the EFTA Surveillance Authority against an EFTA state."[7]

The European Free Trade Association is a striking case study that illustrates decisively three propositions. First, a free trade area has great political and economic flexibility. Second, a free trade area should be appreciated in its own context, not just as the first step on a ladder of economic integration. And, third, a free trade area can provide a common home for countries that may eventually define their futures in very different terms.

West Africa

The largest group in West Africa concerned with regional economic integration is the Economic Community of West African States (ECOWAS). Fifteen countries belong to ECOWAS, which was founded in Nigeria on 28 May 1975. Mauritania left the organization in 2002.

Fourteen have colonial histories. Only Liberia, founded in 1822 by emancipated American slaves, was never a European colony. The Gambia, Ghana, Nigeria, and Sierra Leone are former British colonies. Guinea Bissau and Cape Verde are former overseas territories of the Portuguese colonial empire. The other eight were part of the French colonial empire: Benin, Burkina Faso, Guinea, Ivory Coast, Mali, Niger, Togo, and Senegal.

Liberia and the four former British colonies are Anglophone, with English an official language. Portuguese remains a dominant language in Guinea Bissau and Cape Verde. The eight countries with French heritage are Francophone, with French an official language.

ECOWAS is bilingual, with English and French as its official languages, but ECOWAS embraces many languages and cultures. Besides the three major foreign languages of English, French, and Portuguese, numerous indigenous languages are widely spoken, such as Yoruba and Hausa in Nigeria and Wolof in Senegal.

ECOWAS faces daunting problems. These include military and political conflicts, insufficient diversification of national economies, and different colonial experiences. As to the last, France and Portugal practiced economic assimilation with regard to their colonies. This was a much closer form of colonial economic integration than Great Britain implemented (Chapter 1).

An intriguing legacy of economic assimilation now exists within ECOWAS itself. This is the West African Monetary Union or UEMOA, which stands for *Union Économique et Monétaire Ouest Africaine*. Seven former French colonies and one former Portuguese colony comprise UEMOA. The Francophone countries are Benin, Burkina Faso, *Cote d'Ivoire* (Ivory Coast), Mali, Niger, Senegal, and Togo; the Lusophone country is Guinea Bissau. These countries all share a common currency, the CFA franc, which is guaranteed by France (Chapter 1).[8]

The CFA franc zone extends beyond west Africa and has fourteen members. Besides the eight members of UEOMA, it contains six central African states: Cameroon, Central African Republic, Chad, the Republic of Congo (Brazzaville), Equatorial Guinea, and Gabon. These countries belong to the Central African Economic and Monetary Community or CEMAC, which stands for *Communauté Économique et Monétaire de l'Afrique Centrale* (Chapter 6).

A second monetary union has joined UEOMA within ECOWAS. Five ECOWAS members signed the 2000 Accra Declaration to create this second union, The West African Monetary Zone (WAMZ), which is different from the West African Monetary Union mentioned above. The Gambia, Ghana, Guinea, Nigeria, and Sierra Leone all agreed to reform their economies before introducing their common currency, the eco.

Achieving the eco takes inspiration from the European Union and how that common market launched its single currency, the euro, in 1999. The Accra group promised to meet specific targets in reforming their economies. These targets are called, in the spirit of the European Union, convergence criteria. The eco has four: (1) by 2002 budget deficits were to be no more than 4 percent of Gross Domestic Product; (2) by 2003 inflation was to fall to 5 percent or below; (3) by 2003 central banks were to limit their financing of budget deficits to 10 percent of the previous year's revenue; and (4) by 2003 countries were to have enough foreign reserves to support six months of imports.[9]

This timetable proved unrealistic. The countries of the West African Monetary Zone plan to launch the eco by 2009, within the framework of ECOWAS.

East Africa

This region has narrow and wide definitions. Its core consists of the contemporary states of Kenya, Uganda, and Tanzania, all of which share a British colonial heritage. East Africa has a wider geographical meaning as eastern Africa. This larger region includes the core and adds Somalia to the north, Rwanda and Burundi to the west, Mozambique to the south, and Zambia to the southwest.

Before we discuss current endeavors to promote regional economic integration, let us first sketch the history of economic integration in east Africa.[10] This story is usually told within imperial and colonial categories. These contain the territories imperialism defined and colonialism administered: Kenya, Uganda, Tanganyika, and Zanzibar. Tanganyika and Zanzibar merged in 1964 to create Tanzania.

Efforts at regional economic integration began early in the twentieth century. For Kenya and Uganda the British government established the

East African Currency Board in 1905 (Ch. 1) and a postal union in 1911. During the inter-war period between 1919 and 1939, the British government tried to fashion a regional community that embraced all four of its colonial territories, Kenya, Tanganyika, Uganda, and Zanzibar. After Germany lost World War I, the League of Nations entrusted most of what had been German East Africa to Great Britain as a Class B mandate. The name of the mandate was Tanganyika.

At the outset some hoped this community would be a federation. Indeed, many British settlers in Kenya promoted a Federation of East Africa with its capital in Nairobi. But in 1929 the Hilton-Young Commission on Closer Union opposed this plan. One obstacle was mandate status of Tanganyika; it required that the territory receive special attention. Membership in a federation, especially one under the strong influence of British settlers in Kenya, would dilute and compromise direct British responsibilities for Tanganyika.

With federation no longer feasible politically, the concepts driving the development of the regional community became common services and customs union. Common services flowered as a tradition after 1939, while from the late 1920s a customs union contained Kenya, Tanganyika, and Uganda. The operation of this customs union produced markedly uneven benefits for its members, creating a lesson that contemporary decision-makers ignore at their peril. Let us consider both common services and customs union.

The long-term roots of common services lie in the Currency Board and Postal Union mentioned above. And in 1940 the British government set up a Joint East African Board to supervise tax collection. But it was not until 1948 that the East African High Commission (EAHC) was established. This would prove the crucial agency to inspire and manage common services. Under its aegis would come the flagships of regional common services: East African Railways and Harbours, East African Post and Telegraph, and the regional university, Makerere College in Uganda. Economic integration through expanding common services must rank among the most positive bequests of the British colonial legacy for east Africa.

But after "flag independence" came to east Africa in the early 1960s, common services became politicized in harmful ways. The EAHC was replaced in 1961 by the East Africa Common Services Authority, which lasted until 1967. In that year member countries signed the East African Treaty for Co-operation, which initiated a formal East African Community (EAC).

The regional atmosphere was anything but co-operative. The leaders of Kenya, Tanzania, and Uganda had contrasting visions of what the EAC should be, indeed of what economic development itself meant. The EAC disintegrated under these strains and collapsed by 1977. This unraveling doomed both common services and customs union. It is worthwhile to reflect on the haunting similarities between the colonial and post-independence histories of the East African Customs Union and what they may portend for regional economic re-integration today and in the future.

This customs union began with the British administration of both Kenya and Uganda in the very early 1900s. Kenya and Uganda were part of the same customs administration from the outset; Tanganyika joined in 1927. Two main features characterize the operation of the customs union after 1927. First, it was not a full-fledged customs union in contemporary terms: it had only a partial, not a common, external tariff. So it was, in practice, more a free trade area. There were, for example, no tariffs on the border between Kenya and Tanganyika from 1927 until 1967, when they became a matter for negotiation under that treaty of co-operation mentioned above.[11]

The common external tariff, the signature of a free trade area that has become a full customs union, was breached by the imposition of "suspended duties." These emerged from a conference of the colonial governors of the three East African territories in 1930. Each territory could impose an additional tariff on a wide range of commodities entering it from outside the union. The term "suspended" has misled some scholars into thinking it meant relaxed or removed. In fact, "suspended" has a more parliamentary meaning as "in abeyance." The extra duty was "suspended," until each government in conjunction with its Legislative Council[12] decided to invoke it. The central consequence of "suspended duties" for the common external tariff was jaggedness: "Kenya imposed these duties to the maximum; Tanganyika, in whole or in part on the majority of relevant goods; Uganda, very little."[13]

The second key fact about the customs union, both before and after independence, was that it benefitted Kenya much more than Tanganyika. In fact, the distribution of benefits was so unequal as to constitute an inequity. This statement requires explanation against the wider background of how economic groupings operate.

They cannot be programmed to ensure that all participants receive equal benefits every year. Indeed, the annual distribution of benefits from an economic grouping is rarely, if ever, even close to equality. But gains and losses from participation must over a reasonable term exhibit fundamental equity or fairness for all members. There should be a group consensus as to what constitutes "fairness" and "a reasonable term."

The governing criterion for an effective economic grouping should, therefore, be equity, not equality. If equality were feasible, what a wonderful world it would be. But if inequality is so gross as to perpetrate inequity, what a harmful world it is, for the aggrieved member and, eventually, for the cohesiveness of the group.

This dynamic, which transforms unavoidable inequality into lethal inequity, was at work in the East African Customs Union. The evidence is incontrovertible that Kenya benefitted much more than Tanganyika over the decades and that this imbalance became corrosive. Why? The answer is rooted in an amalgam of history, structure, and power. Kenya had more fledgling industries than Tanganyika. Kenya was also farther along in adding value to its agricultural exports by doing some processing at home. Both situations meant that Kenya would gain more from a higher external tariff around the union on commodities that might compete with its own products. The behavior of the two territories on "suspended duties" provides another laboratory in which to view this dynamic in operation.

But unequal gains, even over many years, would have never become so threatening, had there not been another ingredient that made the amalgam poisonous. The evolution of colonialism in East Africa, which brought a strong community of British settlers first to Kenya, produced a distribution of expatriate power that overwhelmingly favored Kenya. "The whole system," as E. A. Brett concisely notes for the inter-war period, "was based upon the fact that the dominant expatriate interests involved in the East African economy were committed to protectionism and a common market, and worked from bases predominantly concentrated in Kenya."[14] During the post-independence period the East African Customs Union continued to weaken from this dynamic, which had become like arsenic: low doses, administered over a long period, still kill.

The storms that battered regional cooperation gradually abated. During the 1990s there was a revival of interest in the economic integration of East Africa. A more pragmatic leadership came to power in Tanzania. This group muted the ideological divisiveness between African socialism in Tanzania and African capitalism in Kenya that racked the region from the late 1960s into the 1980s.[15] And during the 1990s regional economic integration became a compelling global phenomenon. Times had indeed changed.

Fortunately, not every organization concerned with regional economic cooperation had collapsed. There was a base to build upon. The East African Development Bank (EADB), founded in 1967, survived. It did "lie low" during the desert period of regional rancor, but a new charter in 1980 broadened its mission.[16] The Treaty for East African Co-operation (1967) had established the Bank but limited its mission to "the provision of financial and technical assistance for the promotion of industrial development in Member States." The new charter expanded the responsibilities of the Bank to include agriculture, forestry, tourism, transport, and infrastructure. Preference is given to projects that promote regional cooperation, which makes the Bank a prime instrument of regional economic integration.[17] The EADB is a creation and continuing charge of the governments of Kenya, Tanzania, and Uganda.

In 1996 Kenya, Tanzania, and Uganda agreed to set up a secretariat that would support a new Commission of East African Co-operation. The new secretariat is located in Arusha, a city in northern Tanzania, which was also the headquarters for the old East African Community. This continuity in location is haunting, because it preserves a living historical memory of the old East African Customs Union. Arusha should remind all that the inequities of the old customs union must not be repeated.

In 1999 the presidents of Kenya, Tanzania, and Uganda finally signed, after a year's delay, a treaty that established the new East African Community. This treaty is ambitious. It provides, in sequence, for a customs union, common market, a monetary union, and ultimately a political federation.[18]

The first step – a customs union – is taking shape. In March, 2004, the presidents of Kenya, Tanzania, and Uganda signed a protocol to prepare the ground for a customs union. When all three countries ratify the protocol, the customs union will come into force.

The lessons of the past are influencing the new East African Community. While the old EAC was primarily a government operation, the new EAC accords a major role to the private sector. While the old customs union benefitted Kenya disproportionately, the new customs union contains provisions designed to offset some Kenyan advantages.

Kenya's private sector is more advanced than that of its regional neighbors. The customs union protocol tries to address this imbalance with a "system of asymmetry." Translation: Tanzania and Uganda will open up their markets to Kenyan competition gradually over a period of five years. Kenya will open its markets immediately. In theory, businesses in Tanzania and Uganda will have time to prepare themselves. Some believe they can, but others are worried that the five-year grace period merely postpones Kenyan domination.[19]

The new customs union will have a common external tariff (CET). The "suspended duties" of the old East African Customs Union are gone. Instead, the CET will impose three tariff bands on goods entering the community from outside. Finished goods will be subject to 25 percent tariffs, semi-processed goods to 10 percent, but raw materials enter duty-free.[20]

There is enormous hope and justifiable pride that the new EAC will mean a "new day" for East Africa. Burundi and Rwanda, neighbors to the west, are planning to join. But there is one major complication: the number of regional blocs to which countries already belong. Let us move to the wider geographical meanings of eastern and southern Africa to illustrate this problem.

Eastern and southern Africa

Members of the new East African Community belong to at least three other regional organizations that concern economic integration. Kenya alone belongs to the Intergovernmental Authority on Development (IGAD). This group was established in 1986 formally to coordinate efforts against drought and desertification and informally to discuss regional political and economic issues. Its other members are Djibouti, Ethiopia, Eritrea, Somalia, and Sudan.[21]

Tanzania alone belongs to the Southern African Development Community (SADC). This group was founded in 1992 to "promote regional economic integration and a fully-developed common market."[22] The SADC Trade Protocol, which calls for an 85 percent reduction of internal trade barriers, went into effect on 1 September 2000. Full implementation is on track, and the community hopes to become a free trade area by 2008.[23]

SADC has fourteen members. Many of its fourteen members come from southern Africa and adjacent lands, but it is interregional. In its geographical core are Botswana, Lesotho, Swaziland, and South Africa itself. Just north of the core are Namibia and Angola and to the northeast are Mozambique and Zimbabwe. Fanning out to the northeast are Zambia and Malawi. The Democratic Republic of the Congo (formerly Zaire) and Tanzania are on the outer rings of this system. So are Mauritius and the Seychelles, archipelagoes in the Indian Ocean.

Kenya and Uganda, but not Tanzania, belong to the Common Market for Eastern and Southern Africa (COMESA). Founded in 1993, this group has an even more far-flung membership than SADC. COMESA presently has twenty members, nine of whom also belong to SADC. These are Angola, the Democratic Republic of the Congo, Malawi, Mauritius, Namibia, Seychelles, Swaziland, Zambia, and Zimbabwe. Non-SADC members of COMESA are Burundi, the Comoros islands, Djibouti, Egypt, Eritrea, Ethiopia, Kenya, Madagascar, Rwanda, Sudan, and Uganda.

Members of the Preferential Trade Area (PTA), which included Kenya, Uganda, and Tanzania, set up COMESA. Created in 1981, the PTA served as the forerunner to COMESA. This organization, which has an excellent web site, launched a free trade area in 2000 and is aiming for a customs union in 2004 or later.[24] Tanzania withdrew from COMESA in 1999.[25]

Some argue that multiple regional blocs with overlapping memberships are not the most efficient use of scarce resources.[26] From a strictly economic viewpoint, they may be right. But these organizations are living expressions of political economy. This means that the real question should be, are they the best economic use of scarce resources that contemporary political realities will permit? From this perspective, the answer is, they come close.

Western hemisphere

The great promise and flexibility of the free trade area are evident elsewhere in the world, besides Europe and Africa. In the western hemisphere the old Latin American Free Trade Association (LAFTA) showed that even a free trade area with serious internal conflicts could serve a useful function in stimulating other forms of economic cooperation.

Founded in 1960, LAFTA had eleven members: Argentina, Bolivia, Brazil, Chile, Colombia, Ecuador, Mexico, Paraguay, Peru, Uruguay, and Venezuela. During the 1960s dissension within the group intensified, as some felt that LAFTA was unfairly benefitting its bigger members, like Argentina, Brazil, and Mexico. LAFTA was never able to overcome this split between its "bigger" and "smaller" countries and eventually faded, but out of its ashes rose another organization dedicated to regional integration, on a less sweeping geographical scale but in a tighter economic fashion.

In 1969 five countries left LAFTA to form the Andean Pact, which is codified in the Cartagena (or Andean subregional) Agreement. Bolivia, Chile, Colombia, Ecuador, and Peru are charter members. Chile left in 1976, but another LAFTA dissident, Venezuela, had joined in 1973. The Andean Pact created a customs union on paper, as Article 90 of the Cartagena Agreement pledges creation of a common external tariff. This document resonates with comprehensive pledges to harmonize the economic policies of members on a broad range of issues.

The history of the Andean group shows a striking change in attitudes towards international businesses. In its first fifteen years or so the Andean Community was hostile to international businesses headquartered outside its borders. The Cartagena Agreement, which embodied the strong economic nationalism of the times, forbade foreign investment in the steel industry and sanctioned nationalization as a legitimate weapon for economic self-defense. In the early 1970s Bolivia nationalized Gulf Oil and Peru expropriated the local businesses of International Telephone and Telegraph. A 1971 agreement sharply restricted foreign investment in member states.

By the mid-1980s hostility towards foreign participation had diminished. The United States entered into agreements with some Pact countries to bypass those strict regulations concerning foreign investment in the group. And in May, 1987, members signed the Quito Protocol, which lets each country set its own rules governing foreign participation in its economy.

The group as a whole languished in the 1980s, but greatly revitalized itself in the 1990s. In 1996 members approved the Reform Protocol of the Cartagena agreement, which changed the name and nature of the organization. The Andean Pact became the Andean Community, with a leadership council, a commission, and a secretariat. The Andean Community welcomes international businesses, provided they respect the structures and procedures of the group.

The Andean Community has been advancing along multiple tracks towards greater economic integration. The Andean Free Trade Area, the first track, came into existence in February, 1993. At that time, Bolivia, Colombia, Ecuador, and Venezuela completed the elimination of customs tariffs they levied on each other, while they maintained their own individual tariffs for third parties. Peru joined the Free Trade Area in July, 1997. Since then Peru has been gradually deregulating its trade with its Andean partners. By 2003, Peru had completed more than 90 percent of this undertaking.[27]

The Andean Customs Union, the second track, went into operation in 1995, when the common external tariff (CET) went into effect. Implementation, however, was selective. Colombia, Ecuador, and Venezuela had approved a CET at the basic levels of 5, 10, 15, and 20 percent; but Bolivia receives preferential treatment and only applies levels of 5 and 10 percent. Peru did not sign the CET agreement.[28]

A common market, the third track, is possible. The Andean Community is apparently committed to establish a common market by 2005. Most members are moving incrementally to improve the free circulation of services, capital, and people within the community. Goods have already been circulating freely within the Andean Free Trade Area.[29]

Peru is following its own two-pronged approach to regional economic integration. On the one hand, Peru is an associate member of *mercosur*, an economic community founded in 1991 by Argentina, Brazil, Paraguay, and Uruguay (see Chapter 6). On the other hand, Peru remains a member of the Andean Community, but its participation has not been easy. It threatened to leave in 1997, but remained only after a special agreement was worked out that enabled it to join the Andean Free Trade Area. This agreement allowed Peru to reduce gradually the tariffs it levied on other Community members, a process reported above.

Relations between the Andean Community and *mercosur* remain an ongoing subject of discussion. There is some talk about merging the two communities into order to form a united front in trade negotiations with the North American Free Trade Area.[30] This organization brings together Canada, Mexico, and the United States; it will be analyzed later in this chapter.

In the western hemisphere there is another free trade area that, like LAFTA, experienced serious internal differences. In 1968 the Caribbean Free Trade Area (CARIFTA) came into existence. It had twelve members: Barbados, Guyana, Jamaica, Trinidad and Tobago, Antigua, British Honduras, Dominica, Grenada, Montserrat, St Kitts-Nevis-Anguilla, St Lucia, and St Vincent.[31] In 1973 CARIFTA became the Caribbean Economic Community (CARICOM), now known as the Caribbean Community. In 2002 CARICOM had fifteen members: the original twelve, plus the Bahamas, Haiti, and Suriname.

CARICOM experienced problems moving from a free trade area to a customs union. Attempting to construct a common external tariff highlighted the conflicting needs of its members. Some countries want a higher tariff on incoming manufactured goods in order to protect their fledgling industries. Barbados, Guyana, Jamaica, and Trinidad and Tobago sometimes belong to this camp. Many of the smaller islands in the eastern

Caribbean, regarded in the nomenclature of the international development community as "less advanced," seek a lower tariff on these commodities, because they do not make them locally but still use them. In 1998 CARICOM was described as having a common external tariff, "with exceptions."[32]

In the 2000s CARICOM leaders are concentrating on the CSME, the Caricom Single Market Economy. The CSME "seeks to create a single economic space and allow for the free movement of goods and services, labour and capital" within the Caribbean community.[33] Implementation was staged. Barbados, Jamaica, and Trinidad and Tobago introduced the CSME in 2004. The other countries followed in 2005. On 1 January 2006, the CARICOM Single Market (CSM) formally came into existence.

Challenges continue. September 11 and the removal of preferential markets for major commodities have precipitated a decline in tourism, a slowdown in economic growth, a reduction in investment, and a surge in unemployment. Accepting the free movement of labor and capital may challenge these economies, as high levels of unemployment will act as a "push factor" in the movement of labor.[34]

Unlike LAFTA, whose internal divisions became fatal, CARICOM has managed to live with its differences. This experience gave it the strength to seek an even wider economic integration of the Caribbean and its littoral. CARICOM led the drive to found a new regional group, the Association of Caribbean States (ACS), envisioned as prospective trade bloc of about forty nations in the Caribbean basin. The push for an extended community in the Caribbean came, in part, from the looming presence of the North American Free Trade Area.

The Association of Caribbean States was formally established in July, 1994. In 2003 the ACS had twenty-five full members and three associate members. Full members are Antigua and Barbuda, Bahamas, Barbados, Belize, Colombia, Costa Rica, Cuba, Dominica, Dominican Republic, El Salvador, Grenada, Guatemala, Guyana, Haiti, Honduras, Jamaica, Mexico, Nicaragua, Panama, St Kitts and Nevis, St Lucia, St Vincent and the Grenadines, Suriname, Trinidad and Tobago, and Venezuela. Associate members are Aruba, France (on behalf of French Guiana, Guadeloupe, and Martinique), and the Netherlands Antilles.[35]

The ACS aims to create "an enhanced economic space in the region," to preserve "the environmental integrity of the Caribbean Sea," and to promote "the sustainable development of the Greater Caribbean." Trade, transport, and natural disasters are "its current focal areas."[36]

Seven CARICOM participants also belong to the Organization of Eastern Caribbean States (OECS), which has nine members. The CARICOM seven are Antigua and Barbuda, the Commonwealth of Dominica, Grenada, Montserrat, St Kitts and Nevis, St Lucia, and St Vincent and the Grenadines. Montserrat remains a British Dependent Territory. The other two members of the OECS are also British Dependent Territories. Anguilla, which is the most northerly of the Leeward Islands in the eastern Caribbean, and the British Virgin Islands, an archipelago of thirty-six islands to the east of the US Virgin islands. Anguilla and the British Virgin Islands are associate members of the OECS.

The OECS is a bonded community with its own institutions. It has its own central bank and common currency, which makes it the only cross-border economic grouping in the western hemisphere with these characteristics so far. The Eastern Caribbean Central Bank issues the Eastern Caribbean Dollar. The Eastern Caribbean Supreme Court is a superior court of record for all nine members.[37]

The Central American Common Market (CACM) is another organization with significant potential to strengthen the economic integration of the western hemisphere. Sometimes called the Central American Integration System, the CACM has five members: Costa Rica, El Salvador, Guatemala, Honduras, and Nicaragua.

Bilateral and multilateral agreements are preparing the way for wider economic integration. In April, 1998, the CACM and the Dominican Republic signed a treaty concerning free trade. The Dominican Republic belongs neither to the CACM nor CARICOM but is a member of the ACS. On 1 December 2001, a free trade agreement between CARICOM and the Dominican Republican came into force. On 9 March 2004, CARICOM and Costa Rica, a member of the CACM, signed a free trade agreement. And on 28 May 2004, the five members of the CACM signed a free trade agreement with the United States, the Central American Free Trade Agreement (CAFTA). CAFTA ignited the type of debate that surrounds an earlier free trade agreement, NAFTA, which is our next topic.

North American Free Trade Area (NAFTA)

NAFTA emerged from the free trade area between Canada and the United States that came into being on 1 January 1989. This free trade pact, as some Canadians called it, occasioned little controversy in the United States but provoked a storm of criticism in Canada.[38]

The trade pact was the major issue in the 1988 federal elections in Canada. The Progressive Conservatives, then in power under the leadership of Prime Minister Brian Mulroney, had sponsored this agreement and were its major defenders. Two other parties, the Liberal Party and the New Democratic Party, opposed it. They contended that the free trade pact would benefit the United States more than Canada, hurt Canadian farmers, damage Canadian industries unless protected, and adversely affect Canada's then generous social programs.

These challenges all proved unavailing. The Progressive Conservatives won back-to-back terms for only the second time in 100 years. The political debates among party leaders in the 1988 Canadian elections prefigured one major issue in the debate over NAFTA in the United States: the status of US manufacturing industries and their workers in any wider free trade area.

The United States and Canada decided to bring Mexico into the process of liberalization and all three countries approved NAFTA, which came into existence on 1 January 1994, five years after the establishment of the free trade area between Canada and the United States. Unlike the US–Canada pact, NAFTA unleashed an intense debate in the United States that continues today.

The North American Free Trade Agreement, the legal basis for the free trade area (NAFTA), runs 2,000 pages long and contains many provisions not germane to setting up a free trade area. Their inclusion testifies to the logrolling needed to get this agreement through the United States House of Representatives on 17 November 1993. This document contains side agreements that were added to mollify substantial opposition to NAFTA.

Let us sketch the original agreement, the side agreements, and two other proposals enacted to promote the success of NAFTA. We will then evaluate NAFTA on its tenth anniversary, 1 January 2004.

NAFTA aims to eliminate gradually almost all trade and investment restrictions among Canada, Mexico, and the United States over fifteen years. Tariffs are to be reduced at different rates for different products over this period. Consider agriculture, automobiles, and textiles as three major examples. Most tariffs on agricultural commodities traded between Mexico and the United States were eliminated immediately.

But producers of certain "sensitive" products have the full fifteen years to adjust to duty-free status for their merchandise. In the "sensitive" category are corn and dry beans from Mexico; and orange juice concentrate, melons, sugar, and asparagus from the United States.

The automobile industry is treated under three rubrics: tariffs, quotas, and "local content." Tariffs on autos are to be removed over ten years, as are Mexico's quotas on imports. "Local" in local content here means North American; to qualify for duty-free treatment within NAFTA the North American content of cars had to reach 62.5 percent after eight years.

On textiles the agreement eliminates Canadian, Mexican, and US tariffs over ten years. For clothes to qualify for tariff breaks they must be sewn with fabric woven in North America.[39]

There are important exclusions from the agreement. Legal immigration is excluded, although restrictions on the movement of white-collar workers should lessen. Private sector exploration of Mexican energy, like oil, is excluded, although the state-owned oil company, *Petroleos Mexicanos* or Pemex, opens up procurement to Canadian and US bidders. Mexico is to eliminate all barriers to Canadian and US participation in its financial services sector. And investment restrictions are removed, with four major exceptions: culture in Canada, oil in Mexico, and airline and radio communications in the United States.

NAFTA has two major side agreements. The first concerns the environment. The three countries are liable to fines, and Mexico and the United States are vulnerable to sanctions, if a panel finds a "repeated pattern" of not enforcing environmental laws. The second side agreement deals with labor. All three countries are liable to penalties for "non-enforcement" of child, minimum wage, and health and safety laws.[40]

Two other proposals accompany NAFTA. These are separate items, not part of the NAFTA treaty itself or appended to it as side agreements. The first established the North American Development Bank. Its purpose is to help finance the clean up of the border between Mexico and the United States. The second is US legislation that provides for retraining workers who lose their jobs because of NAFTA.

NAFTA marked its tenth birthday on 1 January 2004, with a mixed record that provokes fierce debate. Discussion is intense, because there is considerable disagreement over how to evaluate NAFTA. Should the historical record of NAFTA be examined only on economic criteria? Or should it be submitted to tests from political economy? Both approaches are necessary, we believe, in order to appreciate why NAFTA is so controversial.

Economic criteria include trade, investment, and jobs. Political economy looks more deeply at the kinds of jobs lost, who did them, and where they live. It also considers popular support, and questions of national strategy and security.

As to the economic criteria of trade and investment, the evidence is irrefutable. During the first ten years of NAFTA, cross-border trade and investment increased substantially. Consider trade first. In 1990 United States exports to, and imports from, Canada and Mexico made up about a quarter of its trade. Now these account for about a third of US trade. This is a "dramatic switch," because the non-NAFTA trade of the US also grew strongly during this time.[41]

NAFTA direct investment rose impressively during the period 1994–2002. For example, US direct investment in Mexico rose about 240 percent, to $58 billion. Mexico's direct investment in the US increased about 270 percent, to $8 billion. Canada's rates of increase were not as great, but Canada already had major two-way investment ties with the US. During 1994–2002, US direct investment in Canada rose about 110 percent, to $153 billion. Canada's direct investment in the US increased about 125 percent, to $92 billion.[42]

The impact of NAFTA on employment is not so straightforward. Between 1994 and 2000 the US economy created more than two million jobs every year. But in the United States jobs in manufacturing have continued to decline.

The precise role of NAFTA in this deterioration is disputed. *The Economist* believes that NAFTA is "one relatively minor cause among many" for job losses in US manufacturing. They conclude that "even NAFTA's highest estimated direct [job] losses can hardly be regarded as crippling."[43] Perhaps this is so, if "crippling" applies only to the US economy as a whole. But that is the macroeconomic level.

One must consider various microeconomic levels in order to assess the full impact of NAFTA. These microeconomic levels reveal that the conclusions advanced by *The Economist* concerning NAFTA and job destruction are incomplete. Consider the following analysis of NAFTA and jobs in US manufacturing.

In this inquiry one generalization is indisputable. Owners of US manufacturing enterprises have gained from easier access to Mexico. They can accelerate the process of locating more of their manufacturing capacity south of the border to take advantage of lower wages paid to Mexican workers, who are not unionized. Mexican workers do not enjoy the legislative protection accorded collective bargaining and the workplace in the United States. In the language of business strategy, NAFTA has intensified the "localization of production" in "developing markets" with lower labor costs and fewer worker protections that is occurring elsewhere in the world.

The "localization" of US production in Mexico has involved two approaches. The first consists of plants, known as *maquilladoras*, that assemble products from imported parts. The finished goods are then exported, largely to the United States.[44] The first approach adds less value to the product on-site and so deprives Mexico of the financial returns that more value adding would bring.

The second approach, which adds more value in Mexico, attempts to manufacture domestically more of the components for finished products. Mexico acknowledges the need to develop processes that add more value at home, but its most dynamic industrial growth still occurs in the *maquilladoras*. In the first nine months of 1998, the *maquilladoras* generated 100,000 new jobs.[45] NAFTA has not similarly empowered workers in US manufacturing industries.[46] In fact, the localization of US production within Mexico has led to job losses in the United States. Two important questions are, what kinds of jobs are disappearing and how substantial are these reductions?

The answers are complicated. Localization began before NAFTA and would have continued without it. NAFTA accelerated an ongoing process by making it easier, so fairness dictates that NAFTA not be blamed entirely for this situation. Several hundred thousand workers in US manufacturing have been "downsized" because of "localization" that is partly attributable to NAFTA; some estimates run into the 300,000s and higher. Some of the jobs eliminated are "lower paid" in US terms.[47] But many are not. The departing jobs go to Mexican workers, who are even more "lower paid" by US standards.

While US manufacturing has lost a significant number of its "lower paid" jobs to Mexico, the financial services industry in the United States has gained a substantial number of new jobs, supposedly because of NAFTA. Ironically, these new jobs, like those lost, are "lower paid" in US terms.

Everyone agrees that NAFTA has created some jobs and destroyed others in the United States. Disagreements arise over the net impact of NAFTA on the US labor force. The Clinton administration, which strongly defended NAFTA, stressed job creation. It asserted in 1997 that 2.3 million jobs in the United States are supported by exports to Mexico and Canada; 311,000 of these jobs can be attributed to increased trade under NAFTA.

The Economic Policy Institute, a demanding critic of NAFTA, argued that the Clinton administration focused on only part of the story. Their analysts stress that the crucial criterion is net job creation, which considers imports as well as exports. The Economic Policy Institute claimed that during the first three years NAFTA has been in place, from 1 January 1994 through 31 December 1996, US exports to Mexico rose by $17 billion, which created 210,000 US jobs. But imports from Mexico into the United States increased by $33 billion, which eliminated 460,000 US jobs. In US–Mexico relations, the net job loss was 250,000; between Canada and the United States, the net US job loss was 170,000. US net job loss, therefore, during NAFTA's first three years was, according to the EPI, 420,000.[48]

The impact of NAFTA on US jobs continues negative in further studies published by the Economic Policy Institute. Robert E. Scott, an economist with the EPI, argues that NAFTA "eliminated 766,030 actual and potential US jobs between 1994 and 2000 because of the growth in the net US export deficit with Mexico and Canada."[49] And in "NAFTA at 10," Jeff Faux, distinguished fellow of the EPI, suggests that since the implementation of NAFTA, "at least a half-million jobs have been lost [in the US], many of them in towns and rural areas where there are no job alternatives."[50]

The preceding argument over NAFTA and jobs remains largely on the macroeconomic level. Microeconomic levels provide deeper insight into the difficulties of assessing the impact of NAFTA on US manufacturing. The experience of agribusiness in the State of Iowa is revealing. Agribusiness designates companies making farm-related products or providing agriculture with financial and other services. During NAFTA's first three years, from 1994 through 1996, Iowa substantially increased its exports of merchandise goods by $740 million, up 38 percent during this period.

This success "rekindled" the NAFTA debate because of the following facts. About 40 percent of this gain in merchandise exports came in machinery, which includes the backhoes, tractors, bailers, and cotton pickers made by John Deere in its Iowa plants. The major destinations for Deere products are Canada, Europe, and Australia. But John Deere's Iowa labor force started shrinking long before NAFTA. One union leader stated that John Deere has less than one-third of the workers in its Waterloo, Iowa, factory than it had in 1979.[51]

The Iowa case underscores the Delphic nature of the evidence concerning NAFTA. How much NAFTA contributed to the shrinking of John Deere's Iowa labor force is impossible to factor out. How much of the increase in Iowa's merchandise exports can be assigned directly to NAFTA is also anybody's guess. Canada, not Mexico, is a major destination for Deere's agribusiness manufactures. Indeed, Canada is the largest market for machinery exports from Iowa. So the issue is not just NAFTA, but the antecedent Canada–US free trade pact and the role this bilateral agreement played in stimulating an increase in Deere's exports to Canada.

A sage once remarked, "all politics is local." This should be an axiom of political economy, but it is sometimes forgotten in the NAFTA debate. Our first two tests from political economy are best understood in light of this axiom.

Total job losses in manufacturing may not "cripple" the US economy, but they devastate particular areas and groups of people. It is the types of jobs destroyed, who lost them, and where they live that show why NAFTA is such a hot political issue. The political economy of lost jobs explains why NAFTA is not popular. In fact, NAFTA can be portrayed as battering the "working poor."

Some of the jobs lost under NAFTA are, to be sure, "lower paid." But they were jobs in industries seen as the vanguard of industrialization in their areas. These were industries with long histories in their regions, providing employment for many generations of workers. Damaging these industries did not just destroy jobs, but struck at the intergenerational families of displaced workers and the social fabric of many communities. The stories of textile workers, in states like North Carolina, give human dimensions to the harms of NAFTA.

The impact of NAFTA varies considerably state-by-state. This unevenness provides another clue as to why NAFTA is so unpopular. A number of states have experienced NAFTA-related job losses disproportionate to their share of the overall US labor force. These are Alabama, Arkansas, Indiana, Michigan, North Carolina, Tennessee, and Texas. Other hard-hit states include Ohio and Pennsylvania.[52]

The State of Ohio provides a striking example of political economy trumping economics. Ohio has lost tens of thousands of manufacturing jobs in recent years. Many were jobs with good benefits that paid working people well. Even though some estimate that NAFTA itself can only be blamed for 10 percent to 15 percent of these lost jobs, dry economics is powerless to assuage human suffering. And economics without a human face cannot compete with political rhetoric, which has made free trade in general and NAFTA in particular in the twin demons of US manufacturing decline.

The electoral arithmetic of NAFTA-related job losses further renders antiseptic economic arguments for free trade politically impotent. The Electoral College is the legal institution that elects the US President. There are 538 electoral votes; 270 are needed to win. Each state has electoral votes equal to the number of its representatives and senators in the Congress. Each state has two senators; population apportions representatives. There are 435 representatives and 100 senators. The District of Columbia has three electoral votes.

Look at the electoral votes of the states that have experienced job losses disproportionate to their share of the overall US labor force: Alabama (9); Arkansas (6); Indiana (11); Michigan (17); North Carolina (15); Tennessee (11); and Texas (34). Add the electoral votes of two other states hit hard by NAFTA: Ohio (20) and Pennsylvania (21). These states yield 144 of the 270 necessary to become the US President. No wonder that the alleged evils of NAFTA and unrestrained free trade have become such potent political issues.

Defenders of NAFTA and free trade, who correctly cite increased trade and investment as macroeconomic benefits, have not been able to invest these trends with the humanity necessary to triumph in the arena of political economy. NAFTA has indeed become a classic case study of a warning concerning free trade. It is not enough to win the debate in economic terms. You must argue your case in the forum of political economy. And you must do a much better job of public relations: show real working people in modest economic circumstances benefitting from NAFTA and free trade. Many voters remain unconvinced that increased growth and investment mean a better future for everyday Americans. That is the monumental task that confronts the proponents of free trade: to present a compelling case in terms of political economy, not just economics.

This challenge will only become more formidable as other trade proposals must be defended. The Central American Free Trade Agreement (CAFTA), mentioned earlier, did pass the US Congress in 2005. President George W. Bush signed CAFTA, which also includes the Dominican Republic, into law on 2 August 2005. But CAFTA passed the US House of Representatives by only two votes, 217–215. The closeness of this vote clouds the prospects for future trade agreements.[53]

The Congressional debate over CAFTA was, in most respects, a re-run of the NAFTA debate in the mid-1990s. Environmental groups, US unions, and others view CAFTA through the NAFTA template, which they regard as defective. NAFTA does not provide, they argue, adequate protections of either the environment or workers' rights.[54] CAFTA is supposedly open to the same charges.[55]

Defenders tried to sell CAFTA as a good economic agreement, with many more winners than losers.[56] But in the aftermath of September 11 there was greater emphasis on the alleged security implications of the agreement. Proponents contend that CAFTA will economically strengthen the fledgling democracies of the region. These could, in turn, play roles in the grand strategy that links, rightly or wrongly, the spread of democracy with winning the global war against terror.

The United States hopes to expand NAFTA and CAFTA to the rest of Latin America by eventually creating a Free Trade Area of the Americas (FTAA). Key countries like Brazil are already skeptical of its benefits. If the advocates of free trade agreements do not realize that they are creating organizations of political economy, the FTAA may not be as lucky as CAFTA was in the US House of Representatives.

Be that as it may, there is a major strategic issue under the rubric of political economy that deserves more attention from both the proponents and opponents of free trade. This concerns the importance of an indigenous manufacturing base for a country that claims to be the one remaining military "superpower" in the world.

A defining moment in the US debate over NAFTA was the famous "dialogue" between Vice-President Al Gore and Ross Perot on the "Larry King Show," broadcast live on the Cable News Network, 9 November 1993.[57] Gore defended NAFTA; Perot opposed it.

This "magic moment" for the proponents of NAFTA, as President Bill Clinton later called it, was disappointing. Gore did an above-average job defending NAFTA, but Perot did not present the strongest case possible against it. In fact, Perot, in his scatter-shot attack on NAFTA, never developed the strategic argument: that however beneficial free trade is in many ways for the United States, there are certain things no country can expose totally to the vagaries of unregulated international competition. To wit, the United States must retain a substantial manufacturing base within its own borders for reasons of self-preservation.

Some suggest that an indigenous manufacturing base is an anachronism in an interdependent global economy. For its own security, they say, the US could still stockpile in advance or import capital goods when needed from friendly countries. Well, the "global economy" contains sovereign nation-states and human beings will always fight over land and other resources.

The "global economy" may not function too well in a regional or world war: air, sea, and land shipping routes will be disrupted. And estimating inventories needed in times of conflict is notoriously problematic. Those who claim an indigenous manufacturing base is not needed place too much faith in the ameliorative effects of economic cooperation on political conflict. Moreover, they forget that all economic groupings are creatures of political economy.

The economic logic of regional integration rests, in part, on the principle of comparative advantage.[58] That is, a country specializes in what it produces most efficiently and then trades with outsiders for everything else it needs. But NAFTA, and all other groupings, must be evaluated, I argue, in the context of political economy, which intertwines economic and political logics. Political logic emphasizes security, which is greatly enhanced by a strategic manufacturing base within the United States. The dictates of security call for a reformulation of the principle of comparative advantage in terms of political economy.

The broader historical question has never been a complete disjunction: either totally "free trade" or completely regulated commerce. Trade has always been subject to some government involvement, and if a grouping wishes to survive, it must reflect the combined economic and political logics of all participants.

A country should never out-source its own security. No one has ever suggested that the United States abandon its agricultural base and depend on outsiders for vital foodstuffs. The same reasoning should apply to crucial manufacturing processes. What constitutes a strategic manufacturing base should be at the top of the US national agenda. During this era of greater economic integration United States should never place its entire economy, especially its strategic manufacturing base, at the mercy of unpredictable international forces.

Asia and the Western Pacific

There are three major groups in the Asia-Western Pacific region that embrace the concept of a free trade area. These are the Association of South East Asian Nations (ASEAN), the South Asian Association for Regional Co-operation (SAARC), and the Forum or Asia-Pacific Economic Cooperation (APEC). A fourth free trade area may emerge that would link ASEAN and the three regional economic powerhouses of China, India, and Japan.

ASEAN was founded in 1967 to promote regional consultation among its members. But it took on a wider economic significance in the 1990s, as it became the cradle for another major free trade area in the world. In January 1992, the six countries that then belonged to ASEAN proposed the ASEAN Free-Trade Area (AFTA). Brunei, Indonesia, Malaysia, the Philippines, Singapore, and Thailand said they wanted a free trade area by 2007. Since then, four new members have joined ASEAN: Burma, Cambodia, Laos, and Vietnam. And since then, ASEAN has striven for closer forms of economic integration than a free trade area implies.

Triggering the development of an enhanced ASEAN was the international financial crisis that began in Thailand in July, 1997, and destroyed much of the value of its currency, the baht. What began as a harsh downward adjustment of one currency maintained at artificially high levels unleashed powerful forces of contraction that engulfed much of Asia and the western Pacific later in 1997 and through 1998.

This regional downturn, which impoverished Indonesia and shook Malaysia, rippled through the rest of the world and destabilized the international financial system. Unfortunately, some called this disease the "Asian contagion." We reject this term because it evokes memories of the historical stereotype known as the "Yellow Peril": hordes of poor Asian immigrants coming to the United States, polluting its Anglo-Saxon genetic stock, and jaundicing the "American Dream."

The global crisis of 1997–98 influenced the process of economic integration worldwide by making some groups eager to strengthen what they had already created. In 1998 ASEAN approved two major initiatives. The first set up "a joint surveillance system to provide early warning of future economic risk in the region..."[59] All ten members provide information on such matters as interest rates, exchange rates, and capital flows to a monitoring committee in Jakarta, Indonesia, the home of the ASEAN Secretariat.

This committee provides a "peer review" of economic and financial stability in each member country. The principle of "peer review" represents a major departure from ASEAN's usual modus operandi, which is based on non-interference in the domestic affairs of its participants.[60]

The second agreement establishes an Asean Investment Area (AIA) in order to reduce barriers to direct investment flows within ASEAN. By 2010 a direct investment from one ASEAN country in another will be treated, from a regulatory standpoint, as if it were a domestic investment originating in the recipient country. By 2020 the same treatment may be applied to all investors, including those from outside the AIA.[61]

ASEAN's target dates for implementing a free trade area have gone back and forth. An earlier plan to have free trade in place by 2007 proved impractical. Then ASEAN determined to implement fully its free trade area by 2020. In October 2003, the ten leaders of ASEAN signed the Bali Concord II, which embodied this pledge. This document also sets out plans for better co-operation on security and social issues.[62] Then in November 2004, ASEAN decided to accelerate its timetable. The six original members – Brunei, Indonesia, Malaysia, the Philippines, Singapore, and Thailand – will scrap tariffs between them and create a free trade zone from 2007, reverting to the original target date. The other four members – Burma, Cambodia, Laos, and Vietnam – will join the free trade area in 2012.[63]

Meanwhile, ASEAN has pursued free trade agreements with China, India, and Japan. In 2002 China agreed to the framework of a free trade deal with ASEAN. On 8 October 2003, China extended its involvement with ASEAN by signing on to ASEAN's 1976 Treaty of Amity and Co-operation. This treaty calls for dialogue-based solutions to both political and economic disputes. A potentially promising outcome of this diplomatic spadework is the landmark trade agreement between ASEAN and China that was signed in November 2004.

This document is a modest but important step forward. China and the original six members of ASEAN promise to lower tariffs on goods they trade by 2010, but thousands of "sensitive goods," such as sugar, iron, steel and cars, are excluded. The other four members of ASEAN have until

2015 to comply.[64] ASEAN and China by themselves contain 1.7 billion people. If India and Japan were to join ASEAN and China, their grouping would cover almost half the population of the world, which exceeds 6.5 billion people.

A second major free trade area is emerging in south Asia. SAARC has been grappling with its creation since the mid-1990s.[65] The seven members of SAARC are Bangladesh, Bhutan, India, the Maldives, Nepal, Pakistan, and Sri Lanka.

Like ASEAN, SAARC encountered early obstacles. The target date for a SAARC free trade area was initially 2001. But conflicts between India and Pakistan and the 1999 military *coup* in Pakistan upset this timetable.

In January 2004, the members of SAARC finally agreed on the design of a free trade area. Major hurdles remain before the SAARC free trade area becomes operational. The bigger countries, especially India, are concerned that poorer SAARC nations could flood their markets with inexpensive goods. Another problem comes from similar export profiles. SAARC members currently export similar types of goods. The group's biggest players compete in exporting textiles, garments, and agricultural commodities like tea, coffee, and sugar.[66]

SAARC has plans to deal with some of its problems. Tariff cuts will be phased in, and countries can nominate industries for special treatment. Smaller economies will have ten years to implement fully the agreement.[67]

The Pacific littoral: Asian-Pacific Economic Cooperation (APEC)

This grouping covers Asia and the western and eastern Pacific regions: in short, the Pacific littoral. In 1989 Bob Hawke, then Prime Minister of Australia, proposed the establishment of what became APEC, which stands for the Asia-Pacific Economic Cooperation forum, sometimes called the Forum.

APEC began with a far-ranging membership that has become more extensive. Its early members included the six countries that then made up ASEAN: Brunei, Indonesia, Malaysia, the Philippines, Singapore, and Thailand. Other pioneering participants were Australia, Canada, Japan, Korea, New Zealand, and the United States.

An expanding membership has reinforced APEC's geographical reach. In 1991 Chinese Taipei (Taiwan), Hong Kong, and the People's Republic of China became members. In 1993 Mexico and Papua New Guinea joined, as did Chile in 1994. In 1998 Peru, Russia, and Vietnam became "members designate."[68] The only two continents presently excluded from APEC's sweep are Africa and Antarctica. Russia has historically been regarded as both European and Asian; so Russia's joining gives APEC an entrée into Europe from the east.

APEC has truly become immense in geographical reach. APEC is intercontinental: it bridges Asia, part of Europe, North America, South America, and Australia. APEC is transoceanic: it embraces the Pacific littoral. In 2003 its twenty-one members account for 45 percent of world trade. APEC began with a modest goal that remains its forte. Its original aim was to foster economic cooperation among its members rather than the structural integration of their economies. APEC was not a free trade area at the outset in either actuality or intent.

APEC advanced in measured steps through the early 1990s. In 1992 it agreed to establish a secretariat and budget system. In 1993 it declared an APEC Trade and Investment framework. Then in 1993 US President Bill Clinton proposed a giant step: APEC should create its own free trade area, as the twenty-first century, he claimed, would be "the Pacific century." So in 1994 APEC set a goal of achieving "free and open trade and investment in the region by 2020."[69] This objective is to be accomplished in two phases depending on whether a country is "developed" or "developing." The "developed" members of APEC are to create a "free trade and investment area" by 2010. "Developing" countries are granted another decade; they should join this regional grouping by 2020.

Creating a free trade area encountered major obstacles in the late 1990s. These challenges threw the 2010–20 timetable into doubt. The Asian economic meltdown in 1997–98, mentioned above, threatened the process of liberalization, or lowering trade and investment barriers, within APEC as a whole. As a response to that turmoil, Malaysia moved to restrict capital flows and ASEAN, as noted above, introduced its joint surveillance system and the Asean Investment Area. Ironically, ASEAN's joint surveillance system is a more focused version of a broader regional system that APEC itself had approved in November, 1997.[70]

Specific trade issues bedeviled APEC in the late 1990s. These disputes sometimes involved the very meaning of liberalization. In 1997, at their annual meeting in Vancouver, Canada, the leaders of APEC began a drive to accelerate liberalization in nine categories of goods and services.

This initiative had three features that did not bode well for successful implementation. It rested on voluntary compliance, lacked a firm timetable, and did not embody a consensus definition of trade liberalization. These three obstacles would have undermined the initiative eventually, but it quickly collapsed under the weight of a continuing Japanese refusal to "approve faster tariff reductions in fish and forestry."[71] In 1998 Japan rejected free trade in forestry and fishery products "as part of a concerted sectoral liberalisation programme."[72] Its opposition on these matters placed Japan in direct conflict with Australia and the United States.

As for what trade liberalization encompasses, Canadian officials insist that it means reducing both tariff and non-tariff barriers. But some Asian governments apparently maintain that liberalization "need only involve 'economic and technical co-operation' with other members."[73] Co-operation is what China, for instance, prefers APEC to facilitate, especially in the area of technology transfer.

Some controversies within APEC relate to the fundamental way in which economic groupings are construed. The 1998 annual meeting in Malaysia took place during a time of intense political turbulence in that country. Its leader had had his major political rival imprisoned on what some thought were false charges.[74] Vice-President Al Gore, representing the United States at the meeting, remarked on this matter in the context of "human rights" and so contributed to further polarization within both Malaysia and APEC. If the meaning of economic liberalization is a problem for APEC members, so also are the definitions of "human rights" and "non-interference in domestic matters."

The Economist provided a comprehensive précis of the Kuala Lampur meeting and treated events under the categories of politics and economics. "Should the annual APEC forum, held this week in Malaysia, be about politics or economics? It seemed to fail on both counts."[75] Politics and economics can be separated for analytical purposes. But all groupings must ultimately be understood in the context of political economy. *The Economist* implied this approach in its review of the Kuala Lampur meeting, but the premise of political economy needs explicit recognition and appreciation.

APEC has learned from its problems. These days important trade decisions are left to the World Trade Organization, whose decisions are at least binding.[76] And the lack of consensus concerning liberalization, the core process creating a free trade area, may not necessarily be a bad thing. It returns APEC to its original mission – as a venue of consultation and reconciliation. APEC acts as an international safety valve by bringing together countries with divergent economic interests, such as Japan and the United States.

Remaining a viable forum will continue as a major accomplishment. Reconciliation may sometimes be as important for economic cooperation as reducing a physical barrier to exchange. APEC provides yet another example of why economic integration should be viewed as a process blending economic with political factors. A modest goal of cooperation without integration can, in fact, be a substantive objective for any grouping, particularly one containing countries with so many disparate interests.

This discussion of APEC completes our panorama of free trade areas. The next chapter turns to customs unions, the second step on the conventional ladder of inter-government economic integration.

6 Customs unions

This chapter features four organizations that provide geographical and historical perspectives on the customs union, the second of the three major steps on the conventional ladder of international economic integration.

Two come from Africa, one from Europe, and one from South America. From Africa we spotlight the Central African Customs and Economic Union (CACEU) and the Southern African Customs Union (SACU). CACEU is significant as a bridge between colonial and post-independence versions of regional economic integration in central Africa. SACU spans the *apartheid* and post-*apartheid* eras in southern Africa.

From Europe we highlight the *Zollverein.* This is the quintessential customs union from the past. It brought together many parts of what would become the unified German nation-state of the 1870s and beyond and so has enormous historical significance. It was the economic incubator of German political unification, and it also serves as a rich case study of the dos and don'ts of inter-government economic integration.

In South America we find *mercosur*, which has the shortest history of our examples, as it was founded in 1991. *Mercosur* contains four core countries from the "southern cone" of South America – Argentina, Brazil, Paraguay, and Uruguay – and has associate members.

The Central African Customs and Economic Union (CACEU)

Formed in 1965, this grouping was also known as *l'Union Douanière et économique de l'Afrique Centrale* (UDEAC). It consisted of Cameroon, the Central African Republic, the Congo (Brazzaville), Chad, and Gabon. The Congo (Brazzaville) was the former French Congo, which is just northwest of the former Belgian Congo, which became Zaire and is now the Democratic Republic of the Congo.

CACEU at the outset brought together five countries that shared a French colonial heritage. The French approach to colonial administration (see Chapter 1) stressed economic assimilation of the colonies with France. In pursuit of this goal the French created two federations that grouped their west and central African colonies geographically: the Federation of West Africa and the Federation of Equatorial Africa. These federations formally disappeared when their members received "flag independence" from France in the 1960s. But some economic ties between France and its former colonies continue strong: the existence of the CFA zone is one such bond (see Chapter 5).

CACEU became "an effective successor" to the Federation of Equatorial Africa and maintained continuity on crucial economic and financial questions.[1] CACEU had its problems: a shifting membership that included a brief association with Zaire in the late 1960s; and the 1969 seizure of its common ports and railroads by the then president of the Congo. But it survived and became one of Africa's "most successful regional organizations." Its effectiveness hinged on its ongoing relationship with the central bank of the Central African states, which was established in 1959 to supervise the flow of CFA francs into the region.[2]

In the 1990s members of CACEU, which now included Equatorial Guinea,[3] decided to transform their customs and economic union into the Central African Economic and Monetary Community (CAEMC). Its French title is *Communauté économique et Monétaire de l'Afrique Centrale* (CEMAC).

CEMAC was supposed to start in 1994, but its launch was delayed until 1998, mainly because of internal difficulties in member states.[4] The new title for CACEU indicates a vision of closer integration.[5]

The six members of the Central African Economic and Monetary Community also belong to another organization, the Economic Community of Central African States (ECCAS). Its French title is *Communauté économiques d'états de l'Afrique Centrale* (CEEAC). This grouping originated in the early 1980s, when interest increased in the economic integration of larger regions within Africa. The United Nations Economic Commission on Africa (ECA) and the 1980 Lagos Plan of Action energized this activity.

In 1981 the leaders of CACEU agreed in principle to found a wider economic community. ECCAS was established on 18 October 1983, with the assistance of members of the Community of the Great Lakes States and other countries. It began functioning officially in 1985, but remained inactive for years because of financial difficulties and the conflict in the Great Lakes area. The war in the Democratic Republic of the Congo was bitterly divisive, as Rwanda and Angola fought on opposing sides. ECCAS came back to life in the late 1990s.[6]

Today ECCAS comprises Angola, Burundi, Cameroon, the Central African Republic, Chad, the Democratic Republic of the Congo (Kinshasa), the Republic of Congo (Brazzaville), Equatorial Guinea, Gabon, Rwanda, and Sao Tomé and Principe. Its ultimate goal is to establish a Central African Common Market.

ECCAS may have an integral significance for CEMAC beyond overlapping memberships. On 24 January 2003 the European Union concluded a financial agreement with ECCAS and CEMAC, conditional on the two merging into one organization. ECCAS is encouraged to take responsibility "for the peace and security of the subregion."[7]

A merger based on this division of labor would be smart administration. ECCAS has focused in recent years on "the peace and security" of central Africa. Sections of the CEMAC bureaucracy could continue to specialize in economics and money.

The Southern African Customs Union (SACU)

This grouping came into existence in 1969, when the Republic of South Africa, a founding member, was still in the *apartheid* era. It is currently the oldest customs union in the world.

Apartheid means "apartness" in the language of Afrikaans and refers to a system of segregation and discrimination that "white" South Africans imposed on South Africans of "color." *Apartheid* began in 1950, with the infamous Population Registration Act, which put every South African in a racial category: "whites," "browns," "blacks," etc.

Apartheid was a program of the Nationalist Party, which had won the national elections in 1948. This party was the home of the Afrikaners, from whose language comes the word *apartheid*. They are "white" South Africans, many of whom trace their lineage back to the Dutch who settled in the country starting in 1652. *Apartheid* did not come to a complete legal end until 1994. In that year Nelson Mandela was elected and became the President of South Africa. There were also elections in 1994 to the South African Parliament, in which his party, the African National Congress, garnered over 60 percent of the popular vote.

SACU has four other members. They are Botswana, Lesotho, Namibia, and Swaziland, or the BLNS countries, as they are sometimes called. Each completed its own journey towards "flag independence."

Botswana, Lesotho, and Swaziland followed a similar route. All were colonial protectorates of Great Britain and under direct control from London. So when Great Britain decolonized most of its African Empire, all received their "flag independence" in 1966. They all, however, remained economically reliant on South Africa, a dependency rooted partly in geography. Lesotho (the former Basutoland) is surrounded by South Africa. Botswana (the former Bechuanaland) is also landlocked, but bordered by South Africa to its south, Zimbabwe to its northeast, and Namibia to its north and west. Swaziland, too, has no opening to the sea. It faces South Africa to its north, west, and south; a portion of its eastern border is with South Africa, but most of it fronts Mozambique, which is on the Indian Ocean.

Namibia took a different and more tortuous path and got its "flag independence" much later. Germany annexed it as German South-West Africa in the 1880s. When Germany lost World War I, South-West Africa became a mandate of the League of Nations and was entrusted to South Africa as a Class C mandate. A Class C mandate was least able to stand on its own. Territories designated as Class B or Class A mandates were closer to that goal.

After World War II, with the founding of the United Nations, the mandates of the old League of Nations became trusteeships. Trusteeship was a more modern term than mandate; it was still patronizing, though not as overtly condescending as the mandate system was. South Africa refused to recognize this change and was accused by the international community of failing in its responsibilities to South-West Africa.

In 1966 the International Court of Justice invalidated the legal position of South Africa in respect to South-West Africa. South Africa ignored this ruling and indeed the exhortations of many countries. For over seventy-five years South-West Africa remained under the control of South Africa, which treated its residents the same way it oppressed the people of "color" in South Africa itself.

Finally, the long nightmare of official discrimination and repression ended, when South-West Africa got its "flag independence" as Namibia on 21 March 1990; but as for Botswana, Lesotho, and Swaziland, legal independence did not end the excessive reliance of Namibia on South Africa itself.

The renaissance of South Africa in 1994 under a majority rule government set in motion forces that have greatly altered the economic landscape of southern Africa. Major changes have occurred between members of SACU and the outside world, and within SACU itself.

South Africa has experienced an economic revolution in its external trade relations. In the mid-1990s about two-thirds of South Africa's African export trade took place within SACU, and South Africa supplied the bulk of the imports of the other four countries. Over the last decade South Africa has greatly diversified the roster of its trading partners and steadily expanded its exports. This sea change resulted from a number of factors. The events of 1994 brought South Africa into the international system and ended the boycotts. South Africa belongs to the free trade agreement of the Southern African Development Community (SADC) and has a free trade agreement with the European Union (EU) that tilts in South Africa's favor. South Africa enjoys preferential access to the US market through the African Growth and Opportunity Act (AGOA) of May 2000. South Africa is negotiating free trade agreements with India, Nigeria, and *Mercosur* in South America.[8]

"Outside of Europe, the US is SACU's second largest trading partner," claimed Alec Erwin, the South African Trade and Industry Minister, in January 2003.[9] This is true, for the grouping as a whole, but Botswana, Lesotho, Swaziland, and Namibia all have different trade profiles, which call for using the acronym BLNS as merely that, and not as jejune analytical shorthand for "the other members of SACU."

Let us consider each country in turn.[10] The calculations are in US dollars. For 2002 Botswana had the following export partners: 87 percent with EFTA (the European Free Trade Association), 7 percent with SACU, and 4 percent with Zimbabwe. For 2000 Botswana had these import partners: 74 percent with SACU, 17 percent with EFTA, and 4 percent with Zimbabwe.

For 2002 Lesotho had the following export partners: 97.5 percent with the US, 0.9 percent with Canada, and 0.6 percent with France. Also for 2002 Lesotho had these import partners: 51.9 percent with Hong Kong, 25 percent with China, and 3.9 percent with France.

For 2001 Namibia had the following export partners: 79 percent with the EU and 4 percent with the US. Also for 2001 Namibia had these import partners: 50 percent with the US and 31 percent with the EU.

For 1999 Swaziland had the following export partners: 72 percent with South Africa, 14.2 percent with the EU, 3.7 percent with Mozambique, and 3.5 percent with the US. Also for 1999 Swaziland had these import partners: 88.8 percent with South Africa, 5.6 percent with the EU, 0.6 percent with Japan, and 0.4 percent with Singapore.

Clearly, Botswana, Lesotho, Namibia, and Swaziland have diversified their trading patterns since 1994. Swaziland still does the greatest shares of its export and import trading with South Africa; and Namibia, while it has increased its trade with the European Union and the United States, pegs the Namibian dollar to the South African rand. But all members of SACU are developing trade ties with many countries that are outside of Africa.

Geography dictates that Botswana, Lesotho, Namibia, and Swaziland maintain close economic and political relations with their neighbor South Africa. This is why a modernized SACU is so important to the region.

Since 1969, SACU has performed its basic functions efficiently. It facilitated the free flow of goods and services among its members. It also collected customs levies on imports that entered SACU from non-member states, as well as various excise taxes, money that it then distributed among the member states according to an agreed formula. Earnings from this pool of customs and excise taxes make up a major part of the revenues of Botswana, Lesotho, Namibia, and Swaziland.[11] Namibia, for instance, drew over 30 percent of its annual revenue from this pool in the late 1990s.[12]

But SACU needed to be renovated to reflect the realities of a democratic South Africa. All SACU members decided that the 1969 Customs Agreement needed a major overhaul. In July 1995, SACU ministers announced plans to make the union "more democratic." They agreed to develop a joint approach to decision-making on important issues. They also decided to set up a council of ministers and a "neutral Secretariat."[13] Negotiations went on for years, but achieved success.

On 21 October 2002, the heads of state of Botswana, Lesotho, Namibia, Swaziland, and South Africa signed a new Southern African Customs Union Agreement (SACUA) in Gaborone, Botswana.[14] This agreement provides for a more democratic institutional structure and sets up a dispute settlement mechanism. It also requires that all members have common policies on industrial development, agriculture, competition, and unfair trade practices. And it proposes a fairer system regarding the common revenue pool and sharing formula.[15]

SACUA thus attempts to make the Southern African Customs Union both efficient and fair. The new common revenue pool and sharing formula illustrate more equitable treatment for all members. Under the 1969 customs formula, South Africa received its share as a residual, but under the new agreement South Africa will share on the same basis as the other four members. The new customs formula tilts towards the BLNS countries. "The intention is clear," Colin McCarthy writes: "to create a favourable regime that will avoid or at least contain a fall in the customs revenue of BLNS."[16] A decline in SACU customs revenue could happen, depending on the impact of the existing free trade agreement between South Africa and the European Union and the prospective FTA between SACU and the US.

As to the latter, the United States and the five members of SACU initiated negotiations toward a free trade agreement in Pretoria, South Africa, on 2 June 2003. The US administration is pushing this FTA, seen as an effort to build on the "success" of the African Growth and Opportunity Act, mentioned above.

According to the web site of the United States Trade Representative (USTR), "free trade with southern Africa is a vital part of the Bush Administration's broader effort to drive global trade liberalization, to lower consumer costs, to create new commercial opportunities for US companies, farmers and workers in fast growing regions of the world, and to draw developing countries into the mainstream of the global economy."[17]

A FTA with SACU could help "level the playing field in areas where US exporters were disadvantaged by the European Union's free trade agreement with South Africa..." The stakes in these negotiations are high: an opportunity for the US to gain guaranteed preferential access to its largest export market in sub-Saharan Africa, worth more than $2.5 billion in 2002.[18]

Not everyone is so enthusiastic about a prospective FTA between the US and SACU. Oxfam America has raised questions about this agreement, as it has about the proposed Free Trade Area of the Americas (Chapter 5) and bilateral trade agreements with Chile and Singapore. Oxfam is concerned that a US–SACU FTA would undermine the ability of SACU governments "to regulate investment, ensure access to affordable medicines, and guarantee food security and the livelihoods of poor farmers."[19]

The OXFAM critique rests on the conviction that "if the US truly wants to help the countries of Southern Africa, it should back provisions on agriculture, investment, and intellectual property in the WTO and elsewhere that will benefit developing countries, not just US business interests."[20]

Whatever happens to the US–SACU Free Trade Agreement, SACU may have great importance for regional economic integration beyond itself. One of the many issues that challenged the negotiators of SACUA was the precise relationship between SACU and other organizations, such as the Southern African Development Community (SADC). All five members of SACU belong to SADC, and relations between a customs union and a free trade area are always intricate.

The "special significance" of SACUA is that "SACU is officially recognized to be a building block in the development of a customs union for the Southern African Development Community (SADC)." SACU has critical roles yet to play: if and when SADC transitions to a customs union and if and when SADC consolidates with other continental groupings, such as the Common Market for Eastern and Southern Africa (COMESA), discussed in Chapter 5. Some, in fact, see SACU as the core of a trade agreement that will cover all of southern Africa.[21]

The *Zollverein*

This grouping transports us from central and southern Africa in the twentieth century back to central Europe in the early 1800s. Germany did not then exist as a unified nation-state. In 1800 a unified Germany was an aspiration and state of mind for many. But in practice there were numerous political entities that made up the *corpus Germanicorum*.

This phrase means "body of the Germanies." In 1789 there were about 314 "Germanies," or separate polities, that comprised the *corpus Germanicorum*. This was political power exercised on many local levels. The *Zollverein* grouped many of these entities, in different sets at different times, and fashioned a customs union that included more and more of the *corpus Germanicorum*. In so doing, the *Zollverein* greatly facilitated the political unification of Germany, a process that unfolded in the 1860s and early 1870s.

The German roots of the name *Zollverein* reveal what the group really became. *Zoll* is a "custom, duty, or tariff," and *verein*, a "union": a customs union. There is an exceptional fit between the name of this group and what it actually was. This perfect congruence has not always happened in the history of international economic integration, which is filled with groups whose titles advertise an economic integration not delivered.

The *Zollverein* sheds great light on the consummate challenge every organization concerned with economic integration faces. This is the problem of "sequencing."

"Sequencing" has three meanings for so-called economic groupings. The first concerns the pace and manner in which its economic integration unfolds. The second deals with the pace and manner of a grouping's political evolution. The third may be the most complicated: the pace and manner in which develops the intertwined dynamic of politics and economics that is the ultimate power source for every grouping.

The *Zollverein* emerged over seven decades in intricate sequences involving its economics, politics, and political economy. We see nine steps in the evolution of the *Zollverein*.[22]

Step 1. Before 1818: creating the intellectual foundation.
Step 2. 1818: Prussia abolished its own internal customs and formed a North German *Zollverein*.
Step 3. 1828: Middle German Commercial Union founded.
Step 4. 1828: South German *Zollverein* founded.
Step 5. 1834: Creation of the German *Zollverein*.
Step 6. 1834: Creation of the *Steuerverein* of central Germany.
Step 7. 1851–54: a series of treaties joined the *Steuerverein* to the *Zollverein*.
Step 8. 1867: New *Zollverein*, New Constitution.
Step 9. 1871: the German Empire legally subsumed the *Zollverein*.

Let us put each step into the contexts of "sequencing" economics, politics, and political economy.

Step 1: before 1818: laying the intellectual foundation

This was done at a time of great fragmentation for the *corpus Germanicorum*. It is crucial to grasp the political situation in Europe in the early 1800s and how it would affect the destinies of the various "Germanies."

This exercise must begin with Napoléon Bonaparte, who was emerging as the leader of France. He became First Consul for life (1802–04) and then emperor of the French (1804–14 and 1815).

Beginning in the 1790s Napoléon engaged in a series of military campaigns. These had evolving goals: first to protect the French Revolution, which had begun in 1789, on its home soil; and then to export his version of the French Revolution to the world. Napoléon and his forces travelled to different parts of Europe and Egypt. The Napoleonic Empire reached its zenith in 1810 and 1811, when it influenced the entire European mainland except the Balkans. Napoléon was eventually defeated on 18 June 1815, at Waterloo, Belgium, by a coalition of European armies. While Napoléon lost militarily in the end, he was, by all accounts, a charismatic leader of panoramic vision, a great reformer of French law, and a military genius who over-reached.[23]

The Congress of Vienna convened in 1814 and 1815 to consider the shape and boundaries of Europe after Napoléon. How this Congress acted with regard to central Europe provides one key to understanding the increasing frustration of those who dreamt of uniting the *corpus Germanicorum* in some way – either economically, administratively, or emotionally. The Congress, in crucial respects, endorsed the status quo and did not return to the status quo ante: central Europe as it existed before Napoléon. The Congress, in short, decided not to rebuild what some have called the "Humpty Dumpty" of the Holy Roman Empire.[24]

This statement is factual, but the figure of speech in which the Holy Roman Empire is wrapped does justice neither to Humpty Dumpty nor to the HRE. Humpty Dumpty was unitary, before he fell and smashed himself into so many pieces that not even an expert restoration group of "all the king's horses and all the king's men" could put him together again.

The HRE lost whatever cohesion it had as it aged. Some acknowledge Charlemagne as its founder and his coronation in AD 800 as its formal beginning. The HRE is usually described as a collection of Germanic states; but the passage of time rendered that collection ever looser. By the 1700s the HRE was at best lines on a map demarcating a surreal entity that could serve as a rallying point for those who wanted to revive the empire of Charlemagne on an even grander scale throughout Europe. So in the decades before Napoléon the Holy Roman Empire was surely not unitary; it was not even confederal. It was much more symbolic and even mystical.

But the "Humpty Dumpty" metaphor does evoke one crucial notion that applies to Germany in the early 1800s: that of pieces. Humpty Dumpty, apparently, was smashed into so many pieces that even a partial reconstruction was impossible. Many Germans could certainly connect with the idea of "pieces," as they lived in so many pieces of the *corpus Germanicorum*.

Yet their pieces were not so tiny or bereft of identity as to discourage thoughts of putting them together. In fact, most "Germanies" yearned to be one *corpus*. And there is a crucial difference between feeling demolished and feeling denied. Humpty Dumpty was demolished. Many living in the *corpus Germanicorum* felt aggrieved by what transpired at the Congress of Vienna.

This convocation did several things to upset those who yearned for some kind of German unification. Writing off the HRE angered those who saw it as a basis for building a pan-Germanic empire. And when the Congress confirmed the French and Napoleonic reorganization of Germany, it endorsed the forces of division in other respects. Napoléon had bestowed crowns on the kings of Bavaria, Saxony, and Württemberg that they were allowed to keep. The Congress acknowledged George III, King of England, as king, not "elector" of Hanover.

But, to be fair, both Napoléon and the Congress consolidated the number of "Germanies." Napoléon significantly streamlined the *corpus Germanicorum* as he organized his European empire. Westphalia is a classic example of Napoleonic reorganization. It was "an entirely new and synthetic state, made up of Hanoverian and Prussian territories and various atoms of the old Germany."[25] And a Confederation of the Rhine encompassed all polities of the *corpus* between what France had seized on the west and what Prussia and Austria embraced on the east. Napoléon regarded Prussia and Austria, major members of the *corpus*, as allies. But they remained independent states outside the Confederation. Though it broke up in 1813, the Confederation of the Rhine hinted at what the Congress of Vienna could do.

The Congress of Vienna consolidated the almost 300 states of the Holy Roman Empire, which dissolved in 1806, into thirty-nine states. It placed them in a new German Confederation, under the leadership of Prussia and Austria. This was a "loose" confederation in which each member retained considerable sovereignty, but it lasted until 1866, when Prussia and Austria went to war against each other.

Streamlining the *corpus Germanicorum* would assist the work of the *Zollverein* in the long run, but in the short run administrative consolidation strengthened the autonomy of the remaining "Germanies" at the expense of a unified *corpus*. This deepened the frustrations of German nationalists.[26]

Besides division, a second political theme dominates the period before 1818, when the intellectual foundation for the *Zollverein* is being laid. This is vagueness. While German nationalists were strong in the clarity of their desires for a unified Fatherland, they were weak in the vagueness of their proposals for governing a unified *corpus*.

The Congress of Vienna endorsed the principle that each German state should have a representative legislative body, but did not elaborate on this suggestion. Whatever its democratic promise, this proposal was, for German nationalists, just another reinforcement of localism. But the nationalists were as vague on the national level. They did not offer specifics on what institutions and constitutions should organize a unified Germany.

The *Zollverein* needs to be appreciated as addressing both division and vagueness. All arrangements of political economy can at times be stressful for their participants, but writing constitutions that embody timeless frameworks and detailing blueprints for entire governments can be decidedly more difficult than agreeing on the first steps for setting up a customs union.

The *Zollverein* concentrated first on its economic sequencing. This was effective strategy, because the economics of the *Zollverein* lent themselves to earlier solutions than its politics or political economy. Tariff disputes can be intractable, but arguments over political ideology can be insoluble. It behooves an economic grouping that wishes to survive to take sometimes the less difficult path. In some situations too much "pain" can mean "no gain."

A customs union rests on clear principles and possesses straightforward structures. Since most German nationalists could not agree for a long time on either political principles or structures, the *Zollverein* had to focus on its economic sequencing, where a consensus over principle and structure was less difficult to achieve.

In concentrating on its economics the *Zollverein* indirectly spoke to its politics and political economy. If one wonders why governments of the "Germanies" went right to a customs union, skipping the first step of a free trade area, the answer lies in the protection a customs union provides: a common external tariff.

This material defense had ramifications far beyond shielding attempts by members to integrate their economies. The tariff wall was also guarding the incubating political unification of the *corpus Gemanicorum* and defending the dream of a unified Fatherland against the hostile forces that swirled around it.

The clear principles that inform a customs union emerge from the writings of many thinkers, but in the German context a writer with great impact on policy was Friedrich List. In his magisterial treatise *History of Economic Analysis*, Joseph Alois Schumpeter, one of the most influential economists of the twentieth century, calls List a "nonprofessional economist."[27] One can evidently be a "nonprofessional economist" and still have a major impact on history. Schumpeter also describes Karl Marx as a "nonprofessional economist." While Marx's influence has been more global, List's contributions to an emerging German nation-state were inestimable.

List developed three themes that have great relevance for the *Zollverein*. The first is the notion of stages. The second is an "infant industry" argument. And the third is the idea of the customs union itself.

To be sure, List did not originate any of these themes and they emerged at different times. The "infant industry" argument, for example, is developed later, in the 1840s, and so technically comes after the pre-1818 period of laying the foundation; but the application together of these three ideas to the German situation was innovative.

The second and third themes are companions. A common external tariff, the core feature of a customs union, can be so deployed as to protect a fledgling or "infant industry" within that grouping. List, who spent time in the United States, owes an intellectual debt to Alexander Hamilton for the "infant industry" argument. Hamilton was a major contributor to the *Federalist Papers* and also wrote *The Report on Public Credit* (1790) and *The Report on Manufactures* (1791). He crafted his thoughts on protection with regard to one country, the United States.[28] List applied Hamilton's ideas on protection to one country not yet in existence, Germany.

The difference between their working environments was vast. The United States was born as a legal common market, when the US Constitution was ratified in 1788. The nation-state of Germany emerged from a customs union that took decades to develop. This is one reason why List's first theme – that of stages – was so important for the other two ideas in his trio: the "infant industry" argument and the customs union itself.

There is a crucial difference between "stage thinking" and "progressing in stages." "Stage thinking" that mandates a universal procedure for all to follow is uncreative, but progress usually comes one step at a time, sometimes in small steps. There is no better model of "progressing in stages" in the history of international economic integration than the *Zollverein*.

The suitability of a customs union for the German situation as the nineteenth century unfolded was extraordinary. The author views a customs union as embodying contrary forces: trade liberalization and trade protection. But that is not how many saw a customs union in those days. The intellectual tradition of "free trade" as it developed in some contemporary writings incorporated elements of protectionism, as if in certain cases trade liberalization could not succeed unless it were protected.[29] This approach just happened to tug at the heartstrings of German nationalists: breaking down barriers to unification in a protected environment.

While the theory of a customs union resonated with the German *Zeitgeist*, the *Zollverein* could have lost its comprehensive appeal with inept implementation. The structures of a customs union are easy to describe: a common external tariff and a common revenue pool that is apportioned to members equitably. But designing that tariff and determining equitable distribution are more difficult matters. Let us discuss these questions in connection with the second step in the evolution of the *Zollverein*.

Step 2: in 1818 Prussia abolished its own internal customs and created a North German **Zollverein**

Just as Prussia under Otto von Bismarck would later take the leading role in the political unification of Germany, so also was Prussia the pioneer in creating the first regional *Zollverein*. In 1818 Prussia not only abolished its own internal customs, it also set up a common external tariff. This would be the tariff that first applied to the North German *Zollverein*.

The design of this exemplary tariff, and what later tarnished it, deserve careful study by anyone interested in customs unions or common markets. In the years 1815–50 Prussia was "never a continuous territory." Nor was Prussia homogeneous. It contained provinces in very different economic circumstances: each had its "own fiscal and tariff history..."[30] Maassen, who created the 1818 tariff, respected these facts as well as principles of sound fiscal management. "The new tariff, then," Professor Clapham writes, "had to be one which all parts of the King's dominions could bear; it had to be arranged to yield a respectable revenue; and it had to be so reasonable as to offer no great temptation to the smugglers."[31]

From the experience of the *Zollverein* and Professor Clapham's analysis, we suggest three principles to guide the design of external tariffs. These are: fairness to all parts of a country or grouping, sufficiency of revenue, and reasonable rates. These principles are equally important.

Moreover, there is a critical relationship between the second and third principles that can be expressed in the following three axioms. First, sufficiency of revenue does not mean revenue maximization. Second, sufficiency of revenue does not require rate maximization. And third, sufficiency of revenue counsels rate moderation. As Professor Clapham again notes: "The sound view was taken that moderate duties are in practice the most productive. Therefore, as revenue was wanted, duties were kept low."[32]

A common external tariff does not mean that every incoming product is taxed. Rather, what is taxed is done so at a uniform rate wherever it enters the grouping. Here are the essentials of the first tariff around the *Zollverein*. Duties on raw materials were very low and, in fact, many were admitted duty-free. Manufactured products paid "modest" duties that did not go much above 10 percent *ad valorem*. Products described as "colonial wares," such as sugar and coffee, paid "stiff" duties of about 20 percent *ad valorem*. Prussia prohibited the import of two commodities, salt and playing cards, because these were both government monopolies.[33]

In 1818, a banner year in German economic history, Prussia also founded the North German *Zollverein*. This regional precursor to the full *Zollverein* was for ten years Prussia itself, along with Schwarzburg-Sonderhausen. This was a state much smaller in size that was located in Thuringia, a region in central Germany.

Then, in 1828, a "decisive" event occurred, when Hesse Darmstadt "was induced to join, the first important recruit."[34] The addition of Hesse Darmstadt was important, because it extended the sphere of the North German *Zollverein* into western Germany; but the presence of Schwarzburg-Sonderhausen as Prussia's only partner for ten years should not be belittled because that state was "tiny" or without major influence.

Schwarzburg-Sonderhausen gave the North German *Zollverein* two significant attributes. The first was an outpost in south-central Germany, which laid the basis for making a northern organization more national. And the second was proof that this *Zollverein* was really a customs union of independent states, not just another name for Prussia itself.

Steps 3 and 4: 1828: the Middle German Commercial Union (Step 3) and the South German Zollverein *(Step 4)*

1828 was "decisive" for the North German *Zollverein* in two other ways, not immediately benign but eventually constructive. Two other economic unions were founded in 1828: the Middle German Commercial Union (Step 3) and the South German *Zollverein* (Step 4).

The presence of these two groups was not helpful right away to the North German *Zollverein*, because they were potential competitors. But they did constitute other amalgamations of Germanic states interested in economic integration. The central challenge for Prussia was to manage this change in ways that benefitted its version of a *zollverein*.

This is exactly what happened over the next several years. Prussia prevailed, in part because both rival unions were unable to mount a compelling challenge to its type of customs union.

The Middle German Commercial Union (Step 3) included Hanover, Saxony, Hesse-Cassel, Nassau, Brunswick, Oldenburg, Frankfurt-am-Main, Bremen, the Saxon duchies, the Reuss principalities, Hesse-Homburg, Schwarzburg-Rudolstadt and the Upper Lordship (*Ober-herrschaft*) of Schwarzburg-Sonderhausen.

The Middle German Commercial Union was aptly named. It was a commercial, not a customs union: it had no common external tariff. And each member went its own way on economic policy. Participants could agree on only two points. The first concerned the other two unions in the north and south: the North and South German *Zollvereins* must not be permitted to expand. The second involved existing trade routes. The main north–south trade routes from Hamburg and Bremen to Frankfurt-am-Main and Leipzig should be kept open for English goods. And traffic on the east–west roads had to be restricted when it ran through Prussian lands.[35]

The program of the Middle German Commercial Union was thus largely negative. There emerged neither policies nor structures promoting a positive vision or constructive cooperation among the membership. The Union could not even agree on what routes new roads through member states should take.[36]

The South German *Zollverein* was also founded in 1828 (Step 4). The tortuous negotiations that produced this union are ably tracked elsewhere.[37] It was a customs union, unlike the Middle German Commercial Union, but it lacked the critical mass to compete. During those negotiations, the larger states, Bavaria and Württemberg, were unable to resolve their differences with the smaller states on the Rhine. As a consequence, Bavaria and Württemberg became the only two members of the South German *Zollverein*.

While larger than other states in the region, they were together still too small to make a customs union work. Professor Henderson notes that "administrative costs were high and absorbed 44 per cent of the receipts." Moreover, "the customs revenue per head of population was only 9 and 1/2 silver groschens as compared with 24 in Prussia."[38]

The South German *Zollverein* had the right concept but the wrong mass, while the Middle German Commercial Union had a weak vision accompanied by understandably inadequate implementation. Both were ripe for absorption by a more powerful organization. Enter the North German *Zollverein* and its driving force, Prussia.

Step 5: creation of the German Zollverein *in 1834, hereafter referred to as the* Zollverein

This is the big one. It resulted from, as one of our sources describes it, the "merger" of the North German *Zollverein* with the Middle German Commercial Union and the South German *Zollverein.* "Merger" does describe the unification of the North and South German *Zollvereins*, since this was accomplished by treaty.

But the North German *Zollverein* did not really "merge" with the Middle German Commercial Union. That union had collapsed and Prussia proceeded to negotiate with its former members to join the North German *Zollverein.* Some members of the Middle German Commercial Union joined other organizations for the express purpose of entering the *Zollverein.*

The new *Zollverein* implemented three policies that made it a full customs union. It removed customs barriers among its members. It created a uniform external tariff against non-members. And it undertook action vital to ensuring the equitable functioning of a customs union. It would collect customs on its external frontiers on a joint account; the proceeds would be distributed to members in proportion to their population and resources.

Let us pause and reflect on steps 2 through 5 in the context of "sequencing." We have already discussed step 1 under this rubric. It is worth noting that steps 1 through 5 pertain to the emergence of the *Zollverein.* Steps 6 through 9 refer to its development: we will present this story shortly.

Recall that step 2 in 1818 included Prussia abolishing its own internal customs. The decision to abolish internal customs dealt with economic and financial matters. But it was also an important political action. Prussia was not going to ask the members of an expanding *Zollverein* to do things it had not already done at home. The abolition of customs within Prussia prepared the way for an ascent to the next level: elimination of all customs within a *zollverein.*

Abolishing its own customs was a decisive act of leadership by Prussia. It was the first major practical melding of politics and economics in the history of the *Zollverein.* It heralds a process of political economy in the emergence of the *Zollverein* that will intensify in the future.

"Sequencing" also concerns groups that appear on what one regards as one's turf. These groups are of two types. The first are those that arise without one's approval and may seem threatening. The second are those that emerge because of one's encouragement and may be helpful. For Prussia in 1828 two groups of the first kind were the Middle German Commercial Union (Step 3) and the South German *Zollverein* (Step 4).

Both types of groups can simplify "sequencing" by offering prefabricated building blocks for one's own edifice. The "block" may have already been disassembled into its components, as in the case of the Middle

German Commercial Union, but it is usually less difficult to combine already existing groupings into an even larger one than to start from scratch.

An example of the second type of group was the case of the Thuringian States in the several years preceding the emergence of the *Zollverein* in 1834. In building the *Zollverein* Prussia preferred, in certain situations, to negotiate with combinations of German states. Prussia suggested that the Thuringian States form their own customs union and then apply together for membership in the *Zollverein*. They did both eventually, although "petty jealousies" among the Thuringian States delayed matters.

Finally, on 10 May 1833, the Customs and Commercial Union of the Thuringian States (*Zoll-Handelsverein der Thüringischen Staaten*) appeared. Its members were Sachse-Weimar, the smaller Saxon duchies, the Reuss principalities, the Prussian districts of Erfurt, Schleusingen and Ziegenrück, and the Hesse-Cassel district of Schmalkalden. On 11 May 1833, one day later, this union entered the Prussian customs union.[39] Some participants in the Customs and Commercial Union of the Thuringian States had been members of the late Middle German Commercial Union, such as the Reuss principalities and the smaller Saxon duchies.

This case shows the value of constructive recombination or repackaging. As members of the Middle German Commercial Union those states were potential roadblocks to Prussia's customs union; but as part of an organization created for the express purpose of joining the *Zollverein*, the Customs and Commercial Union of the Thuringian States, those principalities and duchies had gone from rivalry to close co-operation. The Customs and Commercial Union of the Thuringian States was never abolished and continued as a customs union within a customs union.

This situation had economic as well as political utility: the Thuringian states had one joint vote in the *Zollverein* congress. This body did not follow a "one state, one vote" principle, as numerous smaller states could outvote a few larger ones with substantially more people and other resources. So this "customs union within a customs union," with its one joint vote, preserved a rough proportionality between voting rights and economic strength in the deliberative institutions of the *Zollverein*. This proportionality was another intertwining of politics and economics that nurtured the evolving political economy of the *Zollverein*.

Successful intertwining in political economy requires strength and clarity in both economics and politics. Economics met these criteria, both internally and externally, for the *Zollverein* created in 1834. As to the first, all internal customs barriers were removed. As to the second, a uniform external tariff was erected.

Politics also passed these tests. Customs on the external frontiers would be collected on "joint account." The proceeds would be distributed to members in proportion to population and other resources. This is a most crucial point: the "equitable" treatment of members in distributing proceeds from the customs pool rested on the recognition of their separate political identities. Political economy may eventually give participants a larger political identity, but it need not. And maintaining separate political identities may be good strategy in the short- and medium-term. This is another striking lesson from the *Zollverein* for students of political economy. As far as organizations go, political economy is an arduous process, not something that can be decreed or just hoped for.

While an impressive foundation was laid by 1834, much hard work was ahead for the embryonic *Zollverein*. Some of it involved more negotiations. The Middle German Commercial Union and the South German *Zollverein* were not the only rival organizations to emerge from the *corpus Germanicorum*. The *Zollverein* faced a third group, the *Steuerverein*, that came together in 1834, the year of the *Zollverein*'s own birth.

It is tempting, looking back and knowing how things turned out, to treat the episode of the *Steuerverein* as a footnote in the saga of the *Zollverein*, but that attitude would stunt one's insights into the depth of ultimate *Zollverein* achievement. The *Steuerverein* needs appreciation in its own terms as well as those of the *Zollverein*. That is why we make the *Steuerverein* a separate step in our story.

Step 6: the appearance in central Germany of the Steuerverein *in 1834*

The *Steuerverein* emerged partly because the negotiations that led to the creation of the *Zollverein* in 1834 did not adequately address the concerns of some members of the *corpus Germanicorum*. Having gained a preliminary appreciation of the complexity of these various negotiations, the author is not so sure that these discussions could have dealt satisfactorily with the interests of all the eventual members of the *Zollverein*. There is a level beyond which sophisticated intricacy in negotiation dissolves into excessive and impractical nuance, which wrecks the process. And there are only so many objects the greatest juggler can handle at one time.

The *Steuerverein* was the proverbial "blessing in disguise." In the short-run its appearance testified to the incompleteness of the *Zollverein*, but in the longer-term the *Steuerverein* helped the *Zollverein*. Some prospective members of the *Zollverein* needed more time to clarify their own interests before joining that organization. And the *Steuerverein* simplified the "sequencing" of the *Zollverein*, because it was another grouping of states with which the *Zollverein* could deal. This situation would continue a pattern of the *Zollverein* preferring to work with other groupings, or at least with applicants that had recently been involved in another organization.

Hanover and Brunswick co-founded the *Steuerverein*, which actually came into existence on 1 June 1835. Oldenburg joined in 1836 and Lippe-Schaumburg in 1838. *Steuerverein* means tax union, but it was a real customs union: it had a common external tariff and a joint customs administration. It levied lower duties than the *Zollverein* on manufactured products and imports from tropical countries, but got more revenue per capita from its customs than the *Zollverein*, about a third more per person. This difference continued until 1840, when the per capita revenues for the two customs unions were about the same.[40]

This low tariff policy was presumably based on the wisdom that governed the construction of the North German *Zollverein*'s first tariff, which was the 1818 Prussian tariff. But the *Steuerverein*'s approach, which levied even lower tariffs and got higher per capita revenues for a time, had a special anchor in Hanover's relations with England. The British monarchy had family ties to Hanover, as some members of the Hanoverian dynasty occupied the throne of England. And the English preferred that emerging customs unions have low tariffs, because in the nineteenth century England was the "workshop of the world" and wanted customs barriers to its exports to be as low as possible.

The *Steuerverein* lasted for about twenty years, into the 1850s. During these two decades its relations with the *Zollverein* went through three phases: from uncertainty, to rapprochement, and then to unification. The *Steuerverein* may have learned something from the experience of the failed Middle Union, which was avowedly anti-Prussian. After some initial difficulties, Hanover, which led the *Steuerverein*, took a conciliatory approach to its powerful neighbor.

In fact, in 1837 the two customs unions came to two significant agreements. The first aimed to reduce smuggling. The second, in our language, streamlined the "sequencing" of both groups. The *Steuerverein* and the *Zollverein* agreed to transfer "enclaves" to the customs union in which they were situated. This resolution was essential for the economic unification of the *corpus Germanicorum* to proceed in an orderly fashion. Such transfers also brought geography into a realistic alignment with economic integration, a crucial consideration all emerging groupings should consider.

Step 7 (1851–54): a series of treaties joined the Steuerverein *to the* Zollverein

Those 1837 agreements created a climate favorable for members of the *Steuerverein* to enter the *Zollverein*. Brunswick's scattered territories were incorporated in the 1840s. But it was not until the early 1850s that Brunswick itself and Hanover concluded negotiations that resulted in their joining the *Zollverein*. Oldenburg and Lippe-Schaumburg, the other two members of the *Steuerverein*, came along. The result was that the *Steuerverein* had merged with the *Zollverein*.

This merger was a major event from the perspectives of both economics and politics. Consider politics first. The *Zollverein* now had a membership that comprised almost all the *corpus Germanicorum*, except Austria, the two Mecklenburgs, and some Hanseatic towns. Austria, a major member of the *corpus Germanicorum*, was excluded from the *Zollverein*, because of long-standing conflicts with Prussia that fueled a major rivalry. One source of friction between the two countries came from their different approaches to tariffs, an issue that will be considered in the next paragraph. Austria and Prussia did eventually agree to a separate treaty governing tariffs, but then fought each other in the Austro–Prussia war of 1866, with Prussia winning.

The economic significance of the merger between the *Steuerverein* and the *Zollverein* was also considerable. The *Zollverein* gained access through Hanover and Oldenburg to the North Sea coast, which secured "the commercial future of Prussia and the north of Germany with or without the southern states."[41]

Some have suggested that the entry of Hanover, with its lower-tariff approach, seemingly committed the *Zollverein* to "future liberalization."[42] Not necessarily, the author believes. At the time, one could also have viewed the entry of Hanover as hinting that the *Zollverein* would not embark on greater protection. In any event, the enlarged *Zollverein* stood in sharp contrast to Austria and its allies in the south, which favored a decidedly more protectionist approach.

Step 8: 1867: new **Zollverein***, new Constitution*

After the Austro–Prussian war of 1866, the members of the *Zollverein* approved a new agreement. The new North German Confederation entered the *Zollverein* as a body and other German states negotiated treaties with a victorious Prussia.

The new *Zollverein* had a new constitution (1867), which authorized two important bodies. The first was the *Zollbundesrat*, a federal council of customs, which contained personal representatives of the "several rulers." The second was the *Zollparlament*, which was an elected customs parliament. Prussia, the prime mover of German political unification, dominated both bodies.

The merger between the *Steuerverein* and the *Zollverein* (step 7) had strengthened politics and economics as distinct forces within the *Zollverein*. This result was not divisive, but constructive. Every grouping develops its politics, economics, and political economy in a unique set of sequences. Sometimes, before political economy can advance, an organization needs to clarify or strengthen its forces of politics and economics that still remain separate. Every organization needs to discover its optimum level of integrating politics and economics into political economy and the best time paths to follow to achieve this goal. This process involves "trial and error."

The *Zollverein* was fortunate. While it had its "trials," it committed few "errors." Its relationship with Austria is one major area where one asks, what if? By the time of the Austro–Prussian war of 1866, adversarial politics had long since stifled opportunities to build some kind of creative relationship between Austria and *Zollverein*. The separate treaty on tariffs which Prussia and Austria had negotiated was "too late," if not "too little."

A step-by-step approach over the longer term, which the *Zollverein* used so effectively in so many other cases, might have produced a compromise, not necessarily a resolution, on a wider range of economic and financial issues, including the tariff question. Whether broader economic cooperation might have ameliorated the other conflicts between Austria and Prussia is impossible to say. In the end, the crude urge to dominate that inheres in the territoriality of nation-state politics took over and led to war.

The successes of the *Zollverein* far surpassed its disappointments. It went step by step; but the steps were not uniform in content or duration. Some steps were more concerned with economics and politics as separate forces than with their integration. Others emphasized political economy.

So whereas step 7 dealt with economics and politics as distinct forces, step 8 featured a major upgrading of the organization's political economy. In particular, the two new bodies authorized by the *Zollverein* constitution of 1867, the *Zollbundesrat* and the *Zollparlament*, fostered an even stronger dynamic of political economy for the grouping.

Both new bodies dealt with customs legislation, but in different ways. In so doing each enhanced a distinct dimension of political economy. The *Zollbundesrat* was a federal customs council that replaced the old General Congress. The General Congress embodied the legal status of the *Zollverein* between 1834 and 1867, which consisted of a number of treaties between still sovereign states. After 1867 the legal status of the *Zollverein* became "more complicated."[43]

The commercial relations between members of the North German Confederation, which had entered the new *Zollverein* en masse, rested mainly on the constitution of that Confederation, which continued in force. The economic links between the southern members of the *Zollverein* and the North German Confederation were based on treaties. The "complicated" legal situation thus came from the co-existence within the new *Zollverein* of two different types of contractual relations: constitutional, for the members of the North German Confederation; and treaty-based, between that Confederation and the southern states of the new *Zollverein*.

The General Congress reflected the high degree to which national sovereignties dominated the old *Zollverein*. This was consonant with its legal status, which was based on treaties between sovereign governments. The General Congress "had been a meeting of official delegates who carried out the instructions of their Governments." It required unanimous consent for any proposal. Tariff changes could only result from "wearisome bargaining between the Zollverein Governments."[44]

The customs council (the *Zolbundesrat*) that replaced the General Congress after 1867 began to modify, though not negate, those numerous national sovereignties. The new council was called significantly a "federal" council, which hinted that a stronger central authority was in the future. It operated on the principle of majority rule.

But it was not a "one state, one vote" version of majority rule. The customs council continued the "proportionality" approach to allocating votes that appeared much earlier. As noted, back in 1833, when the Thuringian states joined the old *Zollverein* en masse as the Customs and Commercial Union of the Thuringian States, their union remained intact and they exercised only one joint vote in the General Congress.

Likewise, the new customs council assigned votes in proportion to population and other resources, including political clout. Of the fifty-eight votes in the council, Prussia had seventeen, Bavaria six, Saxony and Württemberg four each, Baden and Hesse-Darmstadt three each, Mecklenburg-Schwerin and Brunswick two each and other states one each. The "other states" commanded seventeen votes.[45]

While the *Zollbundesrat* was appointive, the *Zollparlament*, or customs parliament, was elective. This parliament had limited powers. For instance, it could vote appropriations, but had no control over how the money was spent. And it faced considerable burdens. Its members, for example, were not paid for their services. This made it impossible for some to stand for election.

Bismarck, the leader of Prussia, knew what he was doing. He needed to acknowledge the principle of popular representation in some way for political reasons. Individual citizens of member states had a say in the make-up of the *Zollparlament*. However limited its powers were, this assembly introduced an element of popular participation in an unfolding process of economic integration that had heretofore been mainly the domain of governments in Germany; but Bismarck could not afford to let the *Zollparlament* become stronger than he was, since he saw himself as the primary agent of German political unification and was wary about entrusting a popular assembly with too much authority in any aspect of this process.

The contribution of each new institution to the political economy of the *Zollverein* was distinctive. The customs council embodied a version of qualified majority rule and was the harbinger of more federalism, which is the highest type of integration politics and economics can achieve. The customs parliament broadened participation in economic integration to include citizens from the *Zollverein* states and thus brought crucial private ingredients to a dynamic that needed sources of support beyond those provided by governments themselves.

The year 1867 was a "defining year" for the *Zollverein*. Prussia's already dominant position in the *Zollverein* gained a legal basis. The key was the dissolution of the consensual General Congress and its replacement by a customs council operating on a qualified majority rule in which Prussia already had almost thirty percent of the votes. In the new *Zollverein* the "legal preponderance of Prussia," Professor Henderson observes, "rested upon solid economic foundations." Prussia had ninety percent of the production in mining and metallurgy, half the output in textiles, and two-thirds of all workers employed in the core industries in Germany.[46]

The new Constitution gave the *Zollverein* a "permanence which its predecessor did not possess."[47] Two earlier crises, one lasting from 1849–53 and the other from 1862–65, had rocked the *Zollverein* and revealed how fragile it was. Now its most powerful part, the North German Confederation with its population of twenty-nine million people, was bound together by its own constitution. And its southern members, whose population reached about 8.5 million souls, were most unlikely to renounce the treaty that linked them to the North German Confederation.

This was still a situation of legal inconsistency, but a developing dynamic of political economy need not falter in a legal environment still not standardized. Indeed, it may be best to let time resolve differences in the legal origins of contractual relationships. The crucial point is that all members of the new *Zollverein* were bound to one another by some type of contract, whether by constitution or by treaty. And that was good enough for the *Zollbundesrat* and *Zollparlament* to function as effective agencies of political economy.

A stronger constitutional and legal basis carried the *Zollverein* to a higher level of political economy. This was a nascent federalism in the customs union that would underpin the emergence of the German nation-state itself. The political unification that unfolded in the 1860s and 1870s did create the modern German nation-state, which soon called itself the German Empire.

Step 9: the new German Empire legally subsumed the Zollverein

Everything was now in place for step 9, the last step, when the new German Empire legally subsumed the *Zollverein*. In 1871 the laws and regulations of the *Zollverein* entered the legal corpus of the German Empire. This incorporation acknowledged the major and prerequisite contribution of the *Zollverein* to the birth of modern Germany.

There are two postscripts to this story:

Postscript 1. 1872: Alsace-Lorraine, which Germany seized from France during the Franco–Prussian War of 1870–71, entered what was now known as the imperial customs area, the Empire's version of the *Zollverein*.

Postscript 2. 1888: the Hanseatic cities joined the imperial customs area. The second postscript reveals how much times had changed for those Hanseatic cities. They had belonged to the Hanseatic League centuries ago. This grouping, as noted in Chapter 2, provided some commercial stability on an international scale during the later Middle Ages, when nation-states were too weak to do so. The Hanseatic League declined as nation-states became stronger and more aggressive commercially. It is ironic that a last act in the economic unification of the German nation-state would be inclusion of some Hanseatic cities in the imperial customs area. Those cities, whose historical legacy featured a most decentralized grouping in the Hanseatic League, became part of an imperial customs area that would express a Prussian penchant for tighter centralization.

To be sure, the final administrative unification of the German nation-state was closely related to the policies of Otto von Bismarck. He was a skilled diplomat, but he clearly believed that "war is a continuation of politics by other means" and employed "a blood and iron" approach to national unification. Prussia's war with Denmark (1864) helped Bismarck consolidate his own position in Prussia, and two wars already mentioned – Prussia's war with Austria (1866) and the Prussian/German war with France (1870–71) – left an indelible imprint on the eventual content of the German nation-state.

But without the *Zollverein*, where would Bismarck have been? The short answer is: with an impossible amount of work to do in one lifetime. The *Zollverein* was the foundation of the modern German nation-state. This was a deep foundation, built over decades, and of enormous help to Bismarck. It made the scope of his achievements possible. The *Zollverein* was, as readers know, an organization of economics, politics, and political economy. Bismarck excelled at political economy, as he interrelated his wars and diplomacy with the *Zollverein* itself.

Some suggest that the *Zollverein* was the economic prerequisite for the political unification of Germany. The term "prerequisite" is too strong. A German nation-state could have emerged without the *Zollverein*, but its size and impact can only be matters of speculation. To label the *Zollverein* an "economic prerequisite" and to refer to the "political unification" of Germany leave out the interrelations between economics and politics that mark both *Zollverein* and the multi-faceted process of German unification.

The *Zollverein* as historical muse

To those daunted by problems that bedevil some contemporary groupings pursuing cross-border economic integration, the story of the *Zollverein* may provide hope. The outcome was far from foreordained in 1818; the journey towards completion was neither simple nor easy. Some steps covered more ground than others, but all were important as building blocks in the construction of the final edifice.

The *Zollverein* has left nine general lessons for those searching the past for insights into the process of international economic integration. Each, while numbered separately for study and reflection, can be best appreciated and used as a planning principle in the context of all the others.

(1) It helps to have a central motivating idea. Developed by Friedrich List and others, this idea was that a combination of states could reduce barriers that were limiting trade among them.

(2) It helps to be able to draw on a powerful underlying force with deep emotional wellsprings. This force was German nationalism. The central motivating idea was taking shape in the very early 1800s in an environment of frustrated German nationalism, which found in the idea an outlet for its energy.

(3) It helps to have a vision. The guiding vision was political unification and the major role a customs union could play in this process.

(4) It helps to have leaders, including a major figure, who can implement this vision. The major leader was Otto von Bismarck of Prussia, although there were many others on whose shoulders he stood.

(5) It can help to see your creation overcoming hostile forces. While one prefers not to have enemies, their presence can be turned to one's advantage. The "underdog" or "the threatened" can get major motivation and energy from these self-images. Germans did not lack candidates for their list of "hostile forces."

(6) Align geography and economics. It is less difficult to integrate a grouping if its members are contiguous. This is because geographical contiguity is a powerful ingredient of market continuity. One of the most important, yet least appreciated, events in the history of the *Zollverein* occurred in 1837, when the *Steuerverein* and *Zollverein* agreed to transfer enclaves to their natural geographical grouping. This brought geography and economics into an alignment that facilitated economic integration.

(7) Big things take time. The *Zollverein* took over seven decades to germinate and develop. One looks at the projected timetables of many contemporary economic groupings, especially those begun in recent years, and has to wonder, can one accomplish certain goals in three to five years? The historical record is not enthusiastic about such short-term over zealousness.

(8) Do not do too much at once. This lesson, simply put, has complicated content, because it involves how best to "sequence" the economics, politics, and political economy of a grouping. The *Zollverein* has much to tell us here. First and foremost, sequencing is not a recipe in some historical cookbook. One must go step-by-step, sometimes dealing more with economics, sometimes more with politics, sometimes concentrating on political economy. This journey involves "trial and error," though one hopes that all your errors are those from which you can learn something important. It may be desirable to strive for a situation in which certain strains of politics and economics remain separate and are not fully combined into political economy. As with the "ladder" of inter-government economic integration, one need not reach the top rung or, in this case, achieve total political economy to be successful. It depends on the particular circumstances, both historical and contemporary, that an individual grouping and its members face. In short, there is no optimal sequencing that other

groups can copy, but the preceding reflections can be taken into account as each group works out its own destiny.

(9) Streamline goals. The *Zollverein* is a positive role model in this respect. It concentrated over the years on becoming a more cohesive customs union. At a time when so many groupings of recent vintage seem to want to vault the ladder of economic integration with one giant step, streamlining deserves the deepest reflection. The *Zollverein* never had a single currency, never tried for one, although it "soon established a fixed relationship between its main currencies..."[48] The author strongly believes that streamlining created the focused framework in which members could, if they wanted, expand their cooperation. Indeed, over time *Zollverein* members "made agreements on rail and river transport, on postal arrangements, on bills of exchange and much else."[49] Broader cooperation was not mandated from the center, but developed using the good offices of the *Zollverein*, so to speak.

Streamlining should be tempered by the requirements of "sequencing" and lesson eight: *do not do too much at once.* Every economic grouping has its own strains of economics, politics, and political economy. It is vital that decision-makers strive for the best mix of all three elements during different phases of their group's evolution.

But the *Zollverein* experience suggests that one needs to avoid excessive streamlining. As a group strives to integrate its own politics and economics, it may be prudent to leave certain strains of politics and economics separate so they can reflect the distinctive national cultures and identities of member countries.

In sum, these nine lessons do not constitute an infallible road map, but together they are a powerful searchlight to cast illumination on darkened crossroads ahead.

Mercosur *or* Mercosul

This customs union calls itself a common market. *Mercosur* and *Mercosul* are acronyms for "southern common market" in the two main languages of its members, Spanish and Portuguese. *Mercado Commun del Sur* is Spanish for "southern common market"; hence, *Mercosur. Mercado Commun do Sul* is Portuguese for the same term; thus, *Mercosul.* The Spanish acronym seems more widely used now, but either is acceptable. The term "southern cone common market" is also employed, though "cone" is not literally in the title.

Mercosur has four full members, Argentina, Brazil, Paraguay, and Uruguay. Taken together, they resemble a cone in South America. Their geographical mass does not constitute an exact geometric cone, but the metaphor is suggestive. Brazil and Paraguay are the upper section of a cone, Argentina and Uruguay the lower.

Whatever the shape, the four full members of "the southern common market" make up about two-thirds of the area of South America. Brazil itself, with its area of 3,284,426 square miles, accounts for almost half (47.7 percent) of South America's 6,875,000 square miles. By geographical standards alone, "the southern cone common market" is a major development. When one reviews the resources within this potential market that are under-utilized or not developed at all, *Mercosur* acquires huge significance in the history of international economic integration.

Mercosur in the 1990s and early 2000s: the ABCs

Mercosur was born in the early 1990s, though its intellectual and practical preparation goes back decades.[50] In March 1991, the presidents of Argentina, Brazil, Paraguay, and Uruguay signed the Treaty of Asunción, which called for the formation of a common market with no internal tariffs by January 1995.

Mercosur officially came into being on 1 January 1995. But it was not a common market, in the senses of free factor mobility and community-wide laws. It was well on its way, however, to becoming a free trade area, as it removed tariffs from about 90 percent of intra-regional trade, although the Treaty of Asunción called for 100 percent removal.

The remaining 10 percent of products were to have their tariffs cut progressively to zero by 1 January 1999, for Argentina and Brazil, and by 1 January 2000, for Paraguay and Uruguay. In the 10 percent category Argentina had 221 products, such as paper and textiles; Brazil had 29 products, including peaches and wines; Paraguay had 427 products, including textiles, vegetables, and milk products; and Uruguay had 950 products, ranging from textiles and steel to chemicals.[51]

The common external tariff (CET) of *Mercosur* also went into effect on 1 January 1995. But there was a list of exceptions. These two items of unfinished business – the 10 percent of intra-regional trade that still had tariffs and exceptions to the CET – made *Mercosur* an "incomplete customs union" when it was born.

Mercosur developed a credible plan to have common tariffs for all its imports by 2006. Let us discuss the 1995 exceptions to *Mercosur*'s CET and the plan to phase these out.

On 1 January 1995, about 85 percent of *Mercosur*'s 9,000 product categories adopted the CET. Readers should recall that "common" in a CET means total coverage, not necessarily that every product category has the same tariff in percentage terms. In fact, *Mercosur*'s CET ranged from 0–20 percent, with an average of 13 percent in early 1995.

Two major "exceptions" are capital goods and telecommunications equipment. Brazil and Argentina treat imports of capital goods quite differently: Argentina has a 0 percent tariff, while Brazil assesses a 35 percent tariff. These are to converge gradually to 14 percent in 2001. For telecommunications a 16 percent CET should rule from 2006.

Each government could also exempt temporarily an additional 300 products from the CET. No member took full advantage of this provision. Argentina exempted 232 products, including steel and chemicals; Uruguay, 212, including chemicals and rubber; Paraguay, 210 (chemicals and agricultural products); and Brazil, 175 (chemicals and petroleum derivatives). Finally, members could not agree on vehicles and sugar, which will not come under *Mercosur* rules until 2000. From that year there was to be free trade in cars and car parts.[52]

The plans to achieve a real CET and to eliminate completely all intra-regional tariffs stalled, as two major developments hurt *Mercosur* seriously. The first blow was the crisis in Brazil in 1998 and 1999, epitomized by the collapse of its currency, the *real*. This setback was part of the global turbulence that began in Asia in 1997 but it had its own indigenous roots.[53]

A second crisis then engulfed Argentina. A deep recession was the prelude to economic collapse in 2001, which left more than half the population living in poverty. The country struggled with record debt defaults and currency devaluation.[54]

As Argentina started to recover in 2003 and Brazil continued its comeback, *Mercosur* began to revitalize itself. There was much to re-build on. The storms that battered *Mercosur* left intact its institutional foundations. It is worthwhile to sketch these institutions, because they help *Mercosur* weather the inevitable ups and downs of economics and politics.

While the Treaty of Asunción (1991) embodied a vision and a long-term goal, the Protocol of Ouro Preto (1995) described the institutions that make *Mercosur* work. The main decision-making body is the Common Market Council (*Consejo de Mercado Comun*), which approves changes in regulations, such as adjustments in tariffs.[55] Foreign and finance ministers from the four member countries sit on the Common Market Council.

Underneath the Common Market Council there are two decision-making bodies, the *Mercosur* Group, the "main executive body composed of officials from the four governments," and a Trade Commission, to review trade policy and study complaints.[56]

An annex to the Protocol of Ouro Preto specifies the complaints procedure for the Trade Commission. Members will first try to resolve complaints and trade disputes by a consensus that uses advice from technical committees. If this does not work, the aggrieved can use procedures contained in the 1991 Protocol of Brasilia. These provide for a tribunal of three judges: one from each of the countries at loggerheads, the third is to be an "independent judge." Member governments believe this approach will protect their national sovereignties in legal matters. One institution *Mercosur* does not want is a supranational court independent of national legal systems.[57]

Mercosur also has three other features worth noting: a parliamentary commission represents the legislatures of the four countries; there is a consultative forum for businesses from the private sector and trade unions; and the *Mercosur* Secretariat, based in Montevideo, Uruguay, is the administrative nerve center and official archive of *Mercosur*. There are no plans to transform it into a commission like the one that runs the European Union (see next chapter).[58]

Mercosur was still an "incomplete customs union" in 2004, thirteen years after its birth. But its major institutions survived the turbulence of the late 1990s and early 2000s. And its development potential remained enormous. The *Mercosur* area contains about 200 million people, which makes *Mercosur* the third most important trade bloc in the world, after the European Union and North American Free Trade Area. The *Mercosur* area includes the four full members – Argentina, Brazil, Paraguay, and Uruguay – and two associate members, Bolivia and Chile.

The revitalization of *Mercosur*, which began in 2003, is proceeding slowly, in small steps. The first moves involve discussions, with no concrete proposals. *Mercosur* may expand to include Chile, Bolivia, and Venezuela as full members. Also, "there is talk of creating a *Mercosur* parliament and a joint currency."[59]

The world has heard "talk" about a *Mercosur* currency before. In June 1999, the presidents of Argentina and Brazil agreed to work harder to balance their state budgets and control public debt in order to pave the way for a "common currency" for *Mercosur*.[60] But the description of this currency has shifted from "common" in 1999 to "joint" in 2003. One does not know what "common" or "joint" means here. Without specific proposals, one never will.

Mercosur and the *Zollverein*

But *Mercosur* can take heart from the experience of the *Zollverein*. Let us reflect on *Mercosur* against the background of the *Zollverein*'s nine lessons. This exercise should give advocates of *Mercosur* great hope and perhaps a few ideas.

(1) It helps to have a central motivating idea. Mercosur can have a cluster of motivating ideas. It can draw on a longer corpus of research on the benefits and drawbacks of economic integration than the *Zollverein* could. It can tap into the tradition of regional economic integration in South America that extends back into the 1960s, with the old Latin American Free Trade Association. And *Mercosur* knows that "everyone" or "almost everyone" is doing it. Regional economic integration of countries is *de rigueur* throughout the world today. If the "southern cone" does not become a unified economic force, it will be left out or left behind. The fear of loss is a powerful motive, which leads directly to lesson 2.

(2) It helps to be able to draw on a powerful underlying force with deep emotional wellsprings. For the *Zollverein* the force was German nationalism, surging, aggrieved, and unfulfilled. There is no single leading

candidate in *Mercosur* that has the power and pervasiveness German nationalism had for the *Zollverein*. But there are forces that can drive *Mercosur* forward. These are national and regional pride, the knowledge that *Mercosur* has so much potential economic power, and the fear of losing out if the region does not participate in the global competition that features the development of regional economic blocs.

(3) It helps to have a vision. The panoramic vision for the *Zollverein* was the political unification of most of the *corpus Germanicorum*. *Mercosur* envisions a strong grouping that embraces all or most of South America. This would greatly increase the leverage of the continent in international negotiations. "Bigger" may not always be "better." But "stronger" is always preferable to "weaker," especially in terms of bargaining power in the global arena.

(4) It helps to have leaders, including a major figure, who can implement this vision. There is no Bismarckian figure in the history of *Mercosur*, which may be good for several reasons. *Mercosur* is not likely to be a vehicle for a political federation of its member countries. While Otto von Bismarck was a central personality in the political unification of Germany, his methods involved, in his own words, "blood and iron."

The kind of warfare *Mercosur* will confront is economic, not military, less from within, and more in a world that may be increasingly divided among powerful and more contentious trading blocs. The political skills *Mercosur* needs most are those of persuasion, reconciliation, and co-ordination. Its leaders should concentrate on finding and then expanding the common ground member countries share.

Seminal leaders emerged to help *Mercosur* along its way. Carlos Menem, who was President of Argentina from 1989 to 10 December 1999, is a founding father of *Mercosur*. He is a forceful leader with a distinctive style and flair, and was on the frontiers of economic integration in his region. Fernando Henrique Cardoso was President of Brazil from 1995 to 2003. He made the journey from left-of-center academic to a political centrist in Brazilian terms. With his own considerable intelligence and style, he wrote his name large in the annals of *Mercosur*.

(5) It can help to see your creation overcoming hostile forces. Germans could point to actions taken by international meetings, like the Congress of Vienna, that seem designed to thwart or slow the emergence of a unified German nation-state. The emergence of *Mercosur* can be placed in the context of relations between "north" and "south" as these terms are used today in the international development community. "North" refers to the "developed" world, while "south" designates the "developing" world.

The "developing" world is not always southern in a geographical sense. But for the "southern common market" the term "south" has symbolic significance. The legacies of imperialism and colonialism still partly account for the economic imbalance between "north" and "south." If *Mercosur* needs its own hostile forces, it can highlight the persisting harms reinforced by an imperial "first" and then "second" world taking advantage of less powerful "third" and "fourth" worlds. Europe is the "first" world. North America, especially the United States, is the "second." "Developing" or "underdeveloped" regions constitute the "third." The poorest of the poor make up the "fourth" world.

(6) Align geography and economics. Mercosur has one major asset from its inception that the *Zollverein* did not have. It aligns geography and economics. While the southern "cone" may not be geometrically precise, it embraces contiguous territory and already commands, with its four full members, about two-thirds the landmass of South America. Geographical contiguity facilitates market unification.

By sharp contrast, the *Zollverein* was bedeviled by geographical fragmentation for decades. Its primary sponsor, Prussia, was itself never a continuous territory before 1850, and without the accession of Hanover and Oldenburg in the 1850s, the *Zollverein* would have lacked access to the North Sea. This gave it a major geographical advantage and some insurance against losing southern members, who did in fact stay in the organization once they joined. But this outcome was not certain when Hanover and Oldenburg entered the *Zollverein*.

(7) Big things take time. This lesson should rightly give *Mercosur* enormous hope. So what if *Mercosur* remains an "incomplete customs union" thirteen years after it was founded? Mercosur has survived severe storms intact and is moving into the future. Remember: "run your own race." The finish, not the time, is what counts.

(8) Do not do too much at once. The leaders of *Mercosur* and others should study how the *Zollverein* paced itself. The kinds of treaties the *Zollverein* negotiated with new members or groups of members might also prove useful. We greatly condensed or omitted some technical details that those actually writing treaties might find helpful. We urge those interested to consult our sources, especially Professor Henderson's exemplary book on the *Zollverein*.[61]

(9) Streamline goals. This is the one area where *Mercosur* can go awry. The *Zollverein* was a model of keeping its goal clear and avoiding projects that might undermine its mission. It was a customs union, not a currency union, nor a common market.

Mercosur has a reasonable chance of becoming a "complete customs union" in the fullness of time. But its present leadership speaks what may be the rhetoric of over-reach: about aiming for "a South American alliance based on the model of the European Union."[62]

To appreciate the magnitude of *Mercosur*'s ambition, readers can now turn to a comparative analysis of the two most successful common markets in history, the United States of America and the European Union.

7 Common markets

The two largest common markets to date are the United States of America (US) and the European Union (EU). Both are real common markets. They are complete customs unions that exhibit elements of free factor mobility and legal standardization.

The term "common market," however, embraces a wide range of further economic and political integration. A common market may or may not have a single currency, a central bank, coordinated economic policies, coordinated foreign policies, a common defense policy, and its own military.

There can be significant variations as well within each of the two features that are prerequisite to move from a customs union to a common market – factor mobility and legal standardization.

The US and the EU share common features, but they also embody significant differences. They are, in short, different common markets. There are many ways to compare and contrast the US and the EU. I will concentrate on two areas. The first concerns legal origins and development, while the second highlights a single currency. Law and money are recurring topics in this book and they just happen to reveal some of the most salient contrasts between the two common markets.

Legal origins and development: a comparative overview of the US and the EU

The legal matrix of the US common market is the Constitution of the United States of America, written in 1787 and ratified in 1788. The first empowering document for the EU is the Treaty of Rome, signed in 1957 and implemented on 1 January 1958. This treaty established the European Economic Community (or European Community), out of which came the European Union in 1994.

Both prime documents have important predecessors. The Constitution replaced the Articles of Confederation, signed in 1781. The Treaty of Rome built on The Treaty of Paris, signed in 1951, which established the European Coal and Steel Community. This was a forerunner to the European Economic Community, which incubated the EU.

Both the US Constitution and the Treaty of Rome are "living documents" that have been extended and enriched in various ways. The Constitution has been amended twenty-seven times so far and interpreted in hundreds of consequential decisions by the Supreme Court of the United States. A constitution is inherently more bonding than a treaty. But an organization created by treaty can receive expanded purpose and renewed strength through subsequent treaties and other acts. Defining moments for the EU in this regard include the Single Europe Act of 1986, the Treaty of Maastricht of 1991, the Treaty of Amsterdam of 1997, and the Treaty of Nice of 2000.

The most striking contrast between the US common market and the EU with respect legal origins resides in the following fact: whereas the Constitution contains all the legal provisions necessary to have a complete common market, the Treaty of Rome had to be supplemented substantively over the years to develop a more complete legal matrix for the EU.

To be sure, key Supreme Court decisions made some constitutional provisions for a US common market come alive. But the Court never had to add a substantive provision to the crucial parts of the Constitution that create a common market, such as Article I, Sections 8, 9, and 10, and Article III, Sections 1 and 2. Some critics of federal power in the US may feel that the Supreme Court has, in effect, "added substantive provisions" to the Constitution; but no such judicial amending has, in fact, occurred.

The distinctive legal origins of the US common market and the EU emerge from the documents that give them life and strengthen their mission. For the US this means certain provisions of the Constitution and significant Supreme Court decisions. For the EU this means the Treaties of Rome, Maastricht, Amsterdam, and Nice, and the Single Europe Act. It also means, perhaps, the EU Constitution of 2004. In the early 2000s the EU struggled to write its own constitution. These efforts came to fruition in 2004. Ratification, as of this writing, had not occurred.

Legal origins and development: the United States

The US Constitution created a federal common market, when it set up a federation to succeed the confederation outlined in the Articles of Confederation. The Articles of Confederation were the governing document of the new United States from 1781 into 1788.

The new central or federal government created by the Constitution has more powers than the central government under the Articles of Confederation had. This difference has led some observers to characterize the central government under the Articles of Confederation as "weak" or "ineffectual."

From a "Federalist" or pro-Constitution perspective, the central government under the Articles could not be as effective, because it had "only" one branch of government. This was a unicameral legislature, in which all states, regardless of population, had one vote. The central government under the Articles lacked an executive and an overarching judiciary. The states supposedly had too much power, from a Federalist viewpoint, because they could levy tariffs on goods coming from other states in the Confederation and possibly start trade wars. These would engender an economic disunity to accompany the political disunity inherent in the Articles of Confederation, so pro-Federalist writers state or assume.[1]

The brilliance of the US Constitution does not require the diminution of the Articles of Confederation. The Articles need to be appreciated in their own times and in their own language. The Articles were an effective transitional document. The United States, which officially gained its "flag independence" from Great Britain in 1783, was not eager right away to replace imperial power with a strong central government. So the central government wrought by the Articles was not federal. But confederation does not automatically imply weakness or incompetence.

Public finance provides a clear illustration of how easy it is to criticize unfairly the Articles from a Constitutional perspective. Federalist writers make much of the fact that the central legislature under the Articles had no power to tax: "Congress had no powers to tax and thus was poor. And having no money, it had no power."[2]

Article VIII of the Articles of the Confederation, however, states that "all charges of war, and all other expenses that shall be incurred for the common defense or general welfare, and allowed by the United States in Congress assembled, shall be defrayed out of a common treasury, which shall be supplied by the several States in proportion to the value of all land with each State..."[3] So there was a framework in place for a national treasury, to be supplied by state contributions that if not technically taxes achieved the same revenue result. The national treasury was set up, but states did not honor the rest of Article VIII.

Taxation is not the only technique for getting money. A government, even without the backing of taxation, can borrow money through loans of different kinds, including the issuance of bonds. A government can also issue its own currency, which can then become its own income. And a government can also take innovative action, as when the Congress in December 1781, incorporated the Bank of North America, which started in January 1782.

This bank is the greatest positive legacy from the period of Confederation and remains vastly under-appreciated. It was the first commercial bank of issue and deposit in the United States of America. It helped finance the central government, especially in 1782 and 1783. It never achieved its full promise as a national bank, but it set a valuable precedent that prepared the way for the First Bank of the United States (1791–1811), the Second Bank of the United States (1816–36), and the Federal Reserve System (1913–).[4]

Some revenue streams are more reliable than others. A strong power to tax would have given the central government under the Articles greater financial credibility and made lending to that government less risky. But, when all is said and done, Congress under the Articles "did manage to finance a central government through a trying period..."[5]

The Articles of Confederation were a preliminary stage in the emergence of a federal government and common market in the US. And, in view of the times, they were necessary: a time out from strong direction from the center. But the Articles of Confederation were not suited for constructing a federal common market, which became the bedrock of the US economy.

The legal underpinnings of the US common market rest, first and foremost, on the tripartite system of federal government the US Constitution created. This approach contrasts sharply with a parliamentary system, in which the head of government usually comes from the largest party in the legislature.

The Constitution sets up three branches of government – the executive, legislative, and judicial – that are supposedly coequal but separate. The "separation of powers" creates the "checks and balances" that should guard against the usurpation of authority by any one branch. The tripartite system of government means that the federal common market has three separate yet coequal sources of support. Let us consider in turn the "powers" of each branch of government with respect to a common market.

The US Presidency, which bestrides the executive branch, has its own source of popular legitimization and succession. This is a presidential election held throughout the country every four years. A strong executive can help this common market by proposing or supporting timely legislation and by using the presidency as a "bully pulpit."

The legislative branch – the Congress – receives from the US Constitution a detailed list of powers that can be used to build a common market on a national scale. Article I, Sections 8, 9, and 10, of the US Constitution are the vital texts and complement one other. Section 8 specifies what the Congress can do. Section 9 limits the federal government and the states. Section 10 limits the powers of the states.

Section 8 treats eighteen topics in as many clauses. Not every subject pertains to a common market. Clause 17, for instance, gives the Congress exclusive legislation over the District of Columbia.

Eight clauses deal with military matters. Clause 1, which lists the general powers of Congress, notes its obligation "to provide for the common Defense..." Clause 10 deals with piracies and felonies: Congress can "define and punish Piracies and Felonies committed on the high Seas, and Offences against the Law of Nations..." Clause 11 treats war, and marque and reprisal: Congress can "declare War, grant Letters of Marque and Reprisal, and make Rules concerning Captures on Land and Water..." A letter of marque and reprisal is a license granted by a government to a private citizen to capture the merchant ships of another nation.

Clause 12 enables Congress to "raise and support Armies..." Clause 13 authorizes it to "provide and maintain a Navy..." Clause 14 is an administrative amplification of Clauses 12 and 13: Congress can "make Rules for the Government and Regulation of the land and naval Forces..." Clauses 15 and 16 turn to the Militia and parallel the sequence of Clauses 12, 13, and 14. Clause 15 is enabling: Congress can "provide for calling forth the Militia..." Clause 16 is administrative and concerns the organizing, arming, and disciplining of the Militia.

The military dimensions of Article I, Section 8, deserve attention. The US common market required a military capacity on the federal level from the beginning. There was a crucial need for federal force to deal with insurrections that local security was unable to control.

Outside the country, the US military has played important roles over the years in the development of the US as a world power. This status has extended and shielded the global reach of the US common market.

Other clauses of Article I, Section 8, provide many basics of common market construction. Here is a concise enumeration in the language of the Constitution:

Clause 1: Congress can "lay and collect Taxes, Duties, Imposts and Excises..." and "pay the Debts..." of the United States. "But all Duties, Imposts and Excises shall be uniform throughout the United States..."
Clause 2: Congress can "borrow money on the credit of the United States..."
Clause 3: Congress can "regulate Commerce with foreign Nations, and among the several States, and with the Indian tribes..." This is the "commerce clause."
Clause 4: Congress can "establish an uniform Rule of Naturalization, and uniform Laws on the subject of Bankruptcies throughout the United States..."
Clause 5: Congress can "coin Money, regulate the Value thereof, and of foreign Coin, and fix the Standard of Weights and Measures..."
Clause 6: Congress can "provide for the Punishment of counterfeiting the Securities and current Coin of the United States..."
Clause 7: Congress can "establish Post Offices and post Roads..."
Clause 8: Congress can "promote the Progress of Science and useful Arts, by securing for limited Times to Authors and Inventors the exclusive Right to their respective Writings and Discoveries..."

Two remaining clauses also have their own significance. Clause 9 empowers Congress "to constitute Tribunals inferior to the supreme Court..." Clause 18, the last clause in Section 8, is the "necessary and proper" clause. Congress "can make all Laws which shall be necessary and proper for carrying into Execution the foregoing powers, and all other Powers vested by this Constitution in the Government of the United States, or in any Department or Office thereof."

Certain aspects of Clauses 1–8 have special importance for a common market. Clause 1 addresses a customs union, the foundation for a common market. Congress can "lay and collect" duties and imposts: both are taxes assessed on goods entering the country. The insistence in Clause 1 that duties and imposts be "uniform" throughout the country is critical for a common external tariff. Excises, mentioned in Clause 1 along with duties and imposts, are inland taxes on the manufacture of certain goods, like spirits and tobacco, within a country, and are not part of a CET. But their inclusion here gives Congress power to achieve a tax uniformity that enhances a single national market.

Uniformity appears elsewhere in Article I, Section 8, and relates to the legal standardization that marks a complete common market. Clause 4 mentions a "uniform Rule of Naturalization" and "uniform Laws on the subject of Bankruptcies." A "uniform Rule of Naturalization" affects the factors of labor and entrepreneurial ability and can help transform a labor force of immigrants into one of citizens. Uniformity of bankruptcy law advances legal standardization.

Clause 5 enables Congress to "coin Money" and "regulate its value." Giving Congress the power to regulate the value of the coins it authorizes can produce a uniformity of both intrinsic and extrinsic value among all coins of a certain denomination.

Every coin of a specific denomination has the same extrinsic value, but uniformity in intrinsic value – metallic content – does not always characterize every coin of the same extrinsic value. Batches of coins minted at different times may have the same extrinsic value, but their intrinsic value may have been altered. A credible coinage requires uniformity in both types of value, unless a government has a powerful explanation for manipulating the intrinsic value of its coinage.

Clause 5 also empowers Congress to "fix the Standard of Weights and Measures." Weights and Measures may not be the most riveting subject, but having an honest Standard of Weights and Measures applied consistently is essential for a common market.

Another critical area of legal uniformity concerns patents and copyrights. These are the subjects of Article I, Section 8, Clause 8. This is the "intellectual property" clause in today's terms. Uniform protection on the national level for the forces of innovation is an essential feature of legal standardization.

Clause 8 also has enormous implications for the ideological basis of the US common market. This is to be a common market rooted in private property, which is the essence of capitalism. Clause 8 establishes that specific property rights can attach to "Writings" and "Discoveries." The copyright embodies that right for "Writings"; the patent for "Discoveries."

These are not property rights in perpetuity, as copyrights and patents have fixed time periods. Historically, a US patent lasted seventeen years from the date of issuance. But it is now twenty years, to conform to the international convention of the GATT (General Agreement on Tariffs and Trade), which is now the World Trade Organization (WTO). Under the revised regime, the life of a patent is measured from the date of filing of the earliest application concerning the invention.[6]

Copyrights have no uniform time period. Under today's laws it is almost impossible to lose copyright protection. But a work published before 1978 has to have a valid copyright notice or it enters the public domain. And works published more than seventy-five years ago in the United States are now in the public domain.

Still, even though copyrights and patents are not property rights forever, they do provide substantial protection and create powerful incentives in the best traditions of capitalism. Inventors, artists, and authors are guaranteed long time periods during which they can reap financial gains from their works.

Other aspects of Article I, Section 8 strengthen the federal role in the US common market. The Congress can "borrow Money" (Clause 2) on the credit of the US, which the power to tax (Clause 1) undergirds. The Congress can regulate interstate commerce (Clause 3, the "commerce clause"). This is a decisive power in preserving the federal nature of the US common market. The Congress receives a major role in creating a national infrastructure that transports both people and information in Clause 7. This empowers the Congress to establish post offices and post roads. The prescription for post offices and post roads unleashes other forces of standardization, if not uniformity, within the US common market.[7] Clause 18, the "necessary and proper" clause, shows how deep the federal pillars of this common market are by reinforcing the role of Congress.

Article I, Sections 9 and 10, clarify relations in the US common market between the federal government and the states. Section 9, Clause 5, mandates that "no Tax or Duty shall be laid on Articles exported from any State." In the context of Section 9, which limits the federal government, Clause 5 means that the central government shall not lay taxes or duties on articles exported from any state. Taxes or duties directed by the federal government at specific commodities from particular states would wreck a free trade area.

Section 9, Clause 6, states that "No Preference shall be given by any Regulation of Commerce or Revenue to the Ports of one State over those of another; nor shall Vessels bound to, or from, one State, be obliged to enter, clear, or pay duties in another." The first part of Clause 6 ensures a uniform approach in taxation and other regulation by the federal government towards all ports within the US. This provision would help all three forms of inter-government economic integration. The second part of

Clause 6 prevents any state from taxing or imposing customs procedures on the shipping of another. This denial is key to creating a free trade area.

Article I, Section 10, specifies more limitations on state powers in the US common market. Clause 1 says, among its numerous restrictions, that no state shall "coin Money" nor pass any "Law impairing the Obligation of Contracts." These restrictions advance the integration of the US common market. Congress, not the states, has sole control over coinage, which is not the entire money supply. And the states cannot interfere with contracts. This injunction protects legal forms that transcend state boundaries and express the national character of the common market.

Section 10, Clause 2, states that no state shall, "without the Consent of the Congress, lay any Imposts or Duties on Imports or Exports, except what may be absolutely necessary for executing its inspection Laws..." The "net Produce" of any such actions "shall be for the Use of the Treasury of the United States..." And all such state "Laws shall be subject to the Revision and Control of the Congress." Clause 2 is crucial for a customs union.

All three branches of the federal government have important roles in the US common market. Let us turn to the third branch, the judiciary.

Article III, Section 1, creates a court of last resort, the Supreme Court. This article refers back to Clause 9 of Article I, Section 8, which gives Congress the power to constitute tribunals "inferior" to the Supreme Court. Inferiority here refers to location in a management hierarchy, not to lack of personal worth or organizational importance.

"Inferior" courts are the federal courts grouped in districts throughout the country. Without them the system could not function. An "inferior" court is responsible to a higher power, the Supreme Court.

All federal judges, including the justices of the Supreme Court, "hold their Offices during good Behavior..." They can serve for life, unless removed from the bench by the Congress. The House of Representatives has "the sole Power of Impeachment (Article I, Section 2)." The Senate "has the sole Power to try all Impeachments ... no Person shall be convicted without the Concurrence of two thirds of the Members present (Article I, Section 3)."

Article III, Section 2, details the jurisdiction of Federal courts. Federal courts can hear many types of cases. These include those between two or more states, between a state and citizens of another state, and between citizens of different states.

Article III, Section 2, also shows why the federal judiciary is a prerequisite for holding the US common market together. A court of last resort is essential for a federation, especially for a federation that is also is a common market. Cross-border disputes, and the legal standardization that a complete common market implies, require a final judicial arbiter.

The process of legal standardization is not always linear or swift. Legal standardization thus lends itself to the measured, incremental adjudication that distinguishes the US Supreme Court.

The importance of the federal judiciary for the US common market has received confirmation in legal decisions too numerous for complete consideration here.[8] Selected cases, however, can show the reader why the Supreme Court has had, and continues to have, such an enormous impact on the US common market.

While the Constitution created the legal framework for a common market, the Supreme Court has translated it into practice. The seminal case that affirmed the existence of the US common market as well as its federal nature is *Gibbons* v. *Ogden* (1824). The state of New York had granted a steamboat monopoly on the Hudson River, which touches both New York and New Jersey. The Supreme Court invoked the "commerce clause" (Article I, Section 8, Clause 3) and invalidated that monopoly. Only Congress, it held, could regulate interstate commerce. This decision was doubly monumental: the US common market existed and it was federal.

The Supreme Court also protected one type of business that has played a critical role in developing the US common market as a national and then international phenomenon. This is the corporation, first in its domestic roots and development, and then later in its international guise as the multinational corporation. The corporation was and is the crucial entity that could most effectively move across state and then national borders; but it might not have happened that way without certain legal protections the US Supreme Court accorded corporations.

The corporate form has a long history in Anglo-Saxon common law, which developed in the British Isles and came to the Americas with British colonization. The corporation emerged as a legal vehicle with two important features: liability limits and perpetuity. The owners of a corporation are legally liable only for their resources that are part of their business. A lawsuit directed against their corporation cannot recover damages from their personal funds. This protection is a major asset for the corporation, as is perpetuity or legal immortality. The corporation has a life that transcends human generations.

But the corporation received other assets that helped it develop the US common market. These came in Supreme Court decisions that begin in the nineteenth century. The corporation needed more legal protection. Ideally, it should be able to operate in every state without facing state action intended to destroy or unduly restrict it.

In *Bank of Augusta* v. *Earle* (1839) the Supreme Court took an ambiguous first step in giving the corporation legal protection on the national level. A state could not physically deny access to agents of a corporation chartered in another state, the Court ruled, though it could regulate that corporation and even forbid it to operate as a corporate entity within its own borders.

The opportunities for creative interpretation here are formidable. Agents of a prohibited corporation could still enter that state and conduct business, as long as they were acting on their own. Upon leaving, their personal business could suddenly become corporate business. Still, *Bank of Augusta* accorded only modest protection in theory to the corporation, but it laid important groundwork for increasing federal protection, when it treated the corporation as a "person," "domiciled" in a particular state.[9]

Later decisions built on this approach. In 1844, five years after *Bank of Augusta*, the Court issued a ruling that would have major implications for corporate protection. In *Louisville, Cincinnati, and Charleston Railroad* v. *Letson* (1844), the Court held that the corporation was a "citizen." As such it was entitled to access to federal courts if suing or being sued by a "foreign" person. "Foreign" here can mean outside the state in which a corporation is domiciled or chartered. The corporation was first acknowledged as a "person," and then as a "citizen." This conceptual transformation was crucial in two ways. First, granting access to federal courts in 1844 underpinned the emergence of a national legal identity for the corporation, which was essential for its role in developing the US common market. Second, viewing the corporation as "person" and "citizen" meant that the Court could later consider it in the context of the Fourteenth Amendment to the US Constitution.

This amendment would have major consequences for corporate protection. It was ratified on 9 July 1868, more than three years after the military phase of the US Civil War ended. The primary intent of many of its supporters was to protect African-Americans recently emancipated from slavery. It is one of a trilogy of amendments applying to the US and its jurisdictions: the Thirteenth abolished slavery; the Fifteenth proclaimed that the right to vote "shall not be denied or abridged by the United States or any State on account of race, color, or previous condition of servitude."

The Fourteenth Amendment, in Section 1, contains language that reinforces part of the Fifth Amendment. The Fifth Amendment affirms that no person shall "be deprived of life, liberty, or property, without due process of law..." The Fourteenth Amendment identifies one possible agency of deprivation: "nor shall any State deprive any person of life, liberty, or property, without due process of law; nor deny to any person within its jurisdiction the equal protection of the laws." Specifying state action would eventually give the corporation greater legal recourse.

The route to corporate inclusion within the purview of the Fourteenth Amendment was not straightforward, however. At first the Court refused. In the *Slaughter-House Cases* (1873) it chose to interpret the "due process" clause of the Fourteenth Amendment narrowly; it adhered to the concept of original intent. Since this amendment was crafted to protect emancipated African-Americans, it could not be stretched to cover a wide range of property rights. The corporation was thus left outside.

But exclusion did not last for long. In 1886 the Court held in *Santa*

Clara County v. *Southern Pacific Railroad* that the corporation, like any citizen, was protected from arbitrary state action by the "due process" clause of the Fourteenth Amendment.

One more decision of the Supreme Court must be remarked on here. The US Constitution created a strong federation. But the nineteenth century left the corporation in what, for all practical purposes, was confederal status. That is, the separate states still retained major powers to regulate excessively, even prohibit, the corporation and thereby frustrate its ability to operate as a national entity in every state.

In *Terral* v. *Burke Construction Co.* (1922) the Court took a giant step in protecting a corporation incorporated in another state from retaliatory action by a state in which it was conducting business. The State of Arkansas, acting on state law, revoked the license of the Burke Construction Company, incorporated in Missouri, to do business in Arkansas, because the Company had resorted to the federal courts.

The Court held that this law was unconstitutional. In so doing, the Court underscored an essential right a corporation needs to operate on a national scale: access to the federal courts. *Terral* v. *Burke Construction Co.* enabled the corporation to play more fully its central role in developing the US common market.

In review, the US Constitution and the tripartite system of government it created have left a deep imprint on the nature and development of the US common market. It is a federal common market, with a distinctive type of federalism: three separate but coequal branches of government at the center, each able to have its own impact.

But the Constitution did not eliminate the so-called lower levels of government, like the states, counties, and municipalities. Nor did it render the people subservient to the federal government. The tenth amendment to the US Constitution affirmed two types of rights, those enjoyed by the states and by the people: "The powers not delegated to the United States by the Constitution, nor prohibited by it to the States, are reserved to the States respectively, or to the people."

The states can enact their own laws and establish their own courts, subject to a federal review that may never come. Laws and courts on all "lower levels" of government can limit how far legal standardization can go in the US common market.

Legal standardization, a necessary process for a complete common market, embraces a wide range of possible outcomes. The US experience suggests that there are degrees of standardization, depending on the area of law, and that standardization may not be possible or desirable in every instance. For example, it is neither sensible nor practical to standardize the rules of evidence across every legal jurisdiction.

Legal origins and development: the European Union

The Treaty of Rome (1957), with its 248 articles, is the legal matrix of the European Union. This document established the European Economic Community in 1958, which became the European Union in 1994.

The Treaty of Rome reveals a community that sees a common market as the means to achieve many objectives. In Article 2 the Community pledges "by establishing a Common Market and progressively approximating the economic policies of Member States, to promote . . . a harmonious development of economic activities, a continuous and balanced expansion, an increased stability, an accelerated raising of the standard of living and closer relations between its Member States."[10]

Article 3 details the Community activities necessary to implement Article 2. The eleven clauses of Article 3 specify the essential features of a free trade area, customs union, and common market, as well as numerous other steps a common market can take to become more integrated.

Some aspects of these clauses are noteworthy. Clause b juxtaposes the essence of a customs union – a "common customs tariff" – with a desirable though not integral feature of a common market – a "common commercial policy towards third countries." Clause d mentions a feature that would become one of the Community's most controversial: "the inauguration of a common agricultural policy." And clause h broaches the subject of community-wide laws: "the approximation of their respective municipal law to the extent necessary for the functioning of the Common Market."[11]

Article 4 names key institutions that will run the Community. Four are designated here as "An Assembly, a Council, a Commission, a Court of Justice."[12] The Assembly later became a Parliament. The full names of these four are the European Parliament, the European Council of Ministers, the European Commission, and the European Court of Justice.[13]

There is a fifth institution, not mentioned in Article 4 but specified in Article 3 (clause j), that has important implications for integrating the European Community: the European Investment Bank. And many observers would list a sixth institution that is technically part of the European Commission. This is the civil service of the European Union, which comprises thousands of bureaucrats who do the gritty detail work of making the EU run day to day and who constitute an important force in their own right.

The Treaty of Rome built on an institutional legacy inherited from the European Coal and Steel Community. For example, the Court of Justice was founded in 1952 to deal with disputes arising in connection with the European Coal and Steel Community.

Five subsequent documents develop the organization the Treaty of Rome outlines. This process sometimes enhances economics and politics as individual strains, sometimes attempts to interweave them as political economy. The Single European Act, which went into effect on 1 July 1987, reflects more the first approach. The Treaties of Maastricht (1991), Amsterdam (1997), and Nice (2000) try to promote more the political economy of the community. The EU Constitution of 2004 (EU2004), pending ratification, will also address political economy.

To be sure, all five acknowledge politics and economics as distinctive forces, but Maastricht, Amsterdam, Nice, and EU2004 endeavor to combine politics and economics more than the Single European Act does. This judgment does not in any way diminish the significance of the Single European Act, which prepared the way for a greater integration of economics and politics. Rather, the five documents show the European Community moving towards higher levels of political economy.

Selected examples illustrate the contributions each document made to the development of the European Community. Let us consider each document in chronological order. The Single European Act of 1986 emerged from widespread convictions that the European Community was "resting on its oars" and had to be revitalized.

In this legislation the European Community got serious about establishing a single market. The slogan, popular in its day, encapsulating this objective was EC92. This meant that by 31 December 1992, the European Community was to become "an area without internal frontiers in which the free movement of goods, persons, and services and capital is ensured..."[14]

A single market for goods and services did become a legal reality on 1 January 1993, but it is taking much longer to develop a single market for capital in every one of its dimensions.

A major problem is the absence of standardized definitions throughout the EU for many items that pertain to finance. National laws and regulations concerning taxation, investing, the transfer of assets, estates, the operation of bond and equities markets all may make it impossible for the EU ever to have a single capital market in every respect.

While the Single European Act was most popularized for the push it gave economic integration, it made contributions to the European Community in other areas. Politics and law are two major examples. As to politics, the Single European Act introduced qualified majority voting in the Council of Ministers to replace unanimity. Exceptions were made for measures dealing with taxation, the free movement of persons, and the rights of employed persons. The Act also introduced a "cooperation procedure," which increased the power of the European parliament.

As for the law, the Single European Act made a significant addition to the judicial structures of the community. It established a Court of First Instance under the European Court of Justice. The Court of Justice was dealing with a rapidly increasing caseload in the 1970s and 1980s and requested that a second tier of judicial authority be created. This is the Court of First Instance, which came into existence in 1989.

The Single European Act recognized the beginnings of processes the

Treaties of Maastricht, Amsterdam, and Nice would advance. The Act called for greater cooperation on economic and monetary policy, foreign policy, and on "questions of European security."[15] Monetary union, for instance, was a goal to be "progressively realised."[16]

The Treaty of Maastricht, signed on 10 December 1991, heeded those calls for greater cooperation in the Single European Act in the areas of monetary union, and foreign and defense policies. As to monetary union, Maastricht laid out three stages for its "progressive realisation." We will analyze these stages later in this chapter under the rubric of EU Monetary Integration.

The Treaty of Maastricht did not achieve the dramatic flair in the areas of foreign and defense policies as it did with money and banking. After all, it was hard to top the three-stage approach it sketched for setting up a central bank and a single currency. Still, Maastricht built on the Single European Act in calling for the establishment of "common foreign policies" among members and noting the desirability of a common defense policy under the Western European Union. This is a European defense organization within the context of the North Atlantic Treaty Organization (NATO).[17]

Significant advances in preparing the way for common foreign, defense, and security policies came with the Treaty of Amsterdam (1997).[18] The Treaty of Nice (2000) contains new rules for selecting the members of the European Commission and provides a treaty base for a common defense policy.[19]

In 1999, during the NATO air war over Serbia, the European Union saw first hand how dependent it is on advanced US military technology. This experience prompted calls for the creation of a European Union defense force. A common defense policy is a prerequisite for any EU defense force.

The unknown factor is what role the Constitution of 2004 will play in advancing the political economy of the European Union. At this writing, ratification has encountered obstacles. If the Constitution is not ratified, its drafters may have to revise the document and the following analysis will become totally historical. Still, readers deserve a constitutional primer on the EU Constitution of 2004, courtesy of *The Economist.* Many already refer to the constitution as the "constitutional treaty."

First, why was a constitution written at all? Two forces were at work. The first was a set of criticisms about the way the EU was operating. The second was the enlargement of the EU, which took place on 1 May 2004 and added ten new countries

One place to look for a critique of the EU is the Laeken declaration of December 2001. This started the process of writing a new constitution to replace the existing treaties. The Laeken declaration "talked of popular concerns about too many powers being exercised at [the] European rather than [the] national level, about the lack of democratic scrutiny, and about European institutions and practices being rigid and hard to understand."[20]

On 1 May 2004 the fifteen countries of the EU welcomed ten new members. From northern Europe came the Baltic states of Estonia, Latvia, and Lithuania. From central Europe came the Czech Republic, Hungary, Poland, and Slovakia. From the Balkans came Slovenia. And from the Mediterranean came the islands of Cyprus and Malta.

The EU has not reached the limits of its expansion. Bulgaria and Romania have signed accession treaties, which may enable them to join in January 2007, "if they can reform and modernise fast enough."[21] The list of prospective applicants for the years after 2007 is long. Croatia is a realistic candidate, while a number of other countries have dreams. These include Turkey and the countries of the western Balkans – Albania, Bosnia, Macedonia, Serbia, and Montenegro.

While criticisms of the EU energized the constitutional process, the enlargement issue had more influence on the content of the constitution. Faced with the Laeken critique, "the new constitutional treaty focuses on a genuine but quite different problem: how to make decision-making easier in an enlarged EU."[22]

The draft of the constitution does contain provisions that should make it easier for the EU to legislate. There is a new double-majority voting system. Laws will be passed if 55 percent of countries representing 65 percent of the EU's population approve. Keep those calculators at full power. The European Parliament will receive new powers to amend laws and control the budget.

The draft may make it easier for the EU to legislate, but certain principles are retained that may not make it easier for the EU to operate. For example, the principle of the national veto is preserved in key areas – direct taxation, foreign and defense policy. A country may still "opt out," should a decision displease it.

The draft has important legal implications. It consolidates all EU treaties into a single document called a constitution for the European Union. It incorporates a Charter of Fundamental Rights into EU law for the first time. It gives the EU a formal legal personality for the first time, which will enable it to sign international agreements, and it contains the first formal statement of the primacy of EU law over national law. The European Court of Justice through its jurisprudence had previously established this principle.[23]

All these documents – the Treaties of Rome, Maastricht, Amsterdam, and Nice, the Single European Act, and the 2004 Constitution – embody the legal development of the European Union.

The European Court of Justice, as the constitutional draft recognizes, has played a critical part in shaping the EU.

The European Court of Justice and the US Supreme Court both translate into practice the documents that govern their respective common markets. It would be worthwhile to compare and contrast these two courts as judicial institutions and as shapers of their common markets. Let us first consider the courts as judicial institutions in the areas of personnel, procedures, and jurisdictions.

The US Supreme Court has nine justices. Eight are associate justices and one is the Chief Justice. The US President nominates candidates for the posts of associate justice as well as Chief Justice. The US Senate with a simple majority vote must approve these candidates.

The justices on the Supreme Court, like all federal judges, are "Article III" judges. As discussed above, they are protected by that Article of the US Constitution, which stipulates that they "shall hold their Offices during good Behaviour..." In practice, this means they can serve for life, unless impeached by the House of Representatives and convicted by the US Senate.

The procedures for selecting judges for the European Court of Justice and the Court of First Instance, and the conditions of their service, contrast sharply with those of the US Supreme Court. The Court of Justice has fifteen judges, as does the Court of First Instance. Each member of the EU gets to nominate one for each court. On both EU courts judges serve for six-year terms that can be renewed.

The nomination and approval of judges for both the US Supreme Court and the EU courts are anchored in politics. After all, it was the famous US political humorist Finley Peter Dunne who remarked that the courts follow the election returns. Their composition eventually reflects the realities of political power.

But there is a crucial difference in how the judges of these courts are shielded from political pressures. The "Supremes" can be removed, but only with great difficulty. One navigates the shoals of politics to get on the Supreme Court. But life tenure is excellent protection against the vagaries of politics from outside the Court.

There is no geographical or philosophical balance on the Supreme Court, unless by happenstance. The justices are sometimes labeled "liberal," "conservative," "moderate," "centrist," "middle-of-the-road," "bridges between factions," "compromisers," or "conciliators." But there is no requirement that every region or political ideology in the US have someone on the Supreme Court.

To the contrary, the compositions of the Courts of Justice and First Instance reflect political considerations that partake of geography and the nation-state. National politics are already implanted in the EU courts by their very rules of selection.

Judges on the EU courts have two defenses against the vagaries of politics. The six-year term guards them against political interference from outside the court, but it is not the life tenure US federal judges enjoy. A six-year term may seem long to some, but in judicial time it can be short.

While EU judges are selected and approved by national governments, they have a second defense against short-term political tempests. The publication of decisions by the EU courts does not identify how judges voted.

This is supposed to shield a judge from the United Kingdom, for instance, should he or she vote against the UK in a court proceeding.

These safeguards are meaningful. But if not properly exercised, six-year renewability can amount to judicial recall, which can undermine judicial independence.

The jurisdictions of the European Court of Justice and the US Supreme Court exhibit one striking difference. The European Court of Justice supposedly deals with matters relating to economic integration. The US Supreme Court can consider any issue raised by litigation in the United States. The US Supreme Court is a "full-service" court of last resort.

It would be wrong, however, to regard the European Court of Justice as a single subject tribunal, because of the realities of jurisprudence. Scholars can posit categories of analysis *ex cathedra*, like economics and commerce. But daily life often blurs these distinctions and so matters "mainly" economic in formulation can have all sorts of implications for people's lives in general. Courts frequently have to deal with issues that are tapestries of human concerns, not mosaics of facts compartmentalized in academic categories.

While the European Court of Justice is concerned with economic integration, the complexities of many of these "economic" issues have created opportunities for the Court to adjudicate on a much wider stage. Though not as supreme as the US Supreme Court, the European Court of Justice has emerged as the single most formidable force pushing economic integration in the European Union. For an economic community that shares features of a common market, a federation, and a confederation, as *The Economist* noted, the Court of Justice has implemented a legal framework that promotes cohesion.[24]

Key decisions of this court show the various ways it has promoted economic integration. Before presenting these, we examine how the European Court of Justice and the US Supreme Court achieved the judicial legitimacy necessary to become shapers of their respective common markets.

Both courts first had to establish the principle of judicial review. That is, both had to demonstrate the meaning and reach of their authority. Judicial review is defined somewhat differently for each court. For the Supreme Court it means "the power to refuse to enforce an unconstitutional act of either the state or national government."[25] In the famous case of *Marbury* v. *Madison* (1803) Chief Justice John Marshall laid a deep foundation for the principle of judicial review.[26]

For the European Court of Justice the journey towards judicial review would be as grueling. This Court has fashioned two essential rules in its continuous endeavor to define the European Union as a community governed by the rule of law. These are, first, the direct effect of Community law in member states and, two, the primacy of Community law over national law.[27] These rules make the European Court of Justice indispensable for the European Union.

Judicial review for the European Court of Justice is expressed in language that differs from Professor McCloskey's definition for the US Supreme Court. Whereas the Supreme Court may refuse to enforce an unconstitutional act of either the state or federal government, the European Court of Justice "disapplies" national law if it contradicts Community law.

There is a substantive difference between "refusal to enforce" and "disapplication." The US Supreme Court deems a state or national law unconstitutional. The EU does not yet have a constitution. So the Court of Justice cannot call a national law unconstitutional, but if it decides that a conflict exists between EU law and national law, it can "disapply" the latter. In short, the Supreme Court decides constitutionality, the Court of Justice applicability.

This distinction is more than a nuance. "Refusal to enforce" is strong language that befits a court of last resort in a federal common market. "Disapply" reflects a more indirect approach to contradiction or disharmony, as suits a court of last resort in a common market with confederal tendencies.

In a series of decisions the European Court of Justice fashioned those two basic rules – the direct effect of Community law in member states and the primacy of Community law over national law. Three of the most important are *van Gend en Loos* (1963), *Costa* v. *ENEL* (1964), and *Simmenthal* (1978). These decisions helped define what it means to be a citizen of the Community. In proceedings before their national courts, a citizen of the Community can rely on the written corpus of law and regulation associated with the European Union: all its treaties, regulations, and directives. A citizen of the Community may seek "to have a national law disapplied if it is contrary to Community law."[28]

Both rules underpin the decisions of the Court of Justice relating to the development of a common market. Rulings come in the following areas: the free movement of goods, the free movement of capital, the freedom of movement for persons, and the freedom of competition. Let us consider selected cases in each area.

(a) The free movement of goods. The Court has adjudicated many cases involving the free movement of goods. In the *Cassis de Dijon* judgment (1979) it held that "European consumers may buy in their own country any food product from a country in Community..." as long as that product is "lawfully produced and marketed in that country" and there are no health or environmental obstacles "preventing its importation into the country of consumption."[29] In a case that originated in the protests of some French farmers, the Court held against the French Republic in 1997, because it did not stop those farmers "from obstructing the free passage over French territory of agricultural products from other Member States."[30]

The Court seems to be expanding its definition of "barriers to the free movement of goods." In *Decker*, a 1998 case, the Court considered the plight of a person who had bought spectacles in another member state but was insured for such purchase in the individual's home state. The Court held that national rules that lead to refusing to reimburse a person in those circumstances "constituted an unjustified barrier to the free movement of goods."[31]

(b) The free movement of capital. This area of adjudication illustrates the difficulties that complicate the creation of a single market in capital within the European Union. The Court has decided less complex matters. In the *Bordessa* judgment (1995) the Court ruled that citizens may export the following from one member state to another without having to get prior permission: coins, bank notes, and checks (cheques).[32]

(c) The freedom of movement for persons. A common market fosters, in economic jargon, the mobility of labor and entrepreneurial ability. In simple language, a common market facilitates the movement of persons.

The Court has developed a substantial corpus of law in this area and addressed the freedom of movement for persons in numerous ways. A citizen from one EU country who migrates to another is entitled to the same rights and benefits with regard to employment and working conditions as a national. This principle extends to the rights and benefits of the spouse and children of an EU worker who settles in another EU country. The "same rights and benefits" also covers access to vocational training, as demonstrated in the *Gravier* judgment (1985). The Court held here "that a French student who wanted to study strip cartoon art in Belgium should not have to pay a higher enrolment fee than Belgian students."[33]

(d) The freedom of competition. The Court has made a substantial beginning here. It helped the deregulation of air transport in the *Nouvelles Frontières* case (1986). The Court held here that the rules governing competition in the EU Treaties applied to air transport.[34]

Courts often encounter worthy goals that compete with each other. The European Court of Justice has endorsed at least one principle that can conflict with the free movement of goods: *environmental protection.* It has held that environmental protection is "one of the essential objectives of the Community and, as such, capable of constituting grounds for certain restrictions on the principle of the free movement of goods." In the *Denmark* ruling (1988), the Court said it was legal for Denmark to require that distributors of beer and soft drinks set up a deposit-and-return system for empty containers, despite any adverse effect this might have on trade between member states.[35]

It is a truism that no right or freedom is absolute. In the United States, for example, the First Amendment to the Constitution does not protect one's right to shout "fire" in a crowded theater, when there is no fire. The European Court of Justice is determining just how "free" the "free movement of goods" should be in its common market. It is concluding that there are grounds for legitimate restrictions in some cases on that principle. This is not surprising. Courts of last resort follow their own internal dynamics, which are usually incremental, cautious, and balanced.

A single currency: an overview

The second major topic guiding our comparative analysis of the US common market and the EU is a single currency. A single currency is defined as a single coinage and a single set of paper notes authorized by a single agency. A single currency is not required for a common market. An organization can succeed as a common market without it.

But a single currency is on the menu of options whose implementation can bond members more closely. Adopting a single currency further interweaves politics and economics and can be viewed as a step up the ladder of federalism.

Economics makes powerful arguments for a single currency. Two pertain to exchange rates and involve transactions costs and fluctuations. Currency exchanges cost money: these are transactions costs. If you began a trip in the early 1990s through the then European Community with 100 British pounds and changed that sum progressively into the currencies of the other eleven members of the EC, transactions costs alone would have consumed about 40 percent of your original sum.

Having one currency eliminates the fluctuations in exchange rates among heretofore multiple currencies. This stability, in theory, removes the exchange-rate risk in investing and should facilitate cross-border capital flows. The exchange-rate risk in investing means you can lose a lot if those rates turn against you. You buy stocks or equities denominated in a certain currency with your money. If that currency falls in relation to your money, you lose, in relation to your own money. So currency simplification is enormously efficient in economic terms.

But there are economic arguments against a single currency as well. There is another kind of risk. A single currency does eliminate exchange-rate risk for investors investing in that currency zone, but a single currency is subject to exchange-rate risk for those using it to buy other currencies.

How powerful that single currency will be outside its zone becomes the pivotal question. There are fundamental and technical factors that determine the external strength of a single currency. On the fundamental side, there is the large question of the economic strength of that currency zone in the present and the future. This issue includes the economic strength of individual countries as well as that of the grouping as a whole. Economic strength is always both absolute and relative. The first is in relation to your own standards. The second is in comparison with your competitors.

The technical factors affecting the external strength of a single currency include the quality of the banking infrastructure that supports a single currency. The banking infrastructure encompasses a central bank, if the grouping has one, and relations between that central bank and all other kinds of banks in the single currency zone. If there is no central bank, attention must perforce concentrate on the substitutes for central bank functions that might exist in a mono-money zone. There might, for instance, be central banks or banks that exercise central bank functions within the individual members of that zone.

The experiences of the US common market and the EU with respect to a single currency must be placed within the broader context of monetary integration. Each common market has its own history of monetary integration. Two themes that characterize both histories are the emergence of a single currency as well as a central bank.

While the themes are common, the experiences of the US common market and the EU with these two matters reveal important differences. We will first go through a single currency and central bank for the US, then for the EU. Inspired by the stage analysis of the *Zollverein* in the previous chapter, we divide the development of a single currency and central banking in both the US common market and the EU into phases.

US monetary integration

One major contrast between the US and the EU with respect to monetary integration is based on time. The US experienced much longer apprenticeships with both a single currency and a central bank than the EU.

A single currency emerged in the US in three main phases. The first lasted from the constitutional birth of the US in 1788 until the mid-1860s. It is marked by a single coinage and many paper currencies. The second went from the mid-1860s until 1914. It featured a single coinage and a common paper currency. The third begins with the Federal Reserve System in 1914 and is still ongoing. It implements a complete single currency – single coinage and single paper notes, as the Federal Reserve Bank would authorize its own federal reserve notes. Let us examine each phase in turn.

Phase (1) of the US single currency: single coinage, diversity of paper currencies

The US had a single coinage from its constitutional creation. The US Constitution, as noted earlier in this chapter, empowered the Congress to coin money (Article I, Section 8) and denied that same right to the individual states (Article I, Section 10). Article I, Section 10, also circumscribed the states in other monetary matters. No state could "emit a bill of credit" or make anything except "gold and silver Coin a tender in payment of debts."

But the Constitution did not forbid states from chartering entities that could emit bills of credit, issue paper currency, and accept paper instruments in payment of debts. In fact, during its first eight decades as a federal common market, the US experienced a multiplicity of paper moneys, many issued by banks chartered by the states.

The diversity of paper currency extends well back into the colonial period. During the pre-national era, the US had numerous paper currencies of different types. And the US, both during colonial times and the national era, has had other types of legal money. Wampum, a Native American commodity, was legal tender in Massachusetts until 1790. And gold, a commodity with universal value, could be used as money in the United States until 1934, when it was demonetized.

Phase (2) of the US single currency: single coinage, common paper currency

While the US never gained a single paper currency until the advent of the Federal Reserve System, it did have a common paper currency from the mid-1860s until 1914.

Let us explain how this common paper currency came about. During and after the US Civil War (1861–65) the Congress attempted to make paper currencies in the US more uniform. Ironically, the federal government itself had compounded paper heterogeneity. To finance the Civil War the US Treasury in 1862 issued a new set of US notes called "greenbacks." This was fiat money. Fiat comes from the Latin and means, "let there be." So Congress said, "let there be" more money and it was done. But "greenbacks" circulated below their par or stated value, sometimes way below, because they had no substantive backing.

In 1863 the US Congress passed the National Bank Act, which created a new set of institutions, called national banks. Each national bank was authorized to issue its own national bank notes in the amount of 90 percent of the par or market value (whichever was lower) of US government bonds, which this bank had purchased and then deposited with the US Treasury.[36]

The Congress also launched a major attack on currencies issued by state-chartered banks. Its strategy was to tax those currencies out of existence.[37] In March 1865 the Congress raised from 2 percent to 10 percent a tax on notes issued by state-chartered banks. This increase hastened the conversion of many state banks to federal jurisdiction. Many of the 300 state banks that remained in 1866 were in large cities and had long ago stopped issuing notes when they made loans.[38]

The common paper currency consisted of national bank notes. National bank notes were not a single currency, because each national bank was authorized to issue its own notes in the manner prescribed above. Moreover, the issuing bank had its name and city printed on its own national-bank notes. So efforts to achieve a more uniform paper currency did succeed, but not completely. A common paper currency, consisting of national bank notes, was nonetheless an effective transition between many paper moneys and a single paper currency.

During the 1870s, 1880s, and 1890s, a tumultuous debate unfolded in the US over the roles that gold and silver should play in the US money supply. Should the US money supply be based on gold alone or gold and silver together?

What is striking about the contest between monometallism (gold) and bimetallism (gold and silver) is how political it became. Its supporters portrayed the "gold standard" as the ultimate guarantor of the probity of the currency and even national integrity. Those who backed "bimetallism" argued that silver as legal tender, along with gold, would increase the money supply. There would be more money, bimetallists believed, that could be loaned out or, in the language of economics, there would more loanable funds.

The next step in the reasoning of bimetallism has great political potency. A greater supply of loanable funds would, in turn, supposedly lower interest rates. This would achieve a crucial political and human result: relief for debtor distress, which was especially widespread in US agriculture.

The two major political parties in the US, the Democrats and the Republicans, had chosen sides in the struggle between monometallism and bimetallism. The conflict between approaches to the money standard fueled a growing dichotomy between the two parties. The Republican Party, founded in 1854, pledged to pay the public debt in gold in its platform for the 1868 Presidential election. The association of the Republican Party with gold only strengthened in subsequent decades.

The Democratic Party, to the contrary, served as a tent for people with different views and proposals on bimetallism. The Democrats drew energy from the many agrarian protest movements that are a hallmark of US history in the last third of the nineteenth century. But the Democratic Party was hurt by the emergence of the Populist Party in the early 1890s. The Populist or People's Party (1891–1904) advocated expansion of the money supply by making silver legal tender and so provided an alternative to the Democrats.

The nineteenth-century culmination of this debate in the arena of elective politics was the Presidential campaign of 1896. William Jennings Bryan, the "boy orator of the Platte" from Nebraska, made a stirring speech in Chicago, the site of the Democratic convention, on 8 July 1896. His "Cross of Gold" speech analogized the "gold standard" to the economic crucifixion of the American people: "You shall not press down upon the brow of labor this crown of thorns, you shall not crucify mankind upon a cross of gold."[39] He received the Presidential nomination of his party.

The Republican Party, which had lost two of the last three Presidential elections to conservative Democrat Grover Cleveland, nominated William McKinley, the two-term Governor of Ohio (1892–96). McKinley won decisively, and with him the "gold standard" triumphed politically.

But many in the US still saw the "gold standard" as too rigid. They had as recent evidence the deep recession that followed the Panic of 1893 and lasted about five years. Some argue that this downturn was prolonged by Grover Cleveland's adherence to policies based on the gold standard.

Phase (3) of the US single currency: towards a complete single currency

This phase began with the Federal Reserve Act of 1913, which set up the Federal Reserve System. The Federal Reserve System would authorize its own notes, which over decades would become the dominant paper currency in the US.

Federal Reserve notes qualify as a single paper currency. The Federal Reserve Board authorizes their printing and distribution, even though the twelve regional banks that make up the Federal Reserve System actually issue the notes. Each denomination of Federal Reserve note may seem identical, and it is in most respects, but each note is coded to indicate which regional Federal Reserve Bank issued it. For example, a note with D and 4 on it comes from the Federal Reserve Bank in Cleveland, Ohio.

Some may wonder why Federal Reserve notes constitute a single paper currency when they are differentiated according to issuing bank. After all, we described national bank notes as a common currency, because they were distinguished by the name and city of the issuing national bank.

The crucial issue here is control. National banks were regulated by statute and their ability to issue notes was constrained in the fashion delineated above. But they had more power over how much of their issuing capacity they would use. The twelve regional Federal Reserve Banks issue their notes according to their determination of local needs. But they operate much more within limits set by the Federal Reserve Board, which bestrides the entire system.

Let us now track highlights in the implementation of a single currency in the US. In 1914, currency in circulation – both paper and coin – in the US consisted mainly of the following: gold and gold certificates, silver certificates and silver coin, US notes, and national-bank notes.

Between 1914 and 1933 the components of the currency did not change much, except that gold coins gradually went out of use. Gold certificates, authorized in 1865 and issued by the US Treasury in exchange for gold coin and bullion, circulated until 1933.[40] Gold itself was officially demonetized in 1934. National banks kept issuing their own bank notes, sometimes for advertising purposes, until their issuing privileges were withdrawn in 1935. By 1936, Federal Reserve notes had become the major type of paper currency and indeed the major item of all currency. They accounted for about two-thirds of total cash.[41]

So by 1936 the US was on its way to having a complete single currency. The leading paper currency had become Federal Reserve notes. But achieving a single paper currency, and with that a complete single currency, would take many more decades.

The ascendancy of Federal Reserve notes strengthened. They continued to make up two-thirds of total cash until 1941. On 30 June 1941, there was $9.6 billion worth of currency in circulation: Federal Reserve notes amounted to about $6.6 billion and currency issued by the US Treasury accounted for the remaining $3 billion. Treasury currency included silver and silver certificates, US notes, and other coinage. There was a substantial increase in the cash supply during World War II and the postwar years; Federal Reserve notes made up most of this expansion. In mid-1954, there was $30 billion in currency in circulation: $25 billion were Federal Reserve notes; $5 billion were treasury currency. By mid-1971, currency in circulation exceeded $55 billion: $50 billion were Federal Reserve notes.[42]

By 2004 Federal Reserve notes accounted for about 99 percent of the paper currency in circulation. The rest is made up of US notes and other legal tender notes in circulation but no longer issued. For example, $1 bills that are silver certificates are still in circulation. Silver certificates were authorized in 1878 and issued in exchange for silver dollars. These certificates accounted for almost all the $1 notes in circulation until November 1963, when the Federal Reserve issued its first $1 note.

So in 2004 the US had a single paper currency in the issuing sense. But in circulation there remained a very small fraction of other paper currencies. In sum, a complete, circulating single currency in both coin and paper still eludes the US, but progress has been so great that, for all practical purposes, the US can be said to have reached a single currency, after an apprenticeship of more than two hundred years.[43]

The US experience with a single currency shows just how compelling relations are between getting that currency and having a strong central bank. Indeed, the topics of a single currency and central banking are inextricably interwoven in the histories of both the US common market and the EU. We now turn to the emergence of central banking in the US, which unfolded in four phases. The first concerns the Bank of North America (1780s). The second involves the First Bank of the United States (1791–1811). The third treats the Second Bank of the United States (1816–36). The fourth is the culmination, with the beginning of the Federal Reserve System in 1914.

Phase (1) of US central banking: the Bank of North America

The United States put in a long and sometimes turbulent apprenticeship in central banking, before the Federal Reserve System emerged in 1914. The Continental Congress chartered the Bank of North America in 1781. It opened in January 1782, was rechartered in 1784, but had its charter repealed in 1785.

As noted in our earlier discussion of the Articles of Confederation, the Bank of North America never realized its potential as the first central bank for the fledgling United States. The Bank faced an unfriendly attitude – the distrust of strong central government that characterized much of the period of the Articles of Confederation. And the currency issued by the Bank never reached a volume sufficient to qualify as a national currency. Nonetheless, the Bank of North America should be appreciated as a valuable precursor and important precedent in the history of central banking in the US common market. It was never given enough time.

Phases (2) and (3) of US central banking: the First and Second Bank of the United States

The US had about forty years of monetary governance by two national banks that purported to be central banks. The first was the First Bank of the United States, whose charter ran from 1791 through 1811. The second was the Second Bank of the United States, whose charter went from 1816 through 1836, although it reconstituted itself as the Bank of Pennsylvania of the United States and lasted until 1841. The experiences of both national banks are case studies in political economy.

Both banks originated, operated, and died amidst intense controversy. This debate transformed arguments over the technical merits of central banking into disputes that interwove politics and economics as political economy. The desirability of central banking was associated from the start with a particular political tradition. Hostility came from forces that rejected the core assumption of pro-bank groups: that federal intervention in this manner was appropriate and beneficial.

Some basic facts about early US politics are in order here. Two main political parties were then the Federalists and the Republicans. The latter are, ironically, the ancestors of the modern Democratic Party. Alexander Hamilton, the first Secretary of the US Treasury, was a Federalist and so committed to federal intervention in the national economy. With this conviction he strongly supported the First Bank of the United States.

Opposition to this bank came from those who thought it unconstitutional. The federal government had no power to authorize a central bank, they contended, because it was not explicitly mentioned in the US Constitution. Supporters of a central bank would argue that the "necessary and proper" clause of Article I, Sec. 8, gave the Congress implicit power to set up a national bank.

Many of those who thought the First, as well as the Second, Bank unconstitutional were Republicans and then states' rights Democrats. A central bank, in their opinion, trampled the rights of the states in banking, since the national bank had powers to restrain the activities of banks chartered by the states.

The First and Second Banks of the United States operated in an environment in which the creation of credit was highly visible and, therefore, more amenable to politicization. Unlike today, when credit can be granted through electronic transfer, in these earlier times banks sometimes extended loans by giving their own notes to debtors.

The national bank was concerned with stability and tried to restrain credit growth in order to lessen inflationary pressures. It did this, also in a very visible manner. Its agents would present notes to their issuing banks and ask that they be redeemed in specie, as the note promised. While there were no federally mandated reserve requirements at this time, most bankers were prudent and realized that they needed to maintain their own specie reserves. The actions of the national bank reduced those reserves and, in turn, limited credit creation by banks. So there were twin visibilities in credit creation and credit limitation that helped fuse banks and politics in the early decades of US history into case studies of political economy.

But it was not just any banks and any politics. A crucial issue in the entire constitutional history of the US has been relations between federal powers and states' rights. The First and Second Bank of the United States rested on this great fault line in US political economy. A striking example of the conflict between federal powers and states rights can be seen in the canyon that separated the views of participants in the disputes over these two national banks.

Defenders of the national banks regarded their actions in restraining credit as beneficial. Opponents construed their behavior as meddling, adversarial, and harmful to economic opportunity. These contrary positions crystallized during the run of the first and only charter of the First Bank of the United States. They became more acrimonious during the time of the first and only charter of the Second Bank of the United States.

While both banks were terminated by decisions at the federal level, their experiences with politics reveal important differences. Let us first spotlight the political configurations in the US Congress that the First Bank of the United States faced in the struggle over its charter renewal. Politics here pivots on occupation and geographical section. In 1791 the Bank drew important support from northern and eastern business interests that were Federalist. By 1811 key elements of business had shifted away from supporting a national bank and towards backing state-chartered banks. In fact, between 1791 and 1811 the number of state-chartered banks increased from three to ninety. In the fight to re-charter the First Bank of the United States, there were also strong sectional overtones. The south and west were for renewal, while many members of Congress from the east were against.

The actual votes in the US Congress show just how evenly matched the pro- and anti-Bank forces were. The House of Representatives voted to postpone consideration for good (that is, forever) by a vote of 65–64. The Senate tied, 17–17, until the Vice President, George Clinton of New York, cast the deciding vote against renewal. The First Bank of the United States had lost, but pro-Bank forces had the strength to fight another day. They did, and in 1817 Congress authorized the Second Bank of the United States.[44]

Politics perpetually enveloped all three of our antecedents – the Bank of North America and the First and Second Banks of the US. This politics became more complicated, especially in the latter years of the first Bank of the US and even more so for the Second Bank of the US. It is crucial to remember how the Second Bank of the United States perished. The Second Bank had majority support in both houses of Congress, but not enough votes to override a Presidential veto. A veto override requires a supermajority of two-thirds voting.

The demise of the Second Bank thus came at the hands of a hostile minority in Congress in combination with an adversarial President. Andrew Jackson vetoed the recharter bill on 10 July 1832. There was insufficient Congressional support to override.

The struggle over the Second Bank generated colorful phrases. It was known as the "Bank War"; some opponents of the Bank called it "The Money Monster." There are at least two ways to analyze the political economy of the "Bank War" over "The Money Monster." The first is to consider Jackson's veto message; and the second is to visit what is still the best analysis of this battle, the definitive work by Bray Hammond, which we have already cited.

Summaries of the veto message usually focus on stock ownership and constitutionality. Jackson believed foreign and East Coast ownership of bank stock was excessive and that the Bank was unconstitutional. These are important points, but the entire text of the veto message shows what this fight was all about.[45] In real estate there are three principles: location, location, and location. In the "Bank War" there were three forces: politics, politics, and politics.

The economic and constitutional analysis in the veto message is jejune, but Jackson was consistent in his states' rights approach to economic activity. His veto of the Second Bank followed his veto of the Maysville Road bill in 1830, which would have used federal funds for an interstate road. Jackson favored a state, not federal, approach to infrastructure in finance and transport.

The most comprehensive portrait of the "Bank War" is still found in *Banks and Politics in America from the Revolution to the Civil War*, by Bray Hammond. He identifies five forces that forged a coalition against the Bank. They were: (1) Wall Street's jealousy of Chestnut Street; (2) the business person's dislike of the federal Bank's restraint on bank credit; (3) the hostility of many politicians towards an institution that allegedly interfered with states' rights; (4) the popular identification of the National Bank with the aristocracy of business; and (5) the skillful direction of agrarian antipathy and dislike away from banks in general and towards the National Bank in particular.[46] We have already discussed the second and third elements and will now address the others in order.

(1) New York City (Wall Street) and Philadelphia (Chestnut Street) were competing to become the financial capital of the US. Philadelphia was home to the Second Bank of the United States. The destruction of the Bank would hurt Philadelphia and boost New York.

(4) The leadership of the Second Bank did come disproportionately from the Philadelphia elite; "blue bloods" from the Philadelphia "Main Line." Nicholas Biddle, who became President of the Second Bank in 1823 and led it through its most perilous conflicts with President Jackson, exemplified that aristocratic tradition. But hostile politics unfairly transformed an association with the elite into a total identification, which became a public relations disaster for the Bank.

(5) The first four elements of the coalition accurately describe the situation at the time, but the fifth may be overstated. There was significant agrarian discord with the Second Bank, because it restricted the growth in the money supply and supposedly kept interest rates too high. But to imply that agrarians were manipulated into focusing a general dislike for all banks on the "Money Monster" itself is a stretch. Agrarian discord was not a marionette whose strings could be pulled by superior forces. Nonetheless, agrarian discontent did have a role, and all five elements bonded together in one of the most effective coalitions of its kind in US history.

Those who drafted the Federal Reserve Act of 1913 grasped a central historical lesson from the experiences of the First and Second Banks. Their demises came from politics, politics, and politics. The charter of the Federal Reserve System can be amended, but it is perpetual, unlike the twenty-year charters that the First and Second Banks both had. This is not the same level of protection from politics that federal judges enjoy, but it is substantial insulation.

Phase (4) of US central banking: the Federal Reserve System

The US experienced a series of very volatile business cycles in the nineteenth and early twentieth centuries. Each major financial panic of the nineteenth century – 1837, 1857, 1873, and 1893 – detonated the "boom" or upside of its enveloping business cycle and ushered in a long downturn. The "bankers panic" of 1907, seemingly localized in New York City, generated much wider shocks and aftershocks, since New York was the financial capital of the US.

The Federal Reserve System was created to deal with two endemic problems that fueled this volatility: immobile bank reserves and an inelastic national currency. The immobility of bank reserves was associated with their excessive concentration in New York City, as non-New York banks deposited portions of their own reserves with New York City banks. They did this so they could facilitate their own transactions in the City and also earn interest on their reserves.

This concentration transformed their seemingly "idle" reserves into instruments for economic activity, but it produced an environment fraught with potential peril. Economists describe this arrangement as the "pyramiding of reserves" in order to economize on them. This "pyramid," which should really be turned upside down, placed extraordinary stress on a limited supply of reserves, since these reserves were fulfilling multiple functions.

This situation worked, as long as the reserves had only one role to play at a time, such as serving as loans to people who used them to purchase stock on Wall Street. Should panic materialize anywhere and people want to withdraw their savings from banks that had reserves on deposit in New York City, the vulnerabilities of the system became apparent. New York banks were forced to call in loans made to purchasers of stock in order to get money to return to non-New York banks. Instability intensified, if the owners of stocks had to sell in a collapsing market in order to pay back their loans. They would have to unload more stock to get the money, putting yet more downward pressure on stock prices.

A second major source of instability was an inelastic national currency. This is the economist's concept of elasticity, which refers to how responsive something is to changes that affect it. Currency inelasticity means that there was not enough currency where it was needed, especially in times of economic duress. This imbalance was geographical. Protest groups had long argued, correctly, that those national bank notes mentioned above were unfairly distributed. They clustered in urban areas and were never in sufficient supplies in rural regions of the US.

Contrary to the high expectations of some modern economic historians, the Federal Reserve System was not established to end the business cycle by preventing all downturns in the future. It was set up as a lender of last resort. Institutions in this position, if they perform well, can reduce but never eliminate volatility.

In any event, the "Fed" faced those two other challenges, which were quite formidable. In its earlier years, it made more progress in dealing with currency inelasticity than with the immobility of bank reserves. This is understandable, because immobility of bank reserves reflected the centrality of New York City in US finance. And the Fed, while strong, was not omnipotent and could not by itself reverse that historical trend.

The provision of Federal Reserve notes was an attempt to provide a more geographically balanced supply of paper currency than the old national bank notes furnished. Still, for a long time, these notes were neither plentiful nor diffused enough to satisfy some critics. Be that as it may, the ascendancy of Federal Reserve notes, tracked above, was the crucial development in moving towards a single paper currency. Federal Reserve notes, together with the long-standing single coinage, have produced, practically speaking, a complete single currency for the US common market.

EU monetary integration

The monetary integration of the EU has had far less time to unfold than that of the US common market. The EU was born in 1957; the US common market in 1788.

There is a sharp contrast between them with respect to the prior experiences of their members with monetary integration. The countries that belong to the EU have much longer histories of monetary integration on their own than did the states that make up the US common market. The French and English nation-states, for example, started emerging in the European Middle Ages, before North America experienced the waves of imperial invasion that led to the establishment of European colonies on that continent.

A brief retrospective on the French franc shows how far back the French experience with monetary integration reaches. The name "franc" originated in remarks supposedly made by King Jean le Bon in 1360. On leaving an English prison, he said, "*franc et délivré*." "Franc" became associated with "libre," or free. And "franc" was the name given to a gold coin, called "*franc à cheval*," because it represented the king on a horse. There were other coins, such as "*l'écu, le louis, le liard* [farthing]," but in popular language the word "franc" remained a synonym for the "livre," the unit of royal account.

It was only in 1795, during the French Revolution, that the Convention, which governed France from 21 September 1792, until 26 October 1795, made the franc "*une véritable monnaie*," a real or true money. The "real" franc then underwent its own transformations. In 1960, for instance, the *nouveau franc* or new franc was introduced; it was worth 100 "old francs." The previous franc then became known as the *ancien franc*.[47]

The French franc, as reality, synonym, symbol, and mystique, was thus a powerful bond in French culture. Other European countries had bonding experiences with their national currencies that give the EU a very long-term history of monetary integration, even though the organization itself is relatively youthful in this regard.

There is another kind of historical legacy on which the modern monetary history of the EU stands. These are the earlier experiences of organizations from both continental and offshore Europe that featured monetary integration as one of their concerns. From this perspective, the Hanseatic League of late medieval Europe (Chapter 2) made an important contribution, since its members sought to standardize the forms of exchange. The forms of exchange include not only contracts and other documents, but also the media of exchange. These media involve barter (countertrade) and money itself neoclassically defined (Chapter 1).

This deep historical view emphasizes national as well as cross-border experiences. It is important, because many see European monetary integration as a modern phenomenon, beginning after World War II

(1939–45). The post-WWII period is crucial, but it must be placed in this long-term historical context.

For a saga that has many episodes we propose a framework whose simplicity verges on self-satire.[48] Three developments have special significance for European monetary integration in the last half of the twentieth century. The first is the European Payments Union (EPU). The second is the European Monetary System (EMS) with its Exchange Rate Mechanism (ERM). The third is Economic and Monetary Union (EMU), which emerged from long consultation and planning and is embodied in the Maastricht Treaty of 1991, introduced earlier.

The EPU, EMS, and ERM are all stepping-stones to the euro, the single currency. The euro and the European Central Bank (ECB) are the twin centerpieces of EMU. We first examine the European Payments Union, then the Exchange Rate Mechanism, and lastly Economic and Monetary Union. Since EMU intertwines the euro and the European Central Bank, we consider them together.

This approach differs from our analysis of a single currency and central banking in the US common market. We tracked them separately, because their emergence was not coordinated until 1914, with the foundation of the Federal Reserve System, and their history thus requires separate tracks.

The European Payments Union

The EPU, which came into force in 1950, was crucial for currency transferability and convertibility. Transferability and convertibility are related but distinct processes, and there are degrees of both. Transferability means one currency can be exchanged for another. This exchange may be bilateral, between two countries, or multilateral, among three or more countries. Convertibility implies high levels of transferability, and can apply within and outside a country. External convertibility means that a non-resident of a country can sell that country's currency for any other currency.[49]

It is essential for trade that currencies can be readily exchanged one into another. In some scenarios convertibility means that a currency can also be exchanged for gold of commensurate value. Transferability and convertibility both require an adequate supply of "internationally usable reserves," which are usually gold and dollar holdings.[50] In the aftermath of World War II, there was an acute shortage of holdings in US dollars, which hampered the transferability and convertibility of European currencies.

Convertibility is the more demanding procedure, but transferability can still be daunting. The more practical goal was to pursue transferability, and some countries had developed bilateral arrangements to accomplish these transactions, but the problem of transferability remained severe on the European level. A concerted, multilateral approach was clearly needed.

The EPU emerged as a "clearing union that replaced the existing array of bilateral payment agreements by a multilateral settlement and credit mechanism." A payments union facilitated currency transferability. It did not deal directly with the convertibility of those European currencies, but it bought members time to get up to speed on convertibility.[51] In fact, on 27 December 1958, the EPU "entered into liquidation." That day "a majority of EPU members accepted the obligations of Art. VIII of the IMF [International Monetary Fund] Articles of Agreement and introduced external convertibility for their currencies."[52]

A question has arisen as to whether a payments union was really needed. Some European countries were supposedly reaching a point where they could operate on the convertibility of their current accounts. But this question falsely assumes that a payments union was only an economic instrument.

The EPU was more than an exercise in economics. It embodied powerful political considerations. Convertibility in the early 1950s would have required even more currency devaluations and caused more stress. The EPU was thus an organization of political economy, as it combined appropriate economics and timely politics.

The EPU set precedents across the fabric of political economy. As to economics, the establishment of the euro in the late 1990s presupposed the full transferability of member currencies and the EPU contributed to this achievement. For politics, the EPU highlighted two salient points. The first is how important the cooperation of political leaders is in advancing monetary integration. The second is how vital it is to integrate human considerations into "economic" policy-making. These precedents are why the EPU was pivotal in the modern monetary integration of Europe.

The European Monetary System and its Exchange Rate Mechanism

Started in 1979, the European Monetary System (EMS) consisted "of fixed but adjustable exchange rates." These were "kept within agreed fluctuation margins by 'obligatory intervention.'"[53] The EMS rested on the ERM, an acronym for Exchange Rate Mechanism.

In practice, however, the ERM was the exchange rate *and intervention* mechanism. The *mechanism*, in turn, required the ECU and the divergence indicator. The ECU means European Currency Unit and is a modern creation, but the acronym ECU is the same as the historical French coin *l'ecu*, mentioned above in our capsule on French monetary history. The ECU was introduced as a unit of account for the members of the European Community that participated in the ERM. The ECU was thus on a continental level what the *livre* had been for France.

The modern ECU was to fulfill five official functions. Three were as a denominator: for the ERM; for operations in the intervention and credit mechanisms; and for transactions of the European Monetary Cooperation

Fund (EMCF). A fourth role was as the basis for the divergence indicator, while a fifth was as a reserve asset in settlements among the monetary authorities of European Community countries.[54]

The essentials of the ERM are straightforward, though their application sometimes seemed arcane.[55] Each currency in the ERM had a central rate fixed in terms of the ECU; this was done by mutual consent. A grid of central rates emerged; fluctuation margins of 2.25 percent in either direction were acceptable. There was a more elastic 6 percent margin up or down for currencies that had been floated. The "obligatory intervention" designed to keep a currency within "agreed fluctuation margins" consisted of buying or selling partner currencies in the exchange markets.

The divergence indicator was to serve as an EWS, an early warning system. It linked the market exchange rates of currencies in the ERM to the ECU. It was supposed to signal when the market exchange rate of a currency "diverged" from the weighted average of the others.

Many immediately call the divergence indicator the "rattlesnake." This metaphor built on the "snake" image, which characterized some previous exchange-rate regimes that permitted fluctuations. Evidently these evoked the movements of snakes.

Theory is one thing; practice, another. The divergence indicator had problems "rattling" at the right moments, because the ECU was at the center of the EMS in only a formal sense. Its ambitious program of five official functions was never fully realized. The ECU had a limited role as a means of settlement, since EC central banks preferred other techniques, such as intervening on their own with their own mixes of financial instruments.

Yet the ECU gained substantial acceptance in private transactions. The private ECU was based on the same basket of EC currencies as the official ECU. It became popular as a hedge instrument. Investors could protect themselves against the exchange-rate risks of individual currencies. They could also gain from the higher interest rates for assets denominated in weaker currencies.[56]

Specialists in the modern monetary integration of Europe debate the meaning of the EMS in relation to other regimes of exchange rate coordination. These proceedings are illuminating.[57] We, however, will not dwell on the unrealized potential of the EMS.

We emphasize what the ECU, both the official and private version, actually accomplished. Besides its excellence as a hedge instrument, the ECU was a key agency in monetary standardization, as "it served a number of accounting purposes within the EMS as well as in the EC at large."[58] From a wider perspective, an apprentice unit of account has great value in paving the way for the introduction of a single currency, even if the apprentice currency does not itself become the single currency. The ECU did not get top billing in this phase, as it was part of the EMS and the ERM. Yet the ECU proved an important antecedent to the euro, which also serves as a unit of account.

The EPU and the EMS were both organizations of political economy; but whereas the EPU combined economics and politics effectively, the EMS, especially in the ERM, faced explosive political and economic forces it was not designed to manage.

The early 1990s were a dangerous time for the EMS. The belief spread that its grid of central rates, which expressed each participating currency in terms of the ECU, was unrealistically set. The Maastricht Treaty formalized a monetary regime that would replace the EMS. Heads of government had signed it in December 1991, but it was encountering difficulties in winning approval. The French referendum to approve Maastricht, for instance, passed with a paper-thin majority on 20 September 1992. These were gale warnings of doubt and uncertainty posted for the financial markets. They turned out to understate the strength of the actual storms.

In 1992 and 1993 crises roiled the EMS. Enter currency speculators, with voracious appetites for quick profits and great tolerances for volatility. September 1992 was a microcosm of crisis, especially for Great Britain, which confronted a rising storm surge of speculation against the British pound as the middle of the month approached. September 16, 1992 became known as "Black Wednesday," when the storm surge pounding the British currency did the most damage.

Despite major actions to defend the pound by the Bank of England and the EMS, the British government pulled its currency out of the ERM on 17 September 1992. This debacle, which better management by the British government might have tempered, stoked British ambivalence about having key symbols of national sovereignty "locked" in arrangements sponsored by the European Community which it had joined in 1973.

Economic and Monetary Union

The crises of 1992 and 1993 may also have derived from the problem of expectations. Some expected the EMS to perform as if it were Economic and Monetary Union (EMU), a much stronger set of institutions than those embodied in the EMS. But the EMS, of course, was not the same as EMU.

The Treaty of Maastricht crystallized Economic and Monetary Union, but its origins reach back decades. The Werner Report (1972) contained the original proposals for a single currency. These envisioned monetary union by 1980, but two major events derailed this timetable. The first was the dramatic increase in the price of oil during the 1970s, which came in two spikes, in 1973 and in 1979. The second was the global move to floating exchange rates.[59]

During the early and mid-1980s the desire to complete the single market strengthened in the European Community. The Single European Act (1986), discussed earlier, implemented this conviction. The idea also gathered force that a single market would not be complete without a single currency. This would eliminate exchange-rate fluctuations among member currencies, since they would no longer exist.

A committee chaired by Jacques Delors, then President of the European Commission, issued the definitive report in April 1989. The Delors Report proposed a three-stage progression towards Economic and Monetary Union, which the Treaty of Maastricht codified.

The Treaty of Maastricht laid out three stages for the "progressive realisation" of economic and monetary union. The first was closer coordination of economic policies, which actually started in July 1990. The second stage, begun in 1994, included creation of a European Monetary Institute, a forerunner to the European Central Bank (ECB).

The ECB was founded on 1 June 1998 to regulate monetary policy in the Eurozone, as the EU countries that join monetary union are collectively called. The Eurozone is also known as the Euro-area and Euroland. The ECB began establishing a single set of interest rates for the Eurozone on 1 January 1999. Fiscal policies remain with national governments. The presidents of the central banks of member states sit on the board of directors of the ECB.

The third stage of EMU concerns the single currency, the euro, and had three phases.[60] The first began on 4 January 1999, and launched the transitional period. It was preceded by a "conversion weekend," from 31 December 1998, through 3 January 1999. During "conversion weekend" stock exchanges of participating countries moved to the euro and the domestic debt of those states was redenominated in the euro.

The transitional period was filled with activities. On 4 January 1999, the euro appeared as "written money" in the Eurozone. "Written money" includes checks, travelers' checks, bank transfers, and credit cards. The euro, in its "written forms," circulated along with national currencies in Euroland through December 31, 2001.

Other features of the transitional period included the following: conversion rates between member currencies were irrevocably locked; the euro became the currency of participating states; their national currencies became denominations of the euro; ECU obligations were converted into euro obligations at a 1:1 conversion rate; and new issues of government debt began to be issued in euros. The first phase, or transitional period, ended on 31 December 2001, when obligations denominated in national currency units were redenominated in euros.[61]

The second phase was the introduction of euro notes and coins into circulation on 1 January 2002. Euro notes are in denominations of 500, 200, 100, 50, 20, 10, and 5. Euro coins are in denominations of 2 and 1 euros, and 50, 20, 10, 5, 2, and 1 cent. The designs of the notes commemorate the architectural heritage of Europe. The designs of the common faces of the coins emerged from a European competition. The observe side of each coin can have a unique national imprint for each country.[62]

The national notes and coins of those countries belonging to the Eurozone circulated as legal tender through 30 June 2002, even though the national currencies themselves ceased to exist on 4 January 1999. For example, the French franc ceased to exist on 4 January 1999, but franc notes and coins circulated legally through 30 June 2002. On 1 July 2002, national currencies of Eurozone members became illegal tender and were supposedly withdrawn from circulation and impounded.

In 2004 the Eurozone comprised twelve countries: Austria, Belgium, Finland, France, Germany, Greece, Ireland, Italy, Luxembourg, the Netherlands, Portugal, and Spain. They all met the so-called "convergence criteria." These criteria relate to inflation, long-term interest rates, and debt. Members must maintain price stability, budget deficits within three percent of gross domestic product (GDP), and national debt within 60 percent of GDP.

Three of the fifteen countries that belonged to the EU before "enlargement day" on 1 May 2004 have not entered the Eurozone. They are Denmark, Sweden, and the United Kingdom. Denmark and the United Kingdom have exercised their rights under the Maastricht Treaty to "opt out" of the single currency. Sweden does not technically have the right to "opt out," but it has not joined.

Each country has its own reasons for remaining outside Euroland. Denmark conducted a referendum on joining the euro on 28 September 2000. It failed, with a no vote of 53.2 percent. Whether another referendum will be held is not known.

Denmark has, however, taken an important decision that connects its currency, the Danish krona, to the euro. In 1999, when the euro was created, the krona entered the Second Exchange Rate Mechanism (ERM II). ERM II succeeded ERM I, which crashed in 1993.[63]

The Second European Exchange Rate Mechanism officially replaced the European Monetary System on 1 January 1999. The objective of ERM II is "to set up an appropriate exchange-rate mechanism between the euro and the national currencies of the [EU] countries not participating in the euro area so as to ensure monetary stability and solidarity."[64] While Denmark may never adopt the euro, entering ERM II shows that the country is serious about contributing to "monetary stability and solidarity" as a member of the EU.

Sweden has not, according to some, made a major effort to join. Sweden supposedly does not have a central bank with sufficient independence. To be fair, many Swedes do not see matters that way and characterize their approach to the euro as cautious.

Sweden conducted a referendum on joining the euro on 14 September 2003. It failed, with a no vote of 56.1 percent. A decision on another referendum has apparently been postponed until at least 2012.

The case of the United Kingdom is complicated. There the euro must pass political as well as economic scrutiny. As to politics, three groups – the cabinet, parliament, and the British electorate in a referendum – must approve the euro. In addition, the British government has mandated five economic tests that the single currency must satisfy.

These are convergence, flexibility, investment, financial services, and growth and employment. Convergence refers to whether the business cycles and economic structures of the UK and the Eurozone are compatible. Flexibility introduces the question of whether membership in the Eurozone is supple enough for the British government to deal with any problems that arise. Investment asks whether UK businesses would benefit from membership. Financial services relate to the City of London. This is London's financial district. Can it flourish outside the euro? Would it be better off inside the euro? The fifth and final economic test: will economic growth and the number of jobs increase if the UK joins the euro?

The five economic tests, Tim Weber sums up, "fall into two categories. What are the costs of joining – does the UK economy fit into the eurozone, and can the country cope with any economic turbulence? And what are the benefits of joining – will the UK get more investment, more jobs and a boost for the City if it joins the eurozone?"[65]

The positive evidence for meeting those five tests in 2004 is, apparently, still not compelling. The tests themselves are the subject of much analysis and criticism. One thing is certain, however. The interpretation of the results of those "economic" tests will be political. And it will be political judgments all around that decide whether and when the UK joins the euro.

What about the ten countries that entered the EU on 1 May 2004? They will all eventually join the euro. The single currency is part of their EU membership; they have no right to "opt out." It is unlikely that any will enter the Eurozone before 2007–08. Some states will join earlier than others, depending on when they meet the "convergence criteria."

Single currencies: parallels and guideposts

In review, there are striking parallels between the US single currency and that of the EU in operation and design. In operation each eurozone country decides how much of the single currency it needs. This procedure is analogous to each regional Federal Reserve Bank issuing it own notes in response to local requirements. As to design, each Federal Reserve note is marked to indicate which regional Federal Reserve Bank issued it. Each euro coin, on its obverse side, will show its country of origin. The single coinage in the US also allows room for individual expression. There are, for instance, quarters representing particular states and nickels commemorating the Lewis and Clark expedition.

Two major guideposts stand out from the experiences of the US common market and the EU with a single currency. First, a single currency does not have to be an identical currency. And, second, the emergence of a single currency greatly benefits from the presence of a strong central bank.

The following retrospective summarizes the conclusions that emerge from our study of international economic integration in historical perspective.

Retrospective as prospective

The past does not proffer precise blueprints for present or future conduct. Nor does it reveal everything. But the past can yield insights that may inspire guidelines for action. In this spirit, I summarize the most important conclusions that emerge from the examples in the preceding seven chapters.

(1) *International economic integration is an economic and a political process. But it also involves political economy.* Economics and politics drive organizations pursuing cross-border economic integration, sometimes as separate forces, sometimes interrelated as political economy. Politics and economics must advance together and form interrelations.

Too unbalanced an approach may generate divisive political pressures. Economics cannot get too far ahead of politics and vice-versa. Asia-Pacific Economic Cooperation (APEC), discussed in Chapter 5, shows the problems an organization will face if its economic agenda outruns a political consensus on the meanings of such terms as trade liberalization. The European Union (EU), spotlighted in Chapter 7, underscores the critical importance of laying a strong political foundation to support far-reaching plans for greater federalism in both economics and politics.

I am not suggesting that economics and politics must move forward side by side or in lock step. It is impossible to orchestrate events on the ground with textbook precision. Actually, politics can get ahead of economics and vice-versa, but not too far ahead. How far is "too far"? There is no universal definition. But I am reminded of how Justice Potter Stewart of the US Supreme Court defined pornography: "I'll know it when I see it."

The first conclusion has profound implications for how organizations involved in international economic integration should be understood. Every organization has multiple dynamics as economics, politics, and their interweaving as political economy. Leaders must acknowledge these, because a decision made only on the basis of "economic considerations" may prove ill advised.

Greater awareness of these different dynamics should make decision-making more realistic. It may be prudent not to push for more integration in some controversial area. Sometimes the wisest decision may be acceptance: that a certain "level" of integration is the best that can be achieved without harming an organization.

The previous pages have offered compelling examples of realistic integration. I single out three for special attention in this retrospective. I will immediately reflect on the European Payments Union and the European Economic Area, and then bring back the *Zollverein* under conclusion 3.

The European Payments Union (EPU), presented in Chapter 7, was a major precedent in the emergence of European Monetary Union. It fulfilled a crucial need for a multilateral payments agency, but did not address the full external convertibility of member currencies. There were powerful political reasons for its focus, as convertibility might have required more currency devaluations that would hurt many people. The EPU was, I argued, the best blend of politics and economics that was practical for its times. It was, in the jargon of social science, optimal political economy: that is why I gave an organization that had an eight-year life span so much importance. The European Economic Area (EEA), from Chapter 5, is a "middle way" between the European Free Trade Association and the European Union. Founded in 1994, it gives members of the EFTA two choices. They can get close to the EU without actually joining it, or they can experience the economic integration of a common market as a prelude to applying for membership in the EU. The EEA is creative and flexible, one of the most realistic "middle ways" in the history of international economic integration.

(2) *Define and develop those interrelations between economics and politics that most strengthen your organization.* Each organization should strive to optimize its own political economy. Each grouping has its own strengths and weaknesses in both economics and politics. It should build on its strengths and try to offset its weaknesses. It should take its strengths in economics and politics and interrelate them where possible.

The most basic subject in the study of political economy, as noted in the Introduction, is the relationship between political institutions and economic activity. This general relationship can have numerous interrelations. The following is only a preliminary listing of possibilities. Interrelations can be institutional, when they connect different institutions or agencies within the same organization. They can appear in the decision-making process, when people ask how do economic considerations affect political decisions or how do political factors influence economic policy? Interrelations can be theoretical, as when observers use economic or political theory to analyze government decisions. And interrelations can be structural, as when they bridge or intersect the public and private sectors.

The Hanseatic League, showcased in Chapter 2, provides an excellent illustration of institutional interrelations in political economy. It was an international combination of merchants and cities that had a wide-ranging impact over the northern half of Europe from the thirteenth into the sixteenth centuries.

As the Hanseatic League evolved from associations of merchants into a confederation of towns, economics and politics melded in the life of this organization. The institutional interrelations between merchant associations and towns facilitated the emergence of the League itself. The Hanseatic League is one of the most striking manifestations of institutional political economy in the history of international economic integration.

(3) *History does not provide an infallible road map for cross-border economic integration, but the Zollverein is a good place to start.* Below I summarize from Chapter 6 the lessons the *Zollverein* teaches and then offer my final reflections on this stellar example of realistic integration.[1]

Lesson 1 It helps to have a central motivating idea.
Lesson 2 It helps to be able to draw on a powerful underlying force with deep emotional wellsprings.
Lesson 3 It helps to have a vision.
Lesson 4 It helps to have leaders, including a major figure, who can implement this vision.
Lesson 5 It can help to see your organization overcoming hostile forces.
Lesson 6 Align geography and economics.
Lesson 7 Big things take time.
Lesson 8 Do not do too much at once.
Lesson 9 Streamline goals.

Some may wonder whether all these lessons are equally important. At this point Clio, who usually speaks with clarity, becomes like the Delphic Oracle, who excelled at riddles. A grouping does not require hostile forces to succeed (Lesson 5). But it does not have to seek out enemies, because it either has or will get them. And it can function without aligning geography and economics (Lesson 6). That is, it can operate with members not geographically contiguous to one another.

Every grouping must have its own definitions of the first three lessons, which deal with ideas, emotions, and visions. But a grouping can get by without a "major figure" (Lesson 4) as long as available leadership remains competent, steady, focused, and uncorrupted.

As the first three lessons are related, so are the last three. While the first three concern intangibles, the last three deal with prudent procedures. Lesson 7 – big things take time – is immutable and, therefore, ignored at one's peril. Lesson 8 is a matter of local interpretation, but every grouping has its own limitations. To paraphrase Clint Eastwood in the final moments of *Magnum Force* as Hal Holbrook drives away in a car about to explode, a person has got to know his or her limitations. Every grouping must learn its limitations, but I hope self-knowledge does not come from disaster. Lesson 9 – streamlining goals – is common sense and will help a grouping reach its potential.

(4) *International economic integration has many positives but it has a dark side.* Greater cooperation among nations on economic matters is a good in itself. Many people also benefit, as reducing barriers to cross-border exchange stimulates an increase in business and economic activity. But there is a dark side: economic disintegration, which stands for the harms international economic integration causes.

This is not just an historical phenomenon. Disintegration is very much with us today. Let me first summarize historical instances of economic disintegration and then move to more contemporary manifestations.

The dominant historical exhibit of economic disintegration features the Atlantic slave trade. A number of the chartered companies presented in Chapter 2 played roles in this intercontinental trade, which began in the 1440s and lasted into the twentieth century. Millions of Africans were enslaved and forced to cross the Atlantic to the "New World." They left behind a homeland suffering under the combined assaults of local wars, the depredations of those hunting for people to enslave, and the destabilization of indigenous economies and kinship structures. The Atlantic slave trade did not cause every African woe, but it must bear the greatest share of the blame for economic disintegration in the areas it affected.

A general thrust of European colonialism was to force indigenous economic structures into a particular version of imperial economic integration. This endeavor unleashed other kinds of economic disintegration. I analyzed different examples of imperial economic integration in Chapter 1 and will not retrace every step here. I wish only to re-emphasize the fate of indigenous moneys, a topic I developed in this book because of my earlier published research that combined neo-classical economic analysis with economic anthropology.

Colonial governments defined the legal money supply as their coins and paper money. They demonetized African moneys they perceived as such, and when they suppressed barter, they were sometimes attacking African moneys they did not see as such. The imposition of their "single currencies," which I tracked in Chapter 1, was a major example of economic disintegration on at least two fronts. Colonial bureaucracies required that their taxes be paid in official coinage. Many Africans had to leave their farms and go to work for Europeans to get the requisite coins. This dynamic destabilized African agriculture, which was the first front. The imposition of a "single currency" reduced the amount and diversity of a territory's money supply, which adversely affected exchange and thereby constrained economic growth. This was the second front.

The two organizations not traditionally treated under the rubric of international economic integration are also associated with economic disintegration. The Roman Catholic Church, spotlighted in Chapter 3, in its relentless and widening search for revenue, caused economic disintegration during the Middle Ages and beyond. As specie left England and France to finance the Papacy, the national money supplies of these countries suffered. A specie drain, not the imposition of "single currencies," was the culprit here. But the results were the same: harmful consequences for exchange and economic growth.

And the Mafia, highlighted in Chapter 4, must answer, not surprisingly, for its numerous acts of disintegration. Money laundering, the traffic in illegal drugs, the counterfeiting of legal drugs, stock manipulation schemes, the damage inflicted on legitimate businesses that refuse to pay protection money, the penetration of legalized gambling, and identity theft: this is only a partial listing of the forms of criminal disintegration.

Some contemporary examples of economic disintegration are wrapped in controversy. Free trade agreements always spark vigorous debate. I reviewed in detail the pros and cons of the North American Free Trade Agreement (NAFTA) in Chapter 5 and will not further burden readers here. Suffice it to say there are common themes in these debates. Defenders stress the economic benefits that flow from trade liberalization, because they see these agreements primarily as economic documents. Critics contend that many people lose and argue that free trade agreements must be assessed in a wider context.

Both sides in these debates score telling points. Here are my suggestions. Free trade agreements should be evaluated from three viewpoints: as economic documents, as political statements, and from the perspective of political economy. If agreements were drafted in the context of political economy, losers could be treated with greater fairness. Whether they will or not depends on leadership, which is I argue obligated to repair any damage that results from international economic integration.

The single most disquieting trend for me today is the ongoing disintegration of US manufacturing capacity. I realize that the decline of US manufacturing has many causes, but it behooves policy-makers to pay special attention to any deleterious effects cross-border economic integration may have on US manufacturing.

Those who believe in the power of the "free market" seem unconcerned. In fact, some praise "outsourcing," or transferring jobs outside one's country, as a sign of the efficiency of the US economy. The "free market" may be efficient, but is it wise?

I strongly believe in the critical importance of maintaining a strategic capacity in indigenous manufacturing for any country that wishes to preserve its independence in the world. In times when we may not even foresee what the next lethal threat will be, countries must have the capacity to make things crucial for their defense within their own borders. Never "outsource" your own security.

(5) *There is more than one path forward.* Examine conventional wisdom critically. The ladder of international economic integration for governments, which can have three or more steps, is an opinion, not a prescription. The free trade area, customs union, and common market have

conventional definitions. Some organizations may wish to follow received wisdom, but others may prefer to blaze their own trails.

Creating one's own paradigm may already be happening. Our research has revealed, for example, that "common market" means different things to different organizations. *Mercosur*, presented in Chapter 6, strives to become a common market, but apparently does not view legal standardization as a requirement for achieving that objective. Other groupings, in Africa, Central America, and the Caribbean, deploy similarly idiosyncratic interpretations of common market.

Some may find these definitions deficient from the perspective of western economics, but an organization may want its title to reflect more than economic content. A free trade area or customs union calling itself a common market is not technically correct in terms of the conventional wisdom, but the word "common" has great political value in building a sense of community. So a grouping may decide that politics overrides economics in selecting a name. That is good political economy in the making.

In fact, there is a need to recast the theory and vocabulary of international economic integration in the context of political economy. The economic theory of economic integration is persuasive on paper and often validated in practice. But all our groupings involve people. People experience joys and pains. And people see the same things differently. In short, people mean politics. So, ideally, a theory of international economic integration should emerge that better integrates economics and politics.

A place to begin is with the steps of international economic integration for governments. A major task is to develop an explicit statement of what political conditions should exist in order for an organization to advance through phases of more intense economic bonding. These conditions should be articulated as guidelines, with considerable built-in flexibility, not as prerequisites. These guidelines should not be "one size fits all," but customized to fit the political circumstances in particular countries.

The mixed experience of the European Union with regard to the ratification of its constitution reinforces the need for more systematic attention to the politics of federation. As long as most people look at economics and politics separately, any proposal for greater integration that entails more political losses than economic benefits will fail.

So, in the end, two challenges confront us all, whether we are government leaders, scholars, students, or patient readers. We must analyze and present international economic integration in terms of political economy, not just as separate matters of economics and politics. We must also never forget that international economic integration is only a process. It can be implemented with wisdom or shortsightedness, for good or for ill.

Notes

Introduction

1 Paul M. Johnson, *A Glossary of Political Economy Terms* (1994–2005). Online. Available at: www.auburn.edu/~johnspm/gloss/political_economy (accessed 15 May 2005).

2 Bela Balassa, *The Theory of Economic Integration*, London: Allen and Unwin, 1962, pp. 2–3.

3 See Jeffrey A. Frankel, *Regional Trading Blocs in the World Economic System*, Washington, DC: Institute for International Economics, 1997, pp. 12–17.

1 Colonial empires

1 Rondo Cameron, *A Concise Economic History of the World: From Paleolithic Times to the Present*, Oxford and New York: The Oxford University Press, 1989, p. 82. I am indebted to Professor Cameron for making this point to me in a personal letter as well.

2 See John Komlos, *The Habsburg Monarchy as a Customs Union: Economic Development in Austria–Hungary in the Nineteenth Century*, Princeton, NJ: The Princeton University Press, 1983.

3 Ibid., p. 257.

4 Keith Hopkins, "Introduction," in Peter Garnsey, Keith Hopkins, and C. R. Whitaker (eds) *Trade in the Ancient Economy*, London: Chatto and Windus – the Hogarth Press, 1983, p. xviii.

5 Peter L. Wickins, *An Economic History of Africa From the Earliest Times to Partition*, Capetown: Oxford University Press, 1981, pp. 135–6.

6 Peter Garnsey, "Grain for Rome," in Peter Garnsey, Keith Hopkins, and C. R. Whitaker (eds) *Trade in the Ancient Economy*, London: Chatto and Windus – the Hogarth Press, 1983, p. 118.

7 Ibid., pp. 119–20.

8 Ibid., p. 120.

9 Moses I. Finley, *The Ancient Economy*, Berkeley: University of California Press, 1973, p. 21.

10 Ibid., p. 157.

11 See the entire work *Trade in the Ancient Economy*, Peter Garnsey, Keith Hopkins and C. R. Whitaker (eds), London: Chatto and Windus – the Hogarth Press, 1983. The "Introduction," by Keith Hopkins, is a useful summary of the debate (pp. ix–xxv). "Urban elites and business in the Greek part of the Roman Empire," by H. W. Pleket, analyzes business aspects of the debate with special clarity (pp. 131–44).

12 D. K. Fieldhouse, *The Colonial Empires: A Comparative Survey from the Eighteenth Century*, New York: Delacorte Press, 1967, p. 27.
13 Ibid., p. 27.
14 Ibid., pp. 27–8.
15 According to mercantilism, the accumulation of precious metals – gold and silver – would strengthen a national government. One way to get precious metals was to achieve a positive balance of international trade. If a country exported more than it imported in monetary terms, it would receive an inflow of precious metals, because international trade then operated on movements of bullion to balance things out. A country running a trade deficit had to part with some of its precious metals to pay for its excess of imports over exports. Mercantilism thus emphasized exporting manufactured goods and importing raw materials for processing at home. Colonies were to serve as sources of these raw materials and as markets for those manufactured goods. The classic treatment of mercantilism remains Eli F. Heckscher, *Mercantilism*, 2 vols, authorized translation by Mendel Shapiro, London: Allen & Unwin and New York: Macmillan, 1962.
16 Fieldhouse, *Colonial Empires*, p. 32.
17 Wickins, *An Economic History of Africa*, p. 250.
18 A. Berriedale Keith, *The Belgian Congo and the Berlin Act*, Oxford: The Clarendon Press, 1919, p. 118.
19 Ruth Slade, *King Leopold's Congo*, London: The Oxford University Press, 1962, p. 177.
20 Ibid.
21 Ibid., pp. 130–1.
22 Janet MacGaffey, *Entrepreneurs and Parasites: The Struggle for Indigenous Capitalism in Zaire*, Cambridge: The University Press, 1987, p. 32.
23 Slade, *King Leopold's Congo*, p. 185.
24 See E(dmund) D(ene) Morel, *Red Rubber: The Story of the Rubber Trade Flourishing on the Congo in the Year of grace 1906*, New York: Negro Universities Press, 1969. This is a reprint of the 1906 edition. See also Wm. Roger Louis and Jean Stengers (eds) *E. D. Morel's History of the Congo Reform Movement*, Oxford, UK: Oxford University Press, 1968.
25 Robert Harms, "The world Abir made: The Maringa-Lopori Basin, 1885–1903," *African Economic History*, No. 12 (1983), 125–39. See especially 134–5.
26 I am indebted to Martha Honey for this information.
27 Arthur J. Knoll, *Togo Under Imperial Germany, 1884–1914: A Case Study in Colonial Rule*, Stanford: Hoover Institution Press, 1978, pp. 139–40.
28 Ibid., p. 139.
29 Edward Mortimer, "Empire without profit or prestige," *Financial Times* Weekend, 23/24 August 1997, 7.
30 David K. Fieldhouse, "The Economic Exploitation of Africa: Some British and French Comparisons," in Prosser Gifford and Wm. Roger Louis (eds) *France and Britain in Africa: Imperial Rivalry and Colonial Rule*, New Haven and London: Yale University Press, 1971, p. 607.
31 Ibid.
32 Ibid., p. 608.
33 See Dennis M. P. McCarthy, *Colonial Bureaucracy and Creating Underdevelopment: Tanganyika, 1919–1940*, Ames: The Iowa State University Press, 1982, pp. 11–23, and "Bureaucracy, Business, and Africa During the Colonial Period: Who Did What to Whom and With What Consequences?" in Paul Uselding (ed.) *Research in Economic History*, Vol. 11 (1988), pp. 111–27.
34 A comprehensive framework for studying money is detailed in Dennis M. P.

McCarthy, "A collaboration of history and anthropology: the synergy of economic history and ethnoeconomy in illuminating colonial African moneys," *African Economic History*, 24 (1996), 91–107.

35 For British East Africa, see Dennis M. P. McCarthy, "Money and the underdevelopment of Tanganyika to 1940," *The Journal of Economic History*, 36 (September, 1976), 645–62. For British West Africa, consult Dennis M. P. McCarthy, "Bureaucracy, business, and Africa during the colonial period," pp. 84–100.

36 McCarthy, "Bureaucracy, business, and Africa during the colonial period," pp. 90–1.

37 Sir Harry H. Johnston, *The Story of My Life*, Indianapolis: The Bobbs-Merrill Company, 1923, pp. 176–7.

38 Ibid., p. 178.

39 Ibid., p. 182.

40 Ibid., p. 181.

41 Ibid., p. 182.

42 Ibid.

43 See Richard N. Kottman, *Reciprocity and the North Atlantic Triangle, 1932–1938*, Ithaca, New York: The Cornell University Press, 1968.

44 This is the argument of Barry Eichengreen, endorsed by David Stix, in "History lesson," *Forbes*, 7 January 1991, 89.

45 Fieldhouse, "The economic exploitation of Africa," p. 610.

46 Ibid.

47 Patrick Manning, *Francophone Sub-Saharan Africa, 1880–1985*, Cambridge: Cambridge University Press, 1988, p. 192.

48 Fieldhouse, "The economic exploitation of Africa," p. 612.

49 Manning, *Francophone Sub-Saharan Africa*, p. 192.

50 Ibid.

51 Fieldhouse, "The economic exploitation of Africa," p. 611.

52 For an analysis of this theme in a British colonial context, see Dennis M. P. McCarthy, "Media as ends: money and the underdevelopment of Tanganyika to 1940," *The Journal of Economic History*, 36 (1976), 645–62.

53 Fieldhouse, "The economic exploitation of Africa," p. 604.

54 Ibid., pp. 604–5.

55 Ibid., p. 605.

56 Ibid., p. 634.

57 Manning, *Francophone Sub-Saharan Africa*, pp. 126–7.

2 Merchant associations

1 Charles M. Andrews, *The Colonial Period of American History: The Settlements, Volume I*, New Haven and London: The Yale University Press, 1934 and 1964, pp. 40–1.

2 D. K. Fieldhouse, *The Colonial Empires: A Comparative Survey From the Eighteenth Century*, New York: Delacorte Press, 1967, p. 35.

3 Ibid., pp. 35–6.

4 Ibid., p. 35.

5 Antoin E. Murphy, *John Law: Economic Theorist and Policy-Maker*, Oxford: The Clarendon Press, 1997, p. 164. This book is a comprehensive and balanced interpretation of the multi-faceted career of John Law.

6 See Antoin E. Murphy for a thorough analysis of the bubble and company collapse, especially pp. 188–264.

7 Fieldhouse, *Colonial Empires*, pp. 50–1.

8 Ibid., p. 52.

9 August C. Bolino, *The Development of the American Economy*, Columbus, Ohio: Charles E. Merrill Books, Inc., 1961, pp. 13–14.
10 Ibid., p. 15.
11 A. G. Hopkins, *An Economic History of West Africa*, New York: Columbia University Press, 1973, p. 94.
12 Ibid.
13 Philip D. Curtin, *The Atlantic Slave Trade: A Census*, Madison, Wisconsin: The University of Wisconsin Press, 1969, p. 171.
14 Hopkins, *An Economic History*, p. 92.
15 Curtin, *The Atlantic Slave Trade*, p. 122.
16 Hopkins, *An Economic History*, p. 95.
17 For a basic introduction to early Dutch participation in the Atlantic slave trade that reflects the trends of modern scholarship, see Willie F. Page, *The Dutch Triangle: The Netherlands and the Atlantic Slave Trade, 1621–1664*, New York: Garland Publishing, Inc., 1997.
18 Kenneth G. Davies, *The Royal African Company*, London: Longmans, Green and Co., 1957, p. 225.
19 Fieldhouse, *Colonial Empires*, p. 51. For a comprehensive, richly documented analysis of Dutch participation in the Atlantic slave trade that highlights the West India Company, consult Johannes Menne Postma, *The Dutch in the Atlantic Slave Trade, 1600–1815*, Cambridge, UK: Cambridge University Press, 1990.
20 "Royal Charter granted to the National African Company, later called the Royal Niger Company," as reproduced in J. E. Flint, *Sir George Goldie and the Making of Nigeria*, London: Oxford University Press, 1960, p. 330.
21 Ibid.
22 Ibid., p. 331.
23 Ibid., p. 333.
24 Ibid.
25 Dennis M. P. McCarthy, "The bureaucratic manipulation of indigenous business: a comparative study in legal imposition from colonial Africa," *Business and Economic History*, Second Series, Volume Nineteen, 1990, 126.
26 Roland Oliver and Anthony Atmore, *Africa Since 1800*, 3rd edn, Cambridge, UK: Cambridge University Press, 1981, p. 118.
27 D. M. P. McCarthy, "Language manipulation in colonial Tanganyika, 1919–1940," *Journal of African Studies*, Volume 6, Number 1 (Spring 1979), 9–16.
28 Robert W. Shenton, *The Development of Capitalism in Northern Nigeria*, Toronto: the University of Toronto Press, 1986, pp. 31–3, and *passim* in Chapter 3, "The foundation of colonial capitalism in northern Nigeria," pp. 22–49.
29 Oliver and Atmore, *Africa Since 1800*, p. 123.
30 Fieldhouse, *Colonial Empires*, p. 222.
31 Oliver and Atmore, *Africa Since 1800*, p. 123 and p. 126.
32 For an elegant, compact analysis of British colonialism in Kenya, see Richard D. Wolff, *The Economics of Colonialism: Britain and Kenya, 1870–1930*, New Haven and London: Yale University Press, 1974.
33 Susanna Voyle, "DeBeers hopes small print will give an edge in diamond market," *Financial Times*, 4 March 1998, 1.
34 For a concise, insightful presentation of Dutch foreign trade to 1815, which considers the VOC, see Jan de Vries and Ad van der Woude, *The First Modern Economy: Success, Failure, and Perseverance of the Dutch Economy, 1500–1815*, Cambridge, UK: Cambridge University Press, 1997, pp. 350–504.
35 Fieldhouse, *Colonial Empires*, p. 149.

36 Ibid., p. 145.
37 Ibid., pp. 147–8.
38 Ibid., p. 145.
39 Ibid., p. 149.
40 James D. Tracy, "Introduction," in James D. Tracy (ed.), *The Political Economy of Merchant Empires*, Cambridge, UK: The Cambridge University Press, 1991, pp. 6–7.
41 For an important article that explains how the chartered company prefigured the modern multinational, especially in the areas of managerial hierarchies and the attendant bureaucratization of business procedures, consult Ann M. Carlos and Stephen Nicholas, "'Giants of an earlier capitalism': the chartered trading companies as modern multinationals," *Business History Review*, 62 (Autumn 1988), 398–419. The issues of transactions and their frequency for chartered companies are introduced on 399–403.
42 The most refined analysis of the Hanseatic League in English known to this author is Prof. Rainer Postel, "The Hanseatic League and its Decline," a paper read at the Central Connecticut State University, New Britain, CT, 20 November 1996. Online. Available at: www.hartford-hwp.com/archives/60/039.html (accessed 7 January 2004).
43 Rondo Cameron, *A Concise Economic History of the World: From Paleolithic Times to the Present*, 3rd edn, Oxford and New York: The Oxford University Press, 1997, p. 63.
44 Dennis M. P. McCarthy, "International Business and Economic Integration: Comparative Business Strategies Past and Present," *Business and Economic History*, Second Series, Volume 21, 1992, 241.
45 See Johannes Schildhauer, *The Hansa: History and Culture*, Leipzig: Edition Leipzig, 1985. Translated from the German (*Die Hanse*) by Katherine Vanovitch.
46 Elias H. Tuma, *European Economic History: Tenth Century to the Present*, New York: Harper & Row, 1971, p. 94.
47 Ibid.
48 The title of Chapter III, Book I, of *An Inquiry Into the Nature and Causes of The Wealth of Nations* is "That the division of labour is limited by the extent of the market." See Adam Smith, *The Wealth of Nations*, vol. I, Homewood, Illinois: Richard D. Irwin, Inc., 1963, p. 14. The *Irwin Paperback Classics in Economics* published *The Wealth of Nations* in two volumes. Volume I contains Books I, II, and III of the original; Volume II presents Books IV and V.
49 For a detailed analysis of deteriorating Anglo–Hanseatic relations, see John D. Fudge, *Cargoes, Embargoes, and Emissaries: The Commercial and Political Interaction of England and the German Hanse, 1450–1510*, Toronto: University of Toronto Press, 1995, pp. 51–88. This work is a competent contribution, in every respect, to the literature on the Hanseatic League and shows yet again why the League is such a fascinating subject for students of political economy.
50 For an insightful overview of these conflicts and a penetrating analysis of the decline of the Hanseatic League, see T. H. Lloyd, *England and the German Hanse, 1157–1611: a Study of Their Trade and Commercial Diplomacy*, Cambridge, UK: Cambridge University Press, 1991, pp. 363–77.

3 Religious empires

1 See, for example, the religious empire founded and developed by the Robertson family, father Pat and son Tim, as featured by Mark Robichaux in "Tim Robertson Turns TV's Family Channel into a Major Business," *The Wall Street Journal*, 29 August 1996, A1 and A6.

2 Zenon Grocholewski, "The function of the Sacred Roman Rota and the Supreme Court of the Apostolic Signatura," translated by Dinah Livingstone, in Peter Huizing and Knut Walf (eds) *The Roman Curia and the Communion of Churches*, New York: Seabury Press, 1979, p. 49.
3 For a 1970's perspective on some components of the Curia, see Giancarlo Zizola, "Secretariats and councils of the Roman Curia," translated by Dinah Livingstone, in Peter Huizing and Knut Walf (eds) *The Roman Curia and the Communion of Churches*, New York: Seabury Press, 1979, pp. 42–6.
4 For a highly readable introduction to this influential organization, see Christopher Hollis, *The Jesuits: A History*, New York, New York: Barnes & Noble Books, 1992. The original edition was published by MacMillan, Inc., in 1968.
5 "The Jesuits," article in *The Catholic Encyclopedia*. Online. Available at: www.newadvent.org/cathen/14081a.htm (accessed 24 January 2000). The cyberspace version of this venerable encyclopedia was launched in 1997.
6 Robert B. Ekelund, Jr., Robert F. Hébert, Robert D. Tollison, Gary M. Anderson, and Audrey B. Davidson, *Sacred Trust: The Medieval Church as an Economic Firm*, New York and Oxford: Oxford University Press, 1996, p. 33.
7 Ibid.
8 Ibid., p. 34.
9 Ibid., p. 36.
10 For a concise portrait of the Medici Bank, see Dennis M. P. McCarthy, *International Business History: A Contextual and Case Approach*, Westport, Connecticut: Praeger, 1994, pp. 10–15. The classic treatise on the Bank, from which this portrait is drawn, and one of the best monographs ever written is Raymond de Roover, *The Rise and Decline of the Medici Bank, 1397–1494*, Cambridge, Massachusetts: The Harvard University Press, 1968.
11 Harry A. Miskimin, *The Economy of Early Renaissance Europe, 1300–1460*, Englewood Cliffs, NJ: Prentice-Hall, Inc., 1969, p. 146.
12 Ibid., p. 152.
13 See Harry A. Miskimin, *Cash, Credit, and Crisis in Europe, 1300–1600*, London, UK: Variorum Reprints, 1989, and *Money and Power in Fifteenth-Century France*, New Haven, Connecticut: Yale University Press, 1984.
14 Miskimin, *The Economy of Early Renaissance Europe*, p. 145.
15 Ibid., p. 146.
16 See J. Gilchrist, *The Church and Economic Activity in the Middle Ages*, London: Macmillan, 1969, pp. 62–76.
17 Raymond de Roover, *The Rise and Decline of the Medici Bank*, p. 111.
18 Ibid.
19 Gilchrist, *The Church and Economic Activity*, p. 75.
20 See Chapter 6, "How the Church Gained from Usury and Exchange Doctrines," pp. 113–30, in Ekelund, Jr., *et al.*, *Sacred Trust*. Many consider the usury doctrine part of the broader notion of "just price."
21 See Chapter 7, "How the Church Profited from the Crusades," pp. 131–51, in Ekelund, Jr., *et al.*, *Sacred Trust*.
22 Ekelund, Jr., *et al.*, *Sacred Trust*, pp. 10–11.
23 Ibid. See Chapter 2, note 50.
24 Thomas J. Reese, *Inside the Vatican: The Politics and Organization of the Catholic Church*, Cambridge, Massachusetts: Harvard University Press, 1996, p. 205.
25 Ibid., p. 206.
26 Ibid., p. 207.
27 Ibid.
28 Ibid., p. 206.
29 Ibid.

4 Criminal empires

1 The United States has proved fertile soil for criminal organizations created by many other groups besides the Mafia. See Rich Cohen, *Tough Jews: Fathers, Sons, and Gangster Dreams*, New York, New York: Simon & Schuster, 1998. Cohen also published an article based on this book; see Rich Cohen, "Gun, gangster and the business of crime," *Financial Times*, Weekend, 27/28 June 1998, IV.
2 The *Financial Times* believes that the Mafia itself was created on Sicily in 1282, when a "band of outlaws emerges to revolt against French rule after drunken soldiers attack a woman on her wedding day," (*Financial Times*, "One thousand years of finance," 1 January 2000, 3).
3 For more information on Mafia rituals, consult Diego Gambetta, *The Sicilian Mafia: The Business of Private Protection*, Cambridge, Massachusetts, and London, UK: Harvard University Press, 1993, especially pp. 262–70.
4 Mark Gillispie, "Strollo spills mob secrets," *The Cleveland Plain Dealer*, 4 March 1999, 10-A. Many other details of Mafia life can be found in this article, which includes pp. 1-A and 10-A.
5 For an account of John Gotti, Jr., and his relations with his father that illuminates a nuclear family that ran a "crime" family, see Jeffrey Goldberg, "The Don is done," *The New York Times Magazine*, 31 January 1999, 24–31; 38; 62; 65–6; 71.
6 For information on the *commissione* in Sicily, see Gambetta, *The Sicilian Mafia*, pp. 112–16.
7 David Osterlund *et al.*, *Mafia: the History of the Mob in America*, New York: A & E Home Video, 2001.
8 Joseph Bonanno, *A Man of Honor: the Autobiography of Joseph Bonanno*, with Sergio Lalli, New York: Simon and Schuster, 1983, pp. 159 ff.
9 For an account of Prohibition that is rich in historical detail, see John Kobler, *Ardent Spirits: The Rise and Fall of Prohibition*, New York: G. P. Putnam's Sons, 1973.
10 See Peter Maas, *The Valachi Papers*, New York: G. P. Putnam's Sons, 1968.
11 See Peter Maas, *Underboss: Sammy the Bull Gravano's Story of Life in the Mafia*, New York: HarperCollins Publishers, Inc., 1997.
12 See Fredreka Schouten, Gannett News Service, "Many states put money on gambling," *Des Moines Sunday Register*, 30 May 1999, 1AA.
13 A useful introduction to money, with an article on its history and money laundering, can be found in the October, 1998, issue of *Discover*.
14 For an article with fascinating historical examples of currency fraud, which is akin to money laundering, see Nicholas Leonard, "Scourge of the counterfeiters," *Financial Times*, Weekend 11/12 April 1998, XXIV. Leonard spotlights how Isaac Newton defeated currency fraud in England and references Sir John Craig, *Newton at the Mint*, Cambridge, England: Cambridge University Press, 1946.
15 See Thurston Clarke and John J. Tigue, *Dirty Money: Swiss Banks, the Mafia, Money Laundering, and White Collar Crime*, New York: Simon and Schuster, 1975.
16 A well-organized book with invaluable information on contemporary criminal organizations and modern techniques of "money laundering" is James R. Richards, *Transnational Criminal Organizations, Cybercrime, and Money Laundering: A Handbook for Law Enforcement Officers, Auditors, and Financial Investigators*, Boca Raton, Florida: CRC Press, 1999.
17 US Customs and Border Protection, Department of Homeland Security, "What is Money Laundering?" Online. Available at: www.cbp.gov/xp/cgov/enforce-

ment/ice/investigations/financial_investigations/money (accessed 6 March 2004).

18 For some ABCs of derivatives, see Kenneth M. Morris and Alan M. Siegel, *The Wall Street Journal Guide to Understanding Money & Investing*, New York: Lightbulb Press, Inc., 1993, p. 124 and pp. 146–7.

19 B. H. Liddell Hart inspired the notion of "alternative routes" with his analysis of "alternative objectives." See B. H. Liddell Hart, *Strategy*, 2nd revised edn, New York: Meridian, 1991, pp. 335–6.

20 Sun-tzu, *The Complete Art of War*, translated, with historical introduction and commentary, by Ralph D. Sawyer, with the collaboration of Mei-chún Lee Sawyer, Boulder, Colorado: Westview Press, 1996, p. 41. The quality of the introduction and commentary makes this translation exceedingly valuable and compelling.

21 For a history of international drug trafficking in the first half of the twentieth century, see Kathryn Meyer and Terry M. Parssinen, *Webs of Smoke: Smugglers, Warlords, Spies, and the History of the International Drug Trade*, Lanham, Maryland: Rowman & Littlefield Publishers, 1998.

22 For a fascinating analysis of one case study of this cross-border commerce that is especially disturbing, see Gary Webb, *Dark Alliance: the CIA, the Contras, and the Crack Cocaine Explosion*, 1st edn, New York: Seven Stories Press, 1998.

23 For an investigation of the illegal drugs trade in Iowa that spotlights methamphetamine and notes the key roles of Mexican cartels working through California intermediaries, see Lee Rood, "Mexico Supplies Iowa's Meth," *The Des Moines Register*, 9 March 1999, 1A and 7A. Although many local "mom-and-pop operations" make meth in Iowa, "the drug trade spawned by Mexican cartels is responsible for 90 percent of the meth funneled into the state" (7A). International economic integration has facilitated Mexican penetration of drug traffic in Iowa: "That NAFTA has made it harder to find contraband is irrefutable" (7A). NAFTA, the North American Free Trade Area, is discussed in Chapter 5.

24 For a real case study of BMPE that shows how far its ripples reach, see Michael Allen, "A Tangled Tale of GE [General Electric Co.], Appliance Smuggling and Laundered Money," *The Wall Street Journal*, 21 December 1998, 1A and 6A.

25 Dean Boyd, "Customs alerts U.S. firms to Colombian money laundering scheme." Online. Available at: www.cbp.gov/custoday/jan2000/peso.htm (accessed 11 February 2004).

26 Dean Boyd, "Operation Wire Cutter dismantles major Colombian money laundering network." Online. Available at: www.cbp.gov/xp/CustomsToday/2002/February/custoday_wire_cutter.xml (accessed 11 February 2004).

27 Gary Weiss, "Investors beware: chop stocks are on the rise," *Business Week*, 15 December 1997, 112. The entire article deserves careful reading; it consists of pages 112, 114, 115, 116, 118, 122, 126, and 128.

28 Gary Weiss, "The mob is busier than the Feds think," *Business Week*, 15 December 1997, 130.

29 Other business activities of HealthTech International, Inc., can be found in Kathy Robertson and Kelly Johnson, "Shopping center buyer's CEO is under indictment," *Sacramento Business Journal*, 14(39) (12 December 1997), 1 and 2.

30 Dean Starkman and Deborah Lohse, "Charges Mark Wider Probe of Mob, Wall Street," *The Wall Street Journal*, 26 November 1997, C1.

31 Kenneth M. Morris and Alan M. Siegel, *The Wall Street Journal Guide to*

Understanding Money and Investing, New York: Lightbulb Press, Inc., 1993, p. 49.

32 For a detailed review of the troubled history and legal problems of HealthTech International, Inc., see In the Matter of the Application of HealthTech International, Inc., For Review of Action Taken by the National Association of Securities Dealers, Inc., Securities and Exchange Commission, 26 October 1999. Online. Available at: www.sec.gov/litigation/opinions/34-42060.htm (accessed 6 March 2004).

33 Frances A. McMorris, "HealthTech CEO is convicted in case tied to mob infiltration of Wall Street," *The Wall Street Journal*, 12 May 1999, B8.

34 Ibid.

35 Thomas V. Fuentes, Chief, Organized Crime Section, Criminal Investigative Division, Federal Bureau of Investigation, Statement for the Record on Organized Crime Before the House Subcommittee on Finance and Hazardous Materials, Washington, DC, 13 September 2000, p. 3. Online. Available at: www.fbi.gov/congress/congress00/fuentes.htm (accessed 12 February 2004).

36 "Futures trader convicted," *CNNMoney*, 13 February 2002. Online. Available at: money.cnn.com/2002/02/13/news/union/ (accessed 4 March 2004).

37 Fuentes, Congressional Statement, pp. 3–4.

38 Fuentes, Congressional Statement, p. 4.

39 Peter Maas, *Underboss*, p. 212.

40 Rebecca Buckman, "Cyber-sleuths: dogged on-line investors are SEC's top source in Internet probes," *The Wall Street Journal*, 4 August 1998, C1 and C15.

41 See his obituary by Joseph P. Fried, "Peter Savino, Mafia associate who became an informer, 55," *The New York Times*, 1 November 1997, A24.

42 Joseph P. Fried, "Star witness at Gigante trial admits to 'a life of lies' in the mob," *The New York Times*, 12 July 1997, 20.

5 Free trade areas

1 See Emile Benoit, *Europe at Sixes and Sevens: the Common Market, the Free Trade Association, and the United States*, New York: Columbia University Press, 1961.

2 Rondo Cameron, *A Concise Economic History of the World: From Paleolithic Times to the Present*, 3rd edn, New York and Oxford: Oxford University Press, 1997, p. 391.

3 "EU relations with Switzerland: a special case." Online. Available at: europa.eu.int/comm/external_relations/switzerland/intro/index/htm (accessed 9 March 2004).

4 See "The EFTA Secretariat." Online. Available at: www.secretariat.efta.int/ (accessed 12 March 2004).

5 See "The EFTA Surveillance Authority." Online. Available at: www.eftasurv.int/ (accessed 13 March 2004).

6 See "EFTA Court." Online. Available at: www.eftacourt.lu/ (accessed 12 March 2004).

7 "The European Free Trade Association." Online. Available at: www.efta/int (accessed 12 March 2004).

8 For analysis of the relations between the CFA franc and the euro, the currency of the European Union, see Tony Hawkins, "CFA Zone: Launch of the euro clouds outlook for the 14," in "World Economy and Finance," Special Survey, *Financial Times*, 2 October 1998, XXIV, and Mark Turner, "CFA emerges relatively unscathed," in "African Banking," Special Survey, *Financial Times*, 21 May 1999, 23.

9 "Economic Community of West African States (ECOWAS)." Online. Available at: www.eia.doe.gov/emeu/cabs/ghana.html (accessed 21 March 2004).

10 This sketch draws information from the useful overview by John Githongo, "History of Co-operation: Century of Borderline Deliberations," in "East African Co-operation," Special Survey, *Financial Times*, 5 November 1996, IV.

11 Andrew Coulson, *Tanzania: A Political Economy*, Oxford: Clarendon Press, 1982, p. 73.

12 The Legislative Council was an agency many British colonial territories had. It was primarily a consultative body that contained government officials and unofficial members representing various "interests" within a territory.

13 D. M. P. McCarthy, *Colonial Bureaucracy and Creating Underdevelopment: Tanganyika, 1919–1940*, Ames, Iowa: Iowa State University Press, 1982, p. 19. For a detailed analysis of "suspended duties," see pp. 19–22.

14 E. A. Brett, *Colonialism and Underdevelopment in East Africa: The Politics of Economic Change, 1919–1939*, New York: NOK Publishers, Ltd., 1973, p. 106.

15 Julius K. Nyerere led Tanganyika to independence in 1961 and then was its President until he voluntarily stepped down in 1985. An incorruptible statesman with a high moral purpose, he was also an impractical socialist who inflicted on his country one of the worst experiments in collective living ever devised and implemented: the forcible regrouping of much of the rural population in *ujamaa* (togetherness) villages that accelerated in the 1970s. For a balanced obituary of a leader with great strengths who made some tragic missteps, see "Man of integrity whose policies hurt his country," *Financial Times*, 15 October 1999, 7.

16 The East African Development Bank is one of a number of regional development banks throughout the world. Some operate in larger regions than others. Indeed, the African Development Bank is a regional bank from a global perspective, but its mandate is continental. The Asian Development Bank is in an identical position in these respects. The EADB, however, is a regional development bank in both geography and mission.

Each can play a major role in financial integration, which is part of economic integration. These banks can loan money with conditions that are prudent but not draconian, and they can nurture the development of capital markets in their areas by offering advice and technical assistance. They can make an even greater effort to help private businesses create their own kinds of economic integration. For a valuable study that treats politics as a separate discipline but also recognizes that economic integration also involves political economy, consult Karen A. Mingst, *Politics and the African Development Bank*, Lexington, Kentucky: University Press of Kentucky, 1990.

17 For more information on the East African Development Bank, visit www.transAfrica.org/eadb/ (accessed 8 April 2004).

18 "Viewpoint by Kenya's President Mwai Kibaki on the East African Common Market," 5 November 2003. Online. Available at: www.statehouse.go.ke/commentary.htm (accessed 5 April 2004).

19 "Hopes and fears for Africa trade pact," *BBC News*, 2 March 2004. Online. Available at: news.bbc.co.uk/1/hi/business/3526671.stm (accessed 8 April 2004).

20 "East Africans sign customs pact," *BBC News*, 2 March 2004. Online. Available at: news.bbc.co.uk/1/hi/world/africa/3526195.stm (accessed 8 April 2004).

21 "East African Co-operation," Special Survey, *Financial Times*, 5 November 1996, I.

22 Ibid.

23 "South Africa and the Southern African Development Community," November 2002. Online. Available at: www.eia.doe.gov/emeu/cabs/sadc.html (accessed 10 April 2004).

24 Visit www.comesa.int/ (accessed 13 August 2005).

25 "Comesa loses Tanzania," *BBC News*, 27 July 1999. Online. Available at: news2.this.bbc.co.uk/hi/engl...d/africa/newsid%5F405000/405293.stm (accessed 25 February 2000). An official explanation, given by Iddi Simba, Tanzania's minister for industry and commerce, was that "Tanzania was buying considerably more from other member states than it was in a position to sell." The government "now wanted to concentrate on building up the country's production capacity."

26 Tony Hawkins, "Trade agreement stalled," in "Investing in South Africa," Special Survey, *Financial Times*, 28 March 1996, V.

27 "Customs Union – Andean Community." Online. Available at: www.comunidadandina.org/ingles/union.htm (accessed 12 April 2004).

28 Ibid.

29 "Common Market – Andean Community." Online. Available at: www.comunidadandina.org/ingles/market.htm (accessed 12 April 2004).

30 "Andean nations seek trade boost," *BBC News*, 28 June 2003. Online. Available at: news.bbc.co.uk/1/hi/world/americas/3027720.stm (accessed 12 April 2004).

31 British Honduras became independent as Belize in 1981. St Kitts–Nevis–Anguilla divided. St Kitts–Nevis became an independent two-nation federation in 1983, while Anguilla remained a "dependent territory" within the British Empire (see Ch. 1). Antigua became Antigua and Barbuda; in their previous colonial days, Barbuda had been a dependency of the colony Antigua. St Vincent became known as St Vincent and the Grenadines. In 1998 voters on Nevis voted to remain linked with St Kitts. A referendum on independence needed 66 percent approval to pass, but garnered 62 percent. See "St Kitts and Nevis to stay together," *BBC News*, 11 August 1998. Online. Available at: news2.this.bbc.co.uk/hi/engl...americas/newsid%5F148000/148916.stm (accessed 25 February 2000).

32 "Subregional trading groups," *Economic Perspectives*, USIA Electronic Journal, 3(2), March 1998. Online. Available at: www.usia.gov/journals/ites/0398/ijee/ejsubreg.htm (accessed 23 October 1998).

33 "Towards the implementation of a caricom single market: a long and winding road," *First Citizens Bank Economic Newsletter*, 6(5), March 2003. Online. Available at: www.caricom.org/archives/csmeimplementation.htm (accessed 20 April 2004).

34 Ibid.

35 "About the ACS." Online. Available at: www.acs.aec.org/about.htm (accessed 14 April 2004). Visit http://www.acs.org for more information on the structure and current projects of the ACS.

36 Ibid.

37 The Caribbean Community (www.caricom.org) and the Organization of Eastern Caribbean States both have excellent web sites (www.oecs.org).

38 For an excellent contribution to understanding the background and implications of the free trade agreement between the United States and Canada, consult Mordechai Elihau Kreinin (ed.), *Building a Partnership: the Canada–United States Free Trade Agreement*, East Lansing: Michigan State University Press and Calgary: University of Calgary Press, 2000.

39 "What is NAFTA?" *Financial Times*, 17 November 1993, 6, and "NAFTA Overview," *The Des Moines Register*, 13 November 1993, 11A.

40 "What is NAFTA?" *Financial Times*, 17 November 1993, 6.

41 "Ten years of NAFTA," *The Economist*, 3 January 2004, 13–14.

42 Ibid., 14.

43 Ibid.

44 For detailed information concerning *maquilladora* plants, see *The Complete Twin Plant Guide*. An outline (two pages) of the contents of this guide can be found Online. Available at: www.mexonline.com/solunet.htm (accessed 6 December 1998).

45 Caroline Borders, "Mexico faces challenges despite 5 years free trade," Reuters article in Yahoo Finance, 3 December 1998. Online. Available at: biz.yahoo.com/rf/981203/bqh.html (accessed 6 December 1998).

46 For an article that puts a human face on NAFTA and its impact on US manufacturing, see Rick Wartzman, "In the wake of Nafta, a family firm sees business go south," *The Wall Street Journal*, 23 February 1999, A1 and A10.

47 Allen R. Myerson, "Borderline Working Class: In Texas, Labor Is Feeling Trade Accord's Pinch," *The New York Times*, 8 May 1997, D1 and D23. This is the edition on microfilm.

48 Jeff Faux, President of the Economic Policy Institute, "Administration's NAFTA report seriously misleading," 11 July 1997. Online. Available at: www.epinet.org/naftares.html (accessed 6 December 1998).

49 Robert E. Scott, "NAFTA's hidden costs," April 2001. Online. Available at: www.epinet.org/content.cfm/briefingpapers_nafta01_us (accessed 13 May 2004).

50 Jeff Faux, "NAFTA at 10," 9 February 2004. Online. Available at: www.epinet.org/content.cfm/webfeatures_viewpoints_nafta_legacy_at 10 (accessed 4 May 2004).

51 The Iowa material is found in an excellent article by Kenneth Pins, an agribusiness reporter for *The Des Moines Register*. See "Factory exports up 38 percent: Iowa's success rekindles NAFTA debate," *The Des Moines Sunday Register*, 11 January 1998, 1G and 2G.

52 Jesse Rothstein and Robert Scott, "NAFTA and the States," 19 September 1997. Online. Available at: www.epinet.org/content.cfm/issuebriefs_ib119 (accessed 18 May 2004).

53 Neil King, Jr., Scott Miller and John Lyons, "Cafta vote clouds prospects for other trade deals," *The Wall Street Journal*, 29 July 2005, A1 and A9. See also José DeCórdoba, John Lyons, and David Luhnow, "Despite Cafta, U.S. clout wanes in Latin America," *The Wall Street Journal*, 29 July 2005, A11.

54 "World trade blocs: NAFTA," *BBC News*, 3 September 2003. Online. Available at: news.bbc.co.uk/1/hi/business/3077610.stm (accessed 25 April 2004).

55 Neil King, Jr., "Kerry Would Seek Tighter Standards Governing Cafta," *The Wall Street Journal*, 1 June 2004, A6.

56 For an insightful essay that argues for a middle category between "winners" and "losers" from trade agreements – those "in between" – see David Wessel, "Looking Out for Globalization's Tweeners," *The Wall Street Journal*, 28 July 2005, A2.

57 For a transcript of this debate, go to www.ng.csun.edu/e200sp99/assign/perot.htm (accessed 23 May 2004).

58 Theorists have modified the principle of comparative advantage to take into account "cones" of countries with similar economic characteristics. A new economic geography analyzes different kinds of competition and employs gravity models. There are four types of competition in elementary economic theory: perfect competition, monopolistic competition, oligopoly, and monopoly. In perfect or pure competition many sellers compete using price reductions to gain market share. In monopolistic competition many sellers do not use price as a weapon but rather seek to differentiate their product from their competitors. Oligopoly is competition among the few, usually large-scale corporations, while monopoly features one seller. The new economic geography studies product differentiation in monopolistic and oligopolistic competition. There is a

growing literature on the application of gravity models to economic flows across international borders. These flows can involve people, commodities, investments, etc. A clear introduction to the ABCs of the gravity model, with links to other sites, is Matt T. Rosenberg, "Gravity model: predict the movement of people and ideas between two places," Online. Available at: www.geography.about.com/library/weekly/aa03160a.htm (accessed 14 July 2005). A valuable web site, with more advanced material, is "Gravity models." Online. Available at: www.http://faculty.washington.edu/krumme/systems/gravity.html (accessed 14 July 2005).

59 Tony Tassell, "Asean to monitor looming dangers to region," *Financial Times*, 8 October 1998, 4.

60 To see the surveillance mechanism in action, consult "ASEAN Surveillance Report Confirms Economic Recovery," 26 November 1999. Online. Available at: www.aseansec.org/10819.htm (accessed 28 May 2004).

61 Ibid. For more details concerning the ASEAN Investment Area, see "ASEAN Investment Area: An Update." Online. Available at: www.aseansec.org/10341.htm (accessed 28 May 2004).

62 "Asean leaders agree trade plan," *BBC News*, 7 October 2003. Online. Available at: news.bbc.co.uk/1/hi/world/asia-pacific/3167120.stm (accessed 25 May 2004).

63 "Asean speeds up free trade move," *BBC News*, 29 November 2004. Online. Available at: news.bbc.co.uk/2/asia-pacific/4050563.stm (accessed 15 July 2005).

64 "China in landmark Asean pact," *BBC News*, 29 November 2004. Online. Available at: news.bbc.co.uk/2/hi/asia-pacific/4051653.stm (accessed 15 July 2005).

65 Mark Nicholson, "South Asian states plan free-trade zone," *Financial Times*, 3 May 1995, 5.

66 Mary Hennock, "Uphill task for South Asian trade pact," *BBC News*, 6 January 2004. Online. Available at: www.news.bbc.co.uk/1/hi/business/3370187.stm (accessed 25 May 2004).

67 Ibid.

68 The Secretariat of APEC has a well-organized web site, which contains historical information about APEC. See www.apecsec.org.sg/.

69 "History of Asia-Pacific cooperation," The Ministry of Foreign Affairs, Japan. Online. Available at: www.mofa.go.jp/policy/economy/apec/1995/info/history.html (accessed 21 November 1998).

70 Tony Tassell, "Asean to monitor looming dangers to region," *Financial Times*, 8 October 1998, 4.

71 "APEC's family feud," *The Economist*, 21 November 1998, 41.

72 Peter Montagnon, Gwen Robinson, and Sheila McNulty, "Fingers crossed that leaders can avoid APEC summit fiasco," *Financial Times*, 13 November 1998, 6.

73 Guy de Jonquières, with additional reporting by Gerard Baker, "Elastic approach to free trade," *Financial Times*, 24 November 1997, 3.

74 For details on the internecine rivalry between the Malaysian Prime Minister, Mahathir Mohamad, and his former deputy, Anwar Ibrahim, see Ian Johnson, "How Malaysia's rulers devoured each other and much they built," *The Wall Street Journal*, 30 October 1998, A1 and A11. A shorter article, which summarizes details of Anwar Ibrahim's arrest and treatment, can be found in Sheila McNulty, "Battered Anwar faces court to deny corruption charges," *Financial Times*, 30 September 1998, 16.

75 "APEC's Family Feud," *The Economist*, 21 November 1998, 41.

76 Jonathan Head, "How APEC has changed," *BBC News*, 21 October 2003.

Online. Available at: www.bbc.co.uk/1/hi/world/asia-pacific/32309600.stm (accessed 25 May 2004).

6 Customs unions

1 Patrick Manning, *Francophone Sub-Saharan Africa: 1880–1985*, Cambridge, UK: Cambridge University Press, 1988, p. 160.
2 Ibid., p. 125.
3 Equatorial Guinea, which comprises Rio Muni and Fernando Po, joined CACEU in January, 1984. As a former Spanish colony (Spanish Guinea), it adds diversity in colonial heritage to the all-French backgrounds of the five original and continuing members of CACEU.
4 "Central African common market launched," *BBC News*, 6 February 1998. Online. Available at: www.news.bbc.co.uk/hi/english/world/africa/newsid%5F54000/54257.stm (accessed 1 February 1999).
5 For an early assessment of how Cameroon might gain from the Central African Economic and Monetary Community, see Ferdinand Bakoupa and David Tarr, "How integration into the Central African Economic and Monetary Community affects Cameroon's economy: general equilibrium estimates," Working Paper No. 1872, The World Bank, January, 1998. A summary of this paper is online. Available at: www.worldbank.org/html/iecit/wp1872.html (accessed 1 February 1999).
6 "About us." Online. Available at: www.ceeac-eccas.org/about/index.htm (accessed 10 June 2004). The web site for CEEAC-ECCAS is most informative.
7 Ibid.
8 "An Mbendi Profile: Guide to Exporting from South Africa – South African Trade Statistics." Online. Available at: www.mbendi.co.za/export/sas/trade_statistics.htm (accessed 13 June 2004).
9 "Africa firmly on US agenda," *BBC News*, 20 January 2003. Online. Available at: www.news.bbc.co.uk/l/hi/business/2677923.stm (accessed 12 June 2004).
10 The trade information for Botswana, Lesotho, Swaziland, and Namibia is found in The World Factbook 2004 for each country as compiled and published by the Central Intelligence Agency.
11 "Customs Union." Online. Available at: www.southafrica.net/government/foreign/sacu.html (accessed 1 February 1999).
12 Tabby Moyo, "Sacu trade bid nearing completion," 17 July 1998. Online. Available at: www.woza.co.za/africa/sacuo1.htm (accessed 2 February 1999).
13 Ibid.
14 Colin McCarthy, "The Southern African Customs Union," 5. This paper is an outstanding case study of SACU. It was prepared for a conference, *Intégrations régionales, politiques agricoles communes et sécurité alimentaire, du 26 au 29 Mai 2003*, Ouagadougou, Burkina Faso, with the support of the Food and Agriculture Organization (FAO) of the United Nations.
15 "Trade Policy Review [World Trade Organization]: Southern African Customs Union," 25 April 2003. Online. Available at: www.wto.org/english/tratop_e/tpr_/tp213_e.htm (accessed 18 June 2004).
16 Colin McCarthy, "The Southern African Customs Union," 27. For a detailed analysis of the new formulas for sharing both customs revenue and excise taxes, see 27–8.
17 "U.S.-SACU Free Trade Agreement." Online. Available at: www.ustr.gov/new/fta/sacu.htm (accessed 18 June 2004).
18 Ibid.
19 Oxfam America, "Southern African Customs Union," 10 July 2003. Online.

Available at: www.oxfamamerica.org/advocacy/art5660.html (accessed 18 June 2004).

20 Ibid.

21 Colin McCarthy, "The Southern African Customs Union," 5.

22 This framework builds on the factual summary contained in *Zollverein*, in *The Columbia Encyclopedia*, 5th edn, New York: Columbia University Press, 1993. Online. Available at: www.infoplease.com/ce5/CE057153.html (accessed 25 January 1999). I have incorporated material from this synopsis in my own step analysis of the *Zollverein*.

23 B. H. Liddell Hart, *Strategy*, 2nd revised edn, New York: Meridian, 1991, pp. 94–123.

24 R. R. Palmer and Joel Colton, *A History of the Modern World*, 2nd edn, New York: Alfred A. Knopf, 1956, p. 417.

25 Ibid., p. 389.

26 Ibid., p. 417.

27 Joseph A. Schumpeter, *History of Economic Analysis*, New York: Oxford University Press, 1963, p. 504.

28 John C. Miller gracefully depicts the roles of Alexander Hamilton as a "founding father" of the United States of America in *Alexander Hamilton and the Growth of the New Nation*, New York: Harper & Row: 1964.

29 An analysis, splendid in its salient detail, of the relations between "free trade" and protectionism can be found in Arnold H. Price, *The Evolution of the Zollverein: A Study of the Ideas and Institutions Leading to German Economic Unification Between 1815 and 1833*, New York: Octagon Books, 1973. Chapter 3, "The idea of general German economic unification, 1816–1820," pp. 24–62, is especially helpful here.

30 J. H. Clapham, *The Economic Development of France and Germany, 1815–1914*, 4th edn, Cambridge, UK: Cambridge University Press, 1963, p. 98.

31 Ibid.

32 Ibid.

33 Ibid.

34 Ibid., p. 99.

35 W. O. Henderson, *The Zollverein*, 3rd edn, London, UK: Frank Cass and Company Limited, 1984, pp. 67–8.

36 Ibid., p. 68.

37 Ibid., pp. 57–63.

38 Ibid., p. 63.

39 Ibid., p. 87.

40 Ibid., p. 88.

41 John R. Davis, *Britain and the German Zollverein, 1848–66*, London, UK: MacMillan Press, Ltd., and New York: St Martin's Press, Inc., 1997, p. 85.

42 Ibid.

43 Henderson, *The Zollverein*, p. 315.

44 Ibid., p. 316.

45 Ibid.

46 Ibid., p. 318.

47 Ibid.

48 Ibid., p. 367.

49 Ibid.

50 The better search word is *Mercosul*. Visit www.mercosul.gov.br and www.mercosul.gov.br/textos/?Key=127.

51 Angus Foster, "Most targets have been met," *Financial Times*, 25 January 1995, 14, in *Financial Times Survey: Mercosur*, III.

52 Ibid.

53 See "After Brazil," *The Economist*, 6 February 1999, 18, and "Brazil's slippery slope," 77–8 in the same issue.

54 "Country profile: Argentina," *BBC News*, 3 July 2004. Online. Available at: www.news.bbc.co.uk/1/hi/world/americas/country_profiles/1192478.stm (accessed 6 July 2004).

55 "Subregional Trading Groups," *Economic Perspectives*, USIA Electronic Journal, 3(2), March 1998. Online. Available at: www.usia.gov/journals/ites/0398/ijee/ejsubreg.htm (accessed 23 October 1998).

56 Foster, "Most targets have been met," *Financial Times*, 25 January 1995, 14.

57 Ibid.

58 Ibid.

59 "South American unity pledge," *BBC News*, 19 June 2003. Online. Available at: www.news.bbc.co.uk/1/hi/world/americas/3002586.stm (accessed 6 July 2004).

60 "Argentinian-Brazilian accord to balance public accounts," *BBC News*, 7 June 1999. Online. Available at: www.news2.this.bbc.co.uk/hi/engl...americas/newsid%5F363000/363547.stm (accessed 6 July 1999).

61 For the text of an 1860 treaty, in French, "among France, Prussia and the States of the *Zollverein*," see M. Paul Boiteau, *Traités de Commerce*, New York: Burt Franklin, 1970, pp. 57–98.

62 "South American unity pledge" *BBC News*, 19 June 2003.

7 Common markets

1 A largely Federalist interpretation of the Articles of Confederation can be found in Jeremy Atack and Peter Passell, *A New Economic View of American History from Colonial Times to 1940*, 2nd edn, New York and London: W. W. Norton & Company, 1994, p. 74. The authors acknowledge that there were also "notable successes under the Articles of Confederation," which included the Land Ordinance of 1785 and the Northwest Ordinance of 1787.

A more historically balanced interpretation of the Articles of Confederation appears in Gary M. Walton and Ross M. Robertson, *History of the American Economy*, 5th edn, New York: Harcourt Brace Jovanovich, Inc., 1983, pp. 148–9.

2 Atack and Passell, *A New Economic View of American History*, p. 74.

3 Article VIII, *Articles of Confederation*, 3, The Avalon Project at the Yale Law School. Online. Available at: www.yale.edu.lawweb/avalon/artconf.htm (accessed 23 August 1999). The Avalon Project is a rich repository of primary documents concerning the constitutional history of the United States of America. It is a greatly valued and much appreciated archive.

4 The author found the analysis of the Bank of North America by James Willard Hurst balanced and insightful. See James Willard Hurst, *A Legal History of Money in the United States, 1774–1970*, Lincoln: The University of Nebraska Press, 1973, pp. 6–8.

5 Walton and Robertson, *History of the American Economy*, p. 148.

6 This information can be found in an excellent overall introduction to patents. See Lisa von Bargen Mueller, "An inventor's guide to patents and patenting," *AUTM Educational Series: No. 1*, Norwalk, Connecticut: The Association of University Technology Managers, Inc., 1995, p. 3.

7 For a valuable study of the US post office, see Richard R. John, *Spreading the News: the American Postal System from Franklin to Morse*, Cambridge, Massachusetts: Harvard University Press, 1995.

8 The best introduction to the Supreme Court remains Robert G. McCloskey, *The American Supreme Court*, Chicago and London: The University of

Chicago Press, 1960. An excellent book that focuses on legal aspects of the US common market is Herbert Hovenkamp, *Enterprise and American Law, 1836–1937*, Cambridge, Massachusetts, and London, UK: Harvard University Press, 1991.

9 For a more sophisticated analysis of *Bank of Augusta* v. *Earle*, as well as many other Supreme Court cases that contribute to the evolving legal status of the corporation in the United States, see Herbert Hovenkamp, *Enterprise and American Law, 1836–1937*, pp. 46–9 and *passim*.

10 David Weigall and Peter Stirk (eds), *The Origins and Development of the European Community*, Leicester and London: Leicester University Press, 1992, p. 104.

11 Ibid., pp. 104–5.

12 Ibid., p. 105.

13 The Council of Ministers should not be confused with the European Council. Both are bodies of the EU. The Council of Ministers brings together ministers from member states responsible for different areas of policy and is a decision-making body. The European Council consists of heads of state or government, their ministers of foreign affairs, and the President and one Vice-President of the European Commission. The European Council sets general guidelines for major EU policies. For basic details on EU institutions, see David Weigall and Peter Stirk (eds), *The Origins and Development of the European Community*, pp. 198–200, and *passim*.

14 Weigall and Stirk, *Origins and Development of the European Community*, p. 201.

15 Ibid., pp. 201–2.

16 Ibid., p. 201.

17 See Alfred Cahen, *The Western European Union and NATO: Building a European Defence Identity within the Context of Atlantic Solidarity*, London, UK, and Washington, DC: Brassey's UK, 1989 and G. Wyn Rees, *The Western European Union at the Crossroads: between Trans-Atlantic Solidarity and European Integration*, Boulder, Colorado: Westview Press, 1998.

18 See Part One, Substantive Amendments, of the Treaty of Amsterdam. Article 1 contains amendments to the Treaty on European Union that concern provisions for a common foreign and security policy. Online. Available at: www.ue.eu.int/Amsterdam/en/amsteroc/en/treaty/Partone/amst04.htm (accessed 23 August 1999).

19 "The Union pauses for breath," *The Economist*, 12 February 2000, 49–50.

20 "The right verdict on the constitution," *The Economist*, 26 June 2004, 14.

21 "When east meets west: a survey of EU enlargement," *The Economist*, 22 November 2003, 3. See also "EU candidates sign entry treaty," *BBC News*, 25 April 2005. Online. Available at: www.news.bbc.co.uk/1/hi/world/europe/4480677.stm (accessed 26 April 2005).

22 "The right verdict on the constitution," 14.

23 The provisions in the draft of the EU constitutional treaty are taken from "An EU constitutional primer: What it all means," *The Economist*, 26 June 2004, 54.

24 "The European Revolution," *The Economist*, 9 November 1991, 59–60.

25 Robert G. McCloskey, *The American Supreme Court*, p. 30.

26 For a lucid analysis of John Marshall's opinion in *Marbury* v. *Madison*, consult McCloskey, *The American Supreme Court*, pp. 40–4.

27 "The Court of Justice and the life of European citizens." Online. Available at: www.europa.eu.int/cj/en/pres/cjieu.htm (accessed 8 September 1999).

28 Ibid. For a valuable article on the European Court of Justice, which also highlights a conflict between EU and national law in the area of gender discrimination, see Greg Steinmetz, "In Court of Justice, European Union finds mediator

with clout," *The Wall Street Journal*, 16 March 1999, A1 and A17. For a useful article that discusses conflicts between EU law and the tax rules of member states, see Jonathan Schwarz, "EU Law: Challenging Legal Questions," Survey on World Taxation, *Financial Times*, 24 February 1995, 2 of survey (which is 10 of this edition of the paper). The Schwarz article features an excellent chart with a maze of questions to determine whether an EU national should pay his or her country's tax or consider a challenge to it in the European Court of Justice.

29 "The Court of Justice and the life of European citizens."
30 Ibid.
31 Ibid.
32 Ibid.
33 Ibid.
34 Ibid.
35 Ibid.
36 Gary M. Walton and Hugh Rockoff, *History of the American Economy*, 8th edn, Fort Worth, Texas: Dryden Press, 1998, p. 423.
37 Hurst, *A Legal History of Money in the United States*, p. 49.
38 Walton and Rockoff, *History of the American Economy*, pp. 425–6.
39 William Jennings Bryan, *Speeches of William Jennings Bryan, rev. and arranged by himself, with a biographical introduction by Mary Baird Bryan, his wife*, Vol. 1, New York and London: Funk & Wagnalls, 1913, p. 249.
40 "Fundamental facts about U.S. money," Online. Available at: www.frbatlanta.org/publica/brochure/fundfac/money.htm (accessed 4 November 1999).
41 Ross M. Robertson, *History of the American Economy*, 3rd edn, New York: Harcourt Brace Jovanovich, Inc., 1973, p. 500. While the late Ross Robertson was the principal author of this book, it remained meticulous in its treatment of money and banking in the US.
42 Ibid., p. 501.
43 Information in this paragraph comes from "Fundamental facts about U.S. money."
44 Information in this and the preceding paragraph comes from Bray Hammond, *Banks and Politics in America from the Revolution to the Civil War*, Princeton, New Jersey: Princeton University Press, 1967, p. 219.
45 *President Jackson's Veto Message Regarding the Bank of the United States; July 10, 1832*, The Avalon Project at the Yale Law School. Online. Available at: www.yale.edu/lawweb/avalon/presiden/veto/ajveto01.htm (accessed 31 August 2004).
46 Hammond, *Banks and Politics in America*, p. 329.
47 Information contained in this and the preceding paragraph comes from "*L'arrivée de l'euro*," *Champs-Elysées, série 17, numéro 8 (février 1999), 20.*
48 For an excellent introduction to European monetary integration, see Horst Ungerer, *A Concise History of European Monetary Integration: From EPU to EMU*, Westport, Connecticut: Quorum Books, 1997.
49 Peter Coffey and John R. Presley, *European Monetary Integration*, London: Macmillan, 1971, p. 22.
50 Ungerer, *A Concise History of European Monetary Integration*, p. 27.
51 Details of how the EPU operated can be found in Ungerer, *A Concise History of European Monetary Integration*, pp. 27–8.
52 Ungerer, *A Concise History of European Monetary Integration*, p. 28.
53 Ibid., p. 158.
54 Ibid.
55 The following details concerning the ERM, ECU, and divergence indicator are

from Ungerer, *A Concise History of European Monetary Integration*, pp. 158–67.

56 Ungerer, *A Concise History of European Monetary Integration*, p. 178.

57 Ibid., pp. 164–7.

58 Ibid., p. 163.

59 Clifford Chance, "Road to a single currency – European Monetary Union: the legal framework." Online. Available at: www.1999.cliffordchance.com/...ublications/emu_legal/section1.html (accessed 15 November 1999).

60 A clear, factual introduction to the euro, written in an engaging style, is Lisa DiAntoniis, "The euro dollar," *Ciao*, May/June 1999, 8–11 and 41.

61 Clifford Chance, "Road to a single currency."

62 DiAntoniis, "The euro dollar," 9.

63 See Willem H. Buiter *et al. Financial Markets and European Cooperation: The Lessons of the 1992–1993 Exchange Rate Mechanism Crisis*, Cambridge, UK: Cambridge University Press, 1998.

64 "New exchange-rate mechanism (ERM II)." Online. Available at: www.europa.eu.int/scadplus/leg/en/lvb/125047.htm (accessed 6 August 2004). Readers who want a detailed technical description of how EMR II operates should consult the entire document.

65 Tim Weber, "Assessing the euro assessment," *BBC News*, 9 June 2003. Online. Available at: www.news.bbc.co.uk/1/hi/business/2975790.stm (accessed 8 August 2004). This article is an important critique of the five "economic" tests.

Retrospective as prospective

1 W. O. Henderson presents illuminating comparisons and contrasts between the *Zollverein* and the European Community, from the perspective of the 1970s and early 1980s, in *The Zollverein*, 3rd edn, London, UK, and Totowa, New Jersey: Frank Cass, 1984, pp. 345–69.

Bibliography

The bibliography lists sources cited and consulted. References are to the US edition of the *Financial Times*, and to the Midwestern editions (US) of *The Wall Street Journal* and *The New York Times*, unless otherwise indicated. *BBC News* Online has an outstanding archive of articles on Economic and Monetary Union (European Union); search EMU.

"About the ACS [Association of Caribbean States]." Online. Available at: www.acs.aec.org/about.htm (accessed 14 April 2004).

"About us." Online. Available at: www.ceeac-eccas.org.about/index.htm (accessed 10 June 2004).

"Africa firmly on US agenda." *BBC News*, 20 January 2003. Online. Available at: www.news.bbc.co.uk/1/hi/business/2677923.stm (accessed 12 June 2004).

"After Brazil," *The Economist*, 6 February 1999, 18.

Allen, Michael, "A Tangled Tale of GE, Appliance Smuggling and Laundered Money," *The Wall Street Journal*, 21 December 1998, 1A and 6A.

"An EU constitutional primer: what it all means," *The Economist*, 26 June 2004, 54.

"An Mbendi profile: guide to exporting from South Africa – South African trade statistics." Online. Available at: www.mbendi.co.za/export/sas/trade_statistics.htm (accessed 13 June 2004).

"Andean community discusses further trade integration," *BBC News*, 5 April 1998. Online. Available at: www.news.bbc.co.uk/low/english/world/americas/newsid_74000/74145.stm (accessed 21 September 1998).

"Andean nations seek trade boost," *BBC News*, 28 June 2003. Online. Available at: www.news.bbc.co.uk/1/hi/world/americas/3027720.stm (accessed 12 April 2004).

Anderman, Nancy, *United States Supreme Court Decisions: An Index to Their Locations*, Metuchen, NJ: The Scarecrow Press, Inc., 1976.

Andrews, Charles M., *The Colonial Period of American History: The Settlements, Volume I*, New Haven and London: Yale University Press, 1934 and 1964.

"Apec calls for trade liberalization," *BBC News*, 13 September 1999. Online. Available at: www.news2.this.bbc.co.uk/hi/engl...Feconomy/newsid%5F445000/445628.stm (accessed 25 February 2000).

"APEC's family feud," *The Economist*, 21 November 1998, 41.

"Argentinian-Brazilian accord to balance public accounts," *BBC News*, 7 June 1999. Online. Available at: www.news2.this.bbc.co.uk/hi/engl...americas/newsid%5F363000/363547.stm (accessed 6 July 1999).

Arlacchi, Pino, translated by Jonathan Steinberg, *Mafia, Peasants and Great Estates: Society in Traditional Calabria*, Cambridge, England: Cambridge University Press, 1983.

Articles of Confederation, The Avalon Project at the Yale Law School. Online. Available at: www.yale.edu.lawweb/avalon/artconf.htm (accessed 23 August 1999).

"ASEAN investment area: an update." Online. Available at: www.aseansec.org/1034.htm (accessed 28 May 2004).

"Asean leaders agree trade plan," *BBC News*, 7 October 2003. Online. Available at: www.news.bbc.co.uk/1/hi/world/asia-pacific/3167120.stm (accessed 25 May 2004).

"Asean speeds up free trade move," *BBC News*, 29 November 2004. Online. Available at: www.news.bbc.co.uk/2/hi/asia-pacific/4050563.stm (accessed 15 July 2005).

"ASEAN surveillance report confirms economic recovery," 26 November 1999. Online. Available at: www.aseansec.org/10819.htm (accessed 28 May 2004).

"Asia aims for 'common market,'" *BBC News*, 8 October 2003. Online. Available at: www.news.bbc.co.uk/1/hi/business/3173546.stm (accessed 25 May 2004).

Atack, Jeremy and Passell, Peter, *A New Economic View of American History from Colonial Times to 1940*, 2nd edn, New York and London: W. W. Norton & Company, 1994.

Bakoupa, Ferdinand and Tarr, David, "How integration into the central African Economic and Monetary Community affects Cameroon's economy: general equilibrium estimates." Working Paper No. 1872, The World Bank, January 1998.

Balassa, Bela, *The Theory of Economic Integration*, London: Allen and Unwin, 1962.

Benoit, Emile, *Europe at Sixes and Sevens: the Common Market, the Free Trade Association, and the United States*, New York: Columbia University Press, 1961.

"Bilateral sectorial agreements; Switzerland–EU: timetable." Online. Available at: www.europa.admin.ch/e/int/bilatzeitpl.htm (accessed 17 February 2000).

Boiteau, M. Paul, *Les Traités De Commerce. Texte de Tous Les Traités En Vigueur, Notamment des Traités Conclus avec L'Angleterre, La Belgique, La Prusse (Zollverein) et L'Italie*, New York: Lenox Hill (Burt Franklin), 1970. Originally published, 1863.

Bokhari, Farhan, "Afghanistan doubles opium output," *Financial Times*, 24 February 2000, 4.

Bolino, August C., *The Development of the American Economy*, Columbus, Ohio: Charles E. Merrill Books, Inc., 1961.

Bonanno, Joseph with Lalli, Sergio, *A Man of Honor: the Autobiography of Joseph Bonanno*, New York: Simon & Schuster, 1983.

Borders, Caroline, "Mexico faces challenges despite 5 years free trade," Reuters article in Yahoo Finance, 3 December 1998. Online. Available at: www.biz.yahoo.com/rf/981203/bqh.html (accessed 6 December 1998).

Boudette, Neal E., "In Europe, surfing a web of red tape," *The Wall Street Journal*, 29 October 1999, B1 and B4.

Boyd, Dean, "Customs alerts U.S. firms to Colombian money laundering scheme." Online. Available at: www.cbp.gov/custoday/jan2000/peso.htm (accessed 11 February 2004).

—— "Operation Wire Cutter dismantles major Colombian money laundering network." Online. Available at: www.cbp.gov/xp/CustomsToday/2002/February/custoday_wire_cutter.xml (accessed 11 February 2004).

"Brazil admits Mercosur difficulties," *BBC News*, 25 February 2000. Online. Available at: www.news2.this.bbc.co.uk/hi/engl....americas/newsid%5F656000/656958.stm (accessed 6 March 2000).

"Brazil's slippery slope," *The Economist*, 6 February 1999, 77–8.

Brett, E. A., *Colonialism and Underdevelopment in East Africa: the Politics of Economic Change, 1919–1939*, New York: NOK Publishers, Ltd., 1973.

Bryan, William Jennings, *Speeches of William Jennings Bryan, rev. and arranged by himself, with a biographical introduction by Mary Baird Bryan, his wife*, Vol. 1, New York and London: Funk & Wagnalls, 1913.

Buchan, P. Bruce, "The East India Company 1749–1800: the evolution of a territorial strategy and the changing role of the directors," *Business and Economic History*, Volume 23(1), Fall 1994, 52–61.

Buckman, Barbara, "Cyber-sleuths: dogged on-line investors are SEC's top source in Internet probes," *The Wall Street Journal*, 4 August 1998, C1 and C5.

Buiter, Willem H., Corsetti, Giancarlo and Pesenti, Paolo A., *Financial Markets and European Cooperation: the Lessons of the 1992–1993 Exchange Rate Mechanism Crisis*, Cambridge, UK: Cambridge University Press, 1998.

Cahen, Alfred, *The Western European Union and NATO: Building a European Defence Identity within the Context of Atlantic Solidarity*, London, UK, and Washington, DC: Brassey's (UK), 1989.

Cameron, Rondo, *A Concise Economic History of the World: From Paleolithic Times to the Present*, lst edn, Oxford and New York: Oxford University Press, 1989.

—— *A Concise Economic History of the World: From Paleolithic Times to the Present*, 3rd edn, Oxford and New York: Oxford University Press, 1997.

CARICOM Enterprise Regime. Online. Available at: www.tradepoint.tidco.co.tt/miniti/tragtscaricoment.htm (accessed 28 September 1998).

Carlos, Ann M. and Nicholas, Stephen, " 'Giants of an earlier capitalism': the chartered trading companies as modern multinationals," *Business History Review*, 62 (Autumn 1988), 398–419.

Carlos Ann M., Key, Jennifer and Dupree, Jill L., "Learning and the creation of stock-market institutions: evidence from the Royal African and Hudson's Bay companies, 1670–1700," *The Journal of Economic History*, 58(2) (June 1998), 318–44.

"Central African Common Market Launched," *BBC News*, 6 February 1998. Online. Available at: www.news.bbc.co.uk/hi/english/world/africa/newsid%5F54000/54257/stm (accessed 1 February 1999).

Chance, Clifford, "Road to a single currency – European Monetary Union: the legal framework." Online. Available at: www.1999.cliffordchance.com/...publications/emu_legal/section1.html (accessed 15 November 1999).

"China in landmark Asean pact," *BBC News*, 29 November 2004. Online. Available at: www.news.bbc.co.uk/2/hi/asia-pacific/4051653.stm (accessed 15 July 2005).

Chown, John, *A History of Monetary Unions*, London: Routledge, 2003.

Clapham, J. H., *The Economic Development of France and Germany, 1815–1914*, 4th edn, Cambridge, UK: Cambridge University Press, 1963.

Clarke, Thurston and Tigue, John J., *Dirty Money: Swiss Banks, the Mafia, Money Laundering, and White Collar Crime*, New York: Simon & Schuster, 1975.

Coffey, Peter and Presley, John R., *European Monetary Integration*, London: Macmillan, 1971.

Cohen, Rich, "Gun, gangster and the business of crime," *Financial Times*, Weekend, 27/28 June 1998, IV.

—— *Tough Jews: Fathers, Sons, and Gangster Dreams*, New York: Simon & Schuster, 1998.

"Comesa loses Tanzania," *BBC News*, 27 July 1999. Online. Available at: www.news2.this.bbc.co.uk/hi/engl...d/africa/newsid%5F405000/405293.stm (accessed 25 February 2000).

"Common market – Andean community." Online. Available at: www.comunidadandina.org/ingles/market.htm (accessed 12 April 2004).

"Congo leader in Burundi," *BBC News*, 30 October 1997. Online. Available at: www.news.bbc.co.uk/hi/english/world/africa/newsid%5F19000/19175.stm (accessed 1 February 1999).

Cornwell, Rupert, *God's Banker*, New York: Dodd, Mead, 1984.

Coulson, Andrew, *Tanzania: a Political Economy*, Oxford: Clarendon Press, 1982.

"Country profile: Argentina," *BBC News*, 3 July 2004. Online. Available at: www.news.bbc.co.uk/1/hi/world/americas/country_profiles/1192478.stm (accessed 6 July 2004).

Craig, Sir John, *Newton at the Mint*, Cambridge, UK: Cambridge University Press, 1946.

Creevey, Lucy, Vengroff, Richard, with Gaye, Ibrahima, "Devaluation of the CFA franc in Senegal: the reaction of small businesses," *The Journal of Modern African Studies*, 33(4), 1995, 669–83.

Crooks, Ed, "Target dates [EU] lend weight to aspirations," *Financial Times*, 25/26 March 2000, 2.

Curtin, Philip D., *The Atlantic Slave Trade: a Census*, Madison, Wisconsin: University of Wisconsin Press, 1969.

"Customs union." Online. Available at: www.southafrica.net/government/foreign/sacu.html (accessed 1 February 1999).

"Customs union – Andean community." Online. Available at: www.comunidadandina.org/ingles/union.htm (accessed 12 April 2004).

Davies, Glyn, *A History of Money from Ancient Times to the Present Day*, 3rd edn, Cardiff: University of Wales Press, 2002.

Davies, Kenneth G., *The Royal African Company*, London: Longmans, Green and Co., 1957.

Davis, John R., *Britain and the German Zollverein, 1848–66*, London, UK: Macmillan Press, Ltd., and New York: St. Martin's Press, Inc., 1997.

DeCórdoba, José, Lyons, John and Luhnow, David, "Despite Cafta, U.S. clout wanes in Latin America," *The Wall Street Journal*, 29 July 2005, A11.

de Jonquières, Guy, "Elastic approach to free trade," *Financial Times*, 24 November 1997, 3.

de Roover, Raymond, *The Rise and Decline of the Medici Bank, 1397–1494*, Cambridge, Massachusetts: Harvard University Press, 1968.

de Vries, Jan and van der Woude, Ad, *The First Modern Economy: Success, Failure, and Perseverance of the Dutch Economy, 1500–1815*, Cambridge, UK: Cambridge University Press, 1997.

DiAntoniis, Lisa, "The euro dollar," *Ciao*, May/June 1999, 8–11 and 41.

Drescher, Seymour and Engerman, Stanley L. (eds), *A Historical Guide to World Slavery*, New York: Oxford University Press, 1998.

"East African Co-operation," Special Survey, *Financial Times*, 5 November 1996, I.

East African Development Bank. In International Monetary Fund, *Directory of Economic, Commodity, and Development Organizations*, 20 April 1998. Online. Available at: www.imf.org/external/np/sec/decdo/eadb.htm (accessed 23 October 1998).

"East Africans sign customs pact," *BBC News*, 2 March 2004. Online. Available at: www.news.bbc.co.uk/1/hi/world/africa/3526195.stm (accessed 8 April 2004).

"East Africa's first steps towards union," *BBC News*, 30 November 1999. Online. Available at: www.news2.this.bbc.co.uk/hi/engl...d/africa/newsid%5F543000/523582.stm (accessed 25 February 2000).

Economic Community of Central African States. Online. Available at: www.tradecompass.com/library...ommunityofCentralAfricanStates.html (accessed 1 February 1999).

"Economic Community of West African States (ECOWAS)." Online. Available at: www.eia.doe.gov/emeu/cabs/ghana.html (accessed 21 March 2004).

Economic Policy Institute, *The Failed Experiment: NAFTA at Three Years*, Executive Summary: 3; 1997.

"ECOWAS," Africaland: who is who in African integration. Online. Available at: www.focusintl.com/whos0004.htm (accessed 9 September 1998).

"EFTA Court." Online. Available at: www.eftacourt.lu (accessed 12 March 2004).

Einaudi, Luca, "Monetary unions: history offers a pertinent lesson," In *The Pink Book, quarterly guide: the European economy*, *Financial Times*, 26 February 1999, 15.

Ekelund, Jr., Robert B., Hébert, Robert F., Tollison, Robert D., Anderson, Gary M., and Davidson, Audrey B., *Sacred Trust: The Medieval Church as an Economic Firm*, New York and Oxford: Oxford University Press, 1996.

Epstein, S. R., "Regional fairs, institutional innovation, and economic growth in late medieval Europe," *Economic History Review*, XLVII, 3 (1994), 459–82.

"EU candidates sign entry treaty," *BBC News*, 25 April 2005. Online. Available at: www.news.bbc.co.uk/1/world/europe/4480677.stm (accessed 26 April 2005).

"EU relations with Switzerland: a special case." Online. Available at: www.europa.eu.int/comm/external_relations/switzerland/intro/index/htm (accessed 9 March 2004).

"European business," Survey, *The Economist*, 29 April 2000.

Faux, Jeff, "Administration's NAFTA report seriously misleading," 11 July 1997. Online. Available at: epinet.org/naftares.html (accessed 6 December 1998.)

—— "NAFTA at 10," 9 February 2004. Online. Available www.epinet.org/content.cfm/webfeatures_viewpoints_nafta_legacy_at10 (accessed 4 May 2004).

Fidler, Stephen, "Dead end drugs war," *Financial Times*, 10 June 1998, 14.

Fidler, Stephen and Lapper, Richard, "Summers warns on dollarisation," *Financial Times*, 15 March 1999, 1.

Fieldhouse, D. K., *The Colonial Empires: A Comparative Survey from the Eighteenth Century*, New York: Delacorte Press, 1967.

—— "The economic exploitation of Africa: some British and French comparisons," in Prosser Gifford and Wm. Roger Louis (eds) *France and Britain in*

Africa: Imperial Rivalry and Colonial Rule, pp. 593–662, New Haven and London: Yale University Press, 1971.
Financial Times, "One thousand years of finance," Millennium Special Issue, 1 January 2000, 2–9.
Finley, Moses I., *The Ancient Economy*, Berkeley: University of California Press, 1973.
Fisher, Ian and Onishu, Norimitsu, "Many armies ravage rich land in the 'First World War' of Africa," *The New York Times*, 6 February 2000, 1 and 12–13.
Fleming, Charles, "In the unified Europe, shipping freight by rail is a journey into the past," *The Wall Street Journal*, 29 March 1999, A1 and A8.
Flint, J. E., *Sir George Goldie and the Making of Nigeria*, London: Oxford University Press, 1960.
Foderaro, Lisa W., "A diminishing sisterhood is competing for recruits," *The New York Times*, 16 January 2000, 1 and 44.
Foster, Angus, "Most targets have been met," in *Mercosur*, Special Survey, *Financial Times*, 25 January 1995, III of survey and 14 of entire issue.
Frankel, Jeffrey A., *Regional Trading Blocs in the World Economic System*, Washington, DC: Institute for International Economics, 1997.
Fried, Joseph P., "Star witness at Gigante trial admits to 'a life of lies' in the mob," *The New York Times*, 12 July 1997, 20.
—— "Peter Savino, Mafia associate who became an informer, 55," *The New York Times*, 1 November 1997, A24.
Fudge, John D., *Cargoes, Embargoes, and Emissaries: the Commercial and Political Interaction of England and the German Hanse, 1450–1510*, Toronto: University of Toronto Press, 1995.
Fuentes, Thomas V., Chief, Organized Crime Section, Criminal Investigative Division, Federal Bureau of Investigation. Statement for the Record on Organized Crime Before the House Subcommittee on Finance and Hazardous Materials, Washington, D.C., 13 September 2000. Online. Available at: www.fbi.gov/congress/congress00/fuentes.htm (accessed 12 February 2004).
"Fundamental facts about U.S. money." Online. Available at: www.frbatlanta.org/publica/brochure/fundfac/money.htm (accessed 4 November 1999).
"Futures trader convicted," *CNNMoney*, 13 February 2002. Online. Available at: www.money.cnn.com/2002/02/13/news/union/ (accessed 4 March 2004).
Gailey, Harry A., *Sir Donald Cameron, Colonial Governor*, Stanford: Hoover Institution Press, 1974.
Gambetta, Diego, *The Sicilian Mafia: the Business of Private Protection*, Cambridge, Massachusetts, and London, UK: Harvard University Press, 1993.
Garnsey, Peter, "Grain for Rome," in Peter Garnsey, Keith Hopkins and C. R. Whitaker (eds) *Trade in the Ancient Economy*, London: Chatto and Windus – the Hogarth Press, 1983, pp. 118–30.
Gerschenkron, Alexander, *Economic Backwardness in Historical Perspective: A Book of Essays*, Cambridge, Massachusetts: Belknap Press of Harvard University Press, 1962.
Gilchrist, J., *The Church and Economic Activity in the Middle Ages*, London: Macmillan, 1969.
Gillispie, Mark, "Strollo spills mob secrets," *The Cleveland Plain Dealer*, 4 March 1999, 1–A and 10–A.
Githongo, John, "History of co-operation: century of borderline deliberations," In

"East African co-operation," Special Survey, *Financial Times*, 5 November 1996, IV.

Goldberg, Jeffrey, "The Don is done," *The New York Times Magazine*, 31 January 1999, 24–31, 38, 62, 65–6, 71.

"Gravity models." Online. Available at: www.faculty.washington.edu/krumme/systems/gravity.html (accessed 14 July 2005).

Greene, Kevin, "Technological innovation and economic progress in the ancient world: M. I. Finley re-considered," *Economic History Review*, LIII, 1 (2000), 29–59.

Grocholewski, Zenon, "The function of the Sacred Roman Rota and the Supreme Court of the Apostolic Signatura," translated by Dinah Livingstone, in Peter Huizing and Knut Walf (eds) *The Roman Curia and the Communion of Churches*, New York: Seabury Press, 1979, pp. 47–51.

Hamilton, Alexander, *The Works of Alexander Hamilton* [microform], Henry Cabot Lodge (ed.), 12 vols, New York: G. P. Putnam's Sons, 1904. Microfiche, 60 microfiches, Washington DC: Microcarol Editions, 1969.

Hammond, Bray, *Banks and Politics in America from the Revolution to the Civil War*, Princeton, New Jersey: Princeton University Press, 1967.

Harden, Blaine, "Africa's Gems: Warfare's Best Friend," *The New York Times*, 6 April 2000, A1, A10 and A11.

Harms, Robert, "The World Abir Made: The Maringa-Lopori Basin, 1885–1903," *African Economic History*, No. 12 (1983), 125–39.

Hart, B. H. Liddell, *Strategy*, 2nd revised edn, New York: Meridian, 1991.

Hawkins, Tony, "Trade agreement stalled," in "Investing in South Africa," Special Survey, *Financial Times*, 28 March 1996, V.

—— "CFA Zone: launch of the euro clouds outlook for the 14," in "World Economy and Finance," Special Survey, *Financial Times*, 2 October 1998, XXIV.

—— "Mugabe's mind on foreign adventure as Zimbabwe slides further into mire," *Financial Times*, 5 November 1998, 7.

Head, Jonathan, "How APEC has changed," *BBC News*, 21 October 2003. Online. Available at: www.bbc.co.uk/1/hi/world/asia-pacific/32309600.stm (accessed 25 May 2004).

Heckscher, Eli F., *Mercantilism*, 2 vols, authorized translation by Mendel Shapiro, London: Allen & Unwin and New York: Macmillan, 1962.

Henderson, W. O., *The Zollverein*, 3rd edn, London, UK, and Totowa, New Jersey: Frank Cass and Company Limited, 1984.

Hennock, Mary, "Uphill task for South Asian trade pact," *BBC News*, 6 January 2004. Online. Available at: www.news.bbc.co.uk/1/hi/business/3370187.stm (accessed 25 May 2004).

"History of Asia-Pacific Cooperation," The Ministry of Foreign Affairs, Japan. Online. Available at: www.mofa.go.jp/policy/economy/apec/1995/info/history.html (accessed 21 November 1998).

Hollis, Christopher, *The Jesuits: A History*, New York: Barnes & Noble Books, 1992. Original edition published by MacMillan, Inc., in 1968.

Holman, Michael, "Learning from the past," in "East African co-operation," Special Survey, *Financial Times*, 5 February 1996, I.

"Hopes and fears for Africa trade pact," *BBC News*, 2 March 2004. Online. Available at: www.news.bbc.co.uk/1/hi/world/africa/3526195.stm (accessed 8 April 2004).

Hopkins, A. G., *An Economic History of West Africa*, New York: Columbia University Press, 1973.

Hopkins, Keith, "Introduction," in Peter Garnsey, Keith Hopkins and C. R. Whitaker (eds) *Trade in the Ancient Economy*, London: Chatto and Windus – the Hogarth Press, 1983, pp. ix–xxv.

Hovenkamp, Herbert, *Enterprise and American Law, 1836–1937*, Cambridge, Massachusetts and London, UK: Harvard University Press, 1991.

Hurst, James Willard, *A Legal History of Money in the United States, 1774–1970*, Lincoln: The University of Nebraska Press, 1973.

"Indictment targets Wall Street mobsters," *Yahoo! News*, 2 March 2000. Online. Available at: www.dailynews.yahoo.com/h/ao/20000302/cr/20000302008.html (accessed 3 March 2000).

"Is the UK ready for the euro?" *BBC News*, 14 October 1999. Online. Available at: www.news2.this.bbc.co.uk/hi/engl...Feconomy/newsid%5F474000/474518.stm (accessed 29 March 2000).

James, Canute, "Caribbean states take step nearer trade bloc," *Financial Times*, 5 July 1994, 6.

—— "'Bridge' Treaty: Central America horizons widen," *Financial Times*, 16 April 1998, 7.

John, Richard R., *Spreading the News: the American Postal System from Franklin to Morse*, Cambridge, Massachusetts: Harvard University Press, 1995.

Johnson, Ian, "How Malaysia's rulers devoured each other and much they built," *The Wall Street Journal*, 30 October 1998, A1 and A11.

Johnson, Paul M., *A Glossary of Political Economy Terms* (1994–2005). Online. Available at: www.auburn.edu/~johnspm/gloss/political_economy (accessed 15 May 2005).

Johnston, Sir Harry H., *The Story of My Life*, Indianapolis: The Bobbs-Merrill Company, 1923.

Kahler, Miles, *International Institutions and the Political Economy of Integration*, Washington, D.C.: The Brookings Institution, 1995.

Kaplanis, Costas, "The debasement of the 'dollar of the Middle Ages,'" *The Journal of Economic History*, 63 (September 2003), 768–801.

Keith, A. Berriedale, *The Belgian Congo and the Berlin Act*, Oxford: The Clarendon Press, 1919.

King, Jeanne, "'Sopranos' actor sentenced in New York stock scam," *Yahoo News*, 12 April 2000. Online. Available at: www.dailynews.yahoo.com/h/nm/20000412/re/crime_scam_1.html (accessed 12 April 2000).

King, Jr., Neil, "Kerry would seek tighter standards governing Cafta," *The Wall Street Journal*, 1 June 2004, A6.

King, Jr., Neil, Miller, Scott and Lyons, John, "Cafta vote clouds prospects for other trade deals," *The Wall Street Journal*, 29 July 2005, A1 and A9.

Knoll, Arthur J., *Togo Under Imperial Germany, 1884–1914: A Case Study in Colonial Rule*, Stanford: Hoover Institution Press, 1978.

Kobler, John, *Capone: The Life and World of Al Capone*, Greenwich, Connecticut: Fawcett Publications, Inc., 1972.

—— *Ardent Spirits: the Rise and Fall of Prohibition*, New York: G. P. Putnam's Sons, 1973.

Komlos, John, *The Habsburg Monarchy as a Customs Union: Economic Development in Austria-Hungary in the Nineteenth Century*, Princeton, NJ: Princeton University Press, 1983.

Kottman, Richard N., *Reciprocity and the North Atlantic Triangle, 1932–1938*, Ithaca: Cornell University Press, 1968.

Kreinen, Mordechai Elihau (ed.), *Building a Partnership: the Canada–United States Free Trade Agreement*, East Lansing: Michigan State University Press and Calgary: University of Calgary Press, 2000.

Kuklick, Henrika, *The Imperial Bureaucrat: the Colonial Administrative Service in the Gold Coast, 1920–1939*, Stanford: Hoover Institution Press, 1979.

Langley, Monica, "Nuns' zeal for profits shapes hospital chain, wins Wall Street fans," *The Wall Street Journal*, 7 January 1998, A1 and A11.

Lapper, Richard, "Cocaine supply to Europe, US 'still high,'" *Financial Times*, 24 February 2000, 4.

Lapper, Richard and Bokhari, Farhan, "UN fears growth of heroin trade," *Financial Times*, 24 February 2000, 1.

"*L'arrivée de l'euro,*" *Champs-Elysées, série 17, numéro 8 (février 1999), 20.*

Leibovich, Lori, "That online religion with shopping, too," *The New York Times*, 6 April 2000, D1 and D10.

Leonard, Nicholas, "Scourge of the counterfeiters," *Financial Times*, Weekend, 11/12 April, 1998, XXIV.

"Lesotho elections deal struck," *BBC News*, 15 October 1998. Online. Available at: www.news.bbc.co.uk/hi/english/world/africa/newsid%5F193000/193723.stm (accessed 22 February 1999).

Lloyd, T. H., *England and the German Hanse, 1157–1611: a Study of Their Trade and Commercial Diplomacy*, Cambridge: Cambridge University Press, 1991.

Louis, Wm. Roger, editor in chief, *The Oxford History of the British Empire*, 5 vols, Oxford and New York: Oxford University Press, 1998–99.
v. 1, *The Origins of Empire*, Nicholas Canny (ed.), 1998.
v. 2, *The Eighteenth Century*, P. J. Marshall (ed.), 1998.
v. 3, *The Nineteenth Century*, Andrew Porter (ed.) and Alaine Low (assoc.ed.), 1999.
v. 4, *The Twentieth Century*, Judith M. Brown and Wm. Roger Louis (eds), Alaine Low (assoc.ed.), 1999.
v. 5, *Historiography*, Robin W. Winks (ed.), 1999.

Louis, Wm. Roger and Stengers, Jean (eds), *E. D. Morel's History of the Congo Reform Movement*, Oxford: Oxford University Press, 1968.

Maas, Peter, *The Valachi Papers*, New York: G. P. Putnam's Sons, 1968.

—— *Underboss: Sammy the Bull Gravano's Story of Life in the Mafia*, New York: Harper Collins Publishers, Inc., 1997.

MacGaffey, Janet, *Entrepreneurs and Parasites: The Struggle for Indigenous Capitalism in Zaire*, Cambridge: Cambridge University Press, 1987.

Machlup, Fritz, *A History of Thought on Economic Integration*, New York: Columbia University Press, 1977.

—— (ed.), *Economic Integration: Worldwide, Regional, Sectoral: Proceedings of the Fourth Congress of the International Economic Association held at Budapest, Hungary*, London, New York: Macmillan Press, distributed in the US by Halstead Press: 1976.

"Man of integrity whose policies hurt his country," *Financial Times*, 15 October 1999, 7.

"Mandela hails EU trade deal," *BBC News*, 25 March 1999. Online. Available at: www.news2.thdo.bbc.co.uk/hi/engl....Feconomy/newsid%5F303000/303606.stm (accessed 2 April 1999).

Mandela, Nelson, "Address to the World Economic Forum," Davos, Switzerland, 29 January 1999, in *Mandela Speaks: Speeches, Statements and Writings of Nelson Mandela, 1999*. Online. Available at: www.anc.org.za/ancdocs/history/mandela/1999/ (accessed 5 August 2005).

Manning, Patrick, *Francophone Sub-Saharan Africa, 1880–1985*, Cambridge, UK: Cambridge University Press, 1988.

Marsh, David, "Will someone please explain why Britain should join EMU," Letter to the editor, *Financial Times*, 16 June 1999, 14.

Martin, David, "Gotti [Jr.] plea seen as blow to U.S. crime families," *Yahoo! News*, 6 April 1999. Online. Available at: www.dailynews.yahoo.com/ headline...nm/19990406/ts/crime_gottijr_1.html (accessed 6 April 1999).

McCarthy, Colin, "The Southern African Customs Union," Paper prepared for a conference, *Intégrations régionales, politiques agricoles communes et sécurité alimentaire, du 26 au 29 May 2003*, Ouagadougou, Burkina Faso.

McCarthy, Dennis M. P., "Media as ends: money and the underdevelopment of Tanganyika to 1940," *The Journal of Economic History*, 36 (September, 1976), 645–62.

—— "Language manipulation in Colonial Tanganyika, 1919–1940," *Journal of African Studies*, 6, 1 (Spring 1979), 9–16.

—— *Colonial Bureaucracy and Creating Underdevelopment: Tanganyika, 1919–1940*, Ames: Iowa State University Press, 1982.

—— "Bureaucracy, business, and Africa during the colonial period: who did what to whom and with what consequences?," in *Research in Economic History*, Paul Uselding (ed.), 11 (1988), 81–152.

—— "The bureaucratic manipulation of indigenous business: a comparative study in legal imposition from colonial Africa," *Business and Economic History*, Second Series, 19 (1990), 123–32.

—— "International business and economic integration: comparative business strategies past and present," *Business and Economic History*, Second Series, 21 (1992), 237–46.

—— *International Business History: A Contextual and Case Approach*, Westport, Connecticut: Praeger, 1994.

—— "A collaboration of history and anthropology: the synergy of economic history and ethnoeconomy in illuminating colonial African moneys," *African Economic History*, 24 (1996), 91–107.

—— "International economic integration and business cultures: comparative historical perspectives," *Business and Economic History*, 25, 1 (1996), 72–80.

McCloskey, Robert G., *The American Supreme Court*, Chicago and London: The University of Chicago Press, 1960.

McMorris, Frances A., "HealthTech CEO is convicted in case tied to mob infiltration of Wall Street," *The Wall Street Journal*, 12 May 1999, B8.

McNulty, Sheila, "Battered Anwar faces court to deny corruption charges," *Financial Times*, 30 September 1998, 16.

Mendelson, Edward, "The word and the web," *The New York Times Book Review*, 2 June 1996. Online. Available at: www.nytimes.com/library/cyber/week/0602bookend.html (accessed 26 January 2000).

Meyer, Kathryn and Parssinen, Terry M., *Webs of Smoke: Smugglers, Warlords, Spies, and the History of the International Drug Trade*, Lanham, Maryland: Rowman & Littlefield Publishers, 1998.

Miller, John C., *Alexander Hamilton and the Growth of the New Nation*, New York: Harper & Row, 1964.

Miller, Lisa, "Religious institutions are invoking premiums to inspire the wealthy," *The Wall Street Journal*, 10 March 1999, A1 and A6.

Millman, Joel, "What southeast was to U.S. companies, Mexico is becoming," *The Wall Street Journal*, 29 October 1999, A1 and A6.

—— "The world's new tiger on the export scene isn't Asian; it's Mexico," *The Wall Street Journal*, 9 May 2000, A1 and A10.

Mingst, Karen A., *Politics and the African Development Bank*, Lexington: University Press of Kentucky, 1990.

Miskimin, Harry A., *Money, Prices, and Foreign Exchange in Fourteenth-Century France*, New Haven: Yale University Press, 1963.

—— *The Economy of Early Renaissance Europe, 1300–1460*, Englewood Cliffs, NJ: Prentice-Hall, Inc., 1969.

—— *The Economy of Later Renaissance Europe, 1460–1600*, Cambridge, UK, and New York: Cambridge University Press, 1977.

—— *Money and Power in Fifteenth-Century France*, New Haven: Yale University Press, 1984.

—— *Cash, Credit, and Crisis in Europe, 1300–1600*, London, UK: Variorum Reprints, 1989.

Mobius, Mark, *The Investor's Guide to Emerging Markets*, Burr Ridge, Illinois: Richard D. Irwin, Inc., 1995.

Mole, John, *Mind Your Manners: Culture Clash in the European Single Market*, London: The Industrial Society, 1990.

Montagnon, Peter, Robinson, Gwen and McNulty, Sheila, "Fingers crossed that leaders can avoid APEC summit fiasco," *Financial Times*, 13 November 1998, 6.

Morel, Edmund Dene, *Red Rubber: The Story of the Rubber Trade Flourishing on the Congo in the Year of grace 1906*, New York: Negro Universities Press, 1969. This is a reprint of the 1906 edition.

Morris, Kenneth M. and Siegel, Alan M., *The Wall Street Journal Guide to Understanding Money & Investing*, New York: Lightbulb Press, Inc., 1993.

Mortimer, Edward, "Empire without profit or prestige," *Financial Times* Weekend, 23/24 August 1997, 7.

Moyo, Tabby, "Sacu trade bid nearing completion," 17 July 1998. Online. Available at: www.woza.co.za/africa/sacuo1.htm (accessed 2 February 1999).

Mueller, Lisa von Bargen, "An inventor's guide to patents and patenting," *AUTM Educational Series: No. 1*, Norwalk, Connecticut: The Association of University Technology Managers, Inc., 1995.

Mundell, Robert A., "A theory of optimum currency areas," *American Economic Review*, 51 (September, 1961), 657–65.

Murphy, Antoin E., *John Law: Economic Theorist and Policy-Maker*, Oxford: The Clarendon Press, 1997.

Myerson, Allen R., "Borderline working class: in Texas, labor is feeling trade accord's pinch," *The New York Times*, 8 May 1997, D1 and D23. This is the edition on microfilm.

"NAFTA overview," *The Des Moines Register*, 13 November 1993, 11A.

Neal, Larry and Barbezat, Daniel, *The Economies of the European Union and the Economies of Europe*, New York: Oxford University Press, 1998.

"New exchange-rate mechanism (ERM II)." Online. Available at: www.europa.eu.int/scadplus/leg/en/lvb/125047.htm (accessed 6 August 2004).

Nicholson, Mark, "South Asian states plan free-trade zone," *Financial Times*, 3 May 1995, 5.

"Niger president launches ECOWAS trade fair," PanAfrican News Agency, 6 March 1998. Online. Available at: www.africaonline.com/AfricaOnline/newsstand/PANA/PANA06Mar98.html (accessed 9 September 1998).

Northrup, David (ed.), *The Atlantic Slave Trade*, Lexington, Massachusetts: D. C. Heath and Company, 1994.

Oliver, Roland and Atmore, Anthony, *Africa Since 1800*, 3rd edn, Cambridge: Cambridge University Press, 1981.

Osterlund, David, Royle, David, Kurtis, Bill and Fox, Stephen R., *Mafia: the history of the Mob in America*, New York: A & E Home Video, 2001.

Oxfam America, "Southern African Customs Union," 10 July 2003. Online. Available at: www.oxfamamerica.org/advocacy/art5660.html (accessed 18 June 2004).

Page, Willie F., *The Dutch Triangle: the Netherlands and the Atlantic Slave Trade, 1621–1664*, New York: Garland Publishing, Inc., 1997.

Palmer, R. R. and Colton, Joel, *A History of the Modern World*, 2nd edn, New York: Alfred A. Knopf, 1956.

Peel, Michael, "E. Africa seeks $4.4 bn for roads," *Financial Times*, 18 February 1998, 9.

Pins, Kenneth, "Factory exports up 38 percent: Iowa's success rekindles NAFTA debate," *The Des Moines Sunday Register*, 11 January 1998, 1G and 2G.

Pleket, H. W., "Urban elites and business in the Greek part of the Roman Empire," in Peter Garnsey, Keith Hopkins, and C. R. Whitaker (eds) *Trade in the Ancient Economy*, pp. 131–44, London: Chatto and Windus – the Hogarth Press, 1983.

Postel, Rainer, "The Hanseatic League and its decline." Online. Available at: www.hartford-hwp.com/archives/60/039.html (accessed 7 January 2004).

Postma, Johannes Menne, *The Dutch in the Atlantic Slave Trade, 1600–1815*, Cambridge, UK: Cambridge University Press, 1990.

President Jackson's Veto Message Regarding the Bank of the United States; July 10, 1832, The Avalon Project at the Yale Law School. Online. Available at: www.yale.edu/lawweb/avalon/presiden/veto/ajveto01.htm (accessed 31 August 2004).

Price, Arnold H., *The Evolution of the Zollverein: a Study of the Ideas and Institutions Leading to German Economic Unification Between 1815 and 1833*, New York: Octagon Books, 1973.

Pulliam, Susan, "Stock-Fraud case alleges organized-crime tie: day-care company with dot-com plans turned into target," *The Wall Street Journal*, 15 June 2000, C1 and C21.

Rees, G. Wyn, *The Western European Union at the Crossroads: between Trans-Atlantic Solidarity and European Integration*, Boulder, Colorado: Westview Press, 1998.

Reese, Thomas J., *Inside the Vatican: The Politics and Organization of the Catholic Church*, Cambridge, Massachusetts: Harvard University Press, 1996.

Rhoads, Christopher and Champion, Marc, "As Europe expands, new union faces problems of scale," *The Wall Street Journal*, 29 April 2004, A1 and A8.

Richards, James R., *Transnational Criminal Organizations, Cybercrime, and*

Money Laundering: A Handbook for Law Enforcement Officers, Auditors, and Financial Investigators, Boca Raton, Florida: CRC Press, 1999.

Robertson, Kathy and Johnson, Kelly, "Shopping center buyer's CEO is under indictment," *Sacramento Business Journal*, 14(39), 12 December 1997, 1–2.

Robertson, Ross M., *History of the American Economy*, 3rd edn, New York: Harcourt Brace Jovanovich, Inc., 1973.

Robichaux, Mark, "Tim Robertson turns TV's family channel into a major business," *The Wall Street Journal*, 29 August 1996, A1 and A6.

Rood, Lee, "Mexico Supplies Iowa's Meth," *The Des Moines Register*, 9 March 1999, 1A and 7A.

Rosenberg, Matt T., "Gravity model: predict the movement of people and ideas between two places." Online. Available at: www.geography.about.com/library/weekly/aa031601a.htm (accessed 14 July 2005).

Rothstein, Jesse and Scott, Robert, "NAFTA and the States," 19 September 1997. Online. Available at: www.epinet.org/content.cfm/issuebriefs_ib119 (accessed 18 May 2004).

Schildhauer, Johannes, *The Hansa: History and Culture*, Leipzig: Edition Leipzig, 1985. Translated from the German (*Die Hanse*) by Katherine Vanovitch.

Schlesinger, Jr., Arthur, *The Politics of Upheaval*, Boston: Houghton Mifflin Company, 1960.

Schouten, Fredreka, "Many states put money on gambling," *The Des Moines Sunday Register*, 30 May 1999, 1AA.

Schumpeter, Joseph A., *History of Economic Analysis*, New York: Oxford University Press, 1963.

Schwarz, Jonathan, "EU law: challenging legal questions," in "World Taxation," Special Survey, *Financial Times*, 24 February 1995, 2 of survey, which is 10 of this edition of paper.

Scott, Robert E., "NAFTA's hidden costs," April 2001. Online. Available at: www.epinet.org/content.cfm/briefingpapers_nafta01_us (accessed 13 May 2004).

Securities and Exchange Commission, Washington, D.C., In the Matter of the Application of HealthTech International, Inc., For Review of Action Taken by the National Association of Securities Dealers, Inc., 26 October 1999. Online. Available at: www.sec.gov/litigation/opinions/34-42060.htm (accessed 6 March 2004).

Securities and Exchange Commission, Washington, DC, Litigation Release No. 15572, 25 November 1997; Accounting and Auditing Enforcement Release No. 990, 25 November 1997. *Securities and Exchange Commission v. HealthTech International, Action No. 97 CV 8766 (JSR)*. Online. Available at: www.sec.gov/enforce/litigrel/lr15572.txt (accessed 17 February 2000).

Shenton Robert W., *The Development of Capitalism in Northern Nigeria*, Toronto: University of Toronto Press, 1986.

Sims, Calvin, "Feeling pinch, Japan's mobs struggle for control," *The New York Times*, 2 April 2000, 6.

Sims, G. Thomas and Wessel, David, "European Central Bank can't seem to master art of communication," *The Wall Street Journal*, 27 April 2000, A1 and A10.

Slade, Ruth, *King Leopold's Congo*, London: Oxford University Press, 1962.

Smith, Adam, *An Inquiry Into the Nature and Causes of the Wealth of Nations*, Homewood, Illinois: Richard D. Irwin, Inc., 1963.

Smith, Michael, "Language gridlock fears grow in Brussels," *Financial Times*, 24/25 July 1999, 3.

Smith, Randall and Schroeder, Michael, "Stock-fraud case alleges organized-crime tie: prosecutors say stocks of 19 firms were manipulated," *The Wall Street Journal*, 15 June 2000, C1 and C4.

Sohmen, Helmut, "PBEC's role in APEC," 30 November 1998. Online. Available at: www.pbec.org/speeches/1998/981130sohmen.htm (accessed 25 February 2000).

"South Africa and the Southern African Development Community," November 2002. Online. Available at: www.eia.doe.gov/emeu/cabs/sade.html (accessed 10 April 2004).

"South American unity pledge," *BBC News*, 19 June 2003. Online. Available at: www.news.bbc.co.uk/1/hi/world/americas/3002586.stm (accessed 6 July 2004).

"St Kitts and Nevis to stay together," *BBC News*, 11 August 1998. Online. Available at: www.news2.this.bbc.co.uk/hi/engl...americas/newsid%5F148000/148916.stm (accessed 25 February 2000).

Starkman, Dean and Lohse, Deborah, "Charges mark wider probe of mob, Wall Street," *The Wall Street Journal*, 26 November 1997, C1 and C19.

Stein, Jeff, "The Caribbean connection," *GQ*, August 1999, 164–71, 209–11.

Steinmetz, Greg, "In Court of Justice, European Union finds mediator with clout," *The Wall Street Journal*, 16 March 1999, A1 and A17.

Stix, David, "History lesson," *Forbes*, 7 January 1991, 89.

Strikwerda, Carl, "The troubled origins of European economic integration: international iron and steel and labor migration in the era of World War I," *The American Historical Review*, Volume 98, Number 4 (October, 1993), 1106–29.

"Subregional trading groups," *Economic Perspectives*, USIA Electronic Journal, Vol. 3, No. 2, March 1998. Online. Available at: www.usia.gov/journals/ites/0398/ijee/ejsubreg.htm (accessed 23 October 1998).

Sullivan, Jo and Martin, Jane, *Global Studies: Africa*, 2nd edn, Guilford, Connecticut: The Dushkin Publishing Group, 1985.

Sullivan, John, with Berenson, Alex, "Brokers charged with crime figures in complex fraud," *The New York Times*, 15 June 2000, A1 and C27.

Sun-tzu, *The Complete Art of War*, translated, with historical introduction and commentary, by Ralph D. Sawyer, with the collaboration of Mei-chún Lee Sawyer, Boulder, Colorado: Westview Press, 1996.

Tassell, Tony, "Asean to monitor looming dangers to region," *Financial Times*, 8 October 1998, 4.

"Ten years of Nafta," *The Economist*, 3 January 2004, 13–14.

The Complete Twin Plant Guide, Outline. Online. Available at: www.mexonline.com/solunet.htm (accessed 6 December 1998).

"The [European] Court of Justice and the life of European citizens." Online. Available at: www.europa.eu.int/cj/en/pres/cjieu.htm (accessed 8 September 1999).

"The EFTA Secretariat." Online. Available at: www.secretariat.efta.int/ (accessed 12 March 2004).

"The EFTA Surveillance Authority." Online. Available at: www.eftasurv.int/ (accessed 13 March 2004).

"The European Free Trade Association." Online. Available at: www.efta/int (accessed 12 March 2004).

"The European Revolution," *The Economist*, 9 November 1991, 59–60.

"The Jesuits," in *The Catholic Encyclopedia*. Online. Available at: www.newadvent.org/cathen/14081a.htm (accessed 24 January 2000).

"The right verdict on the constitution," *The Economist*, 26 June 2004, 14.

"The Union pauses for breath," *The Economist*, 12 February 2000, 49–50.

Tierney, John, "Javits center's chronic woes seen as going beyond mob," *The New York Times*, 19 March 1995, 1 and 15.

"Towards the implementation of a caricom single market: a long and winding road," *First Citizens Bank Economic Newsletter*, vol. 6, no. 5, March 2003. Online. Available at: www.caricom.org/archives/csmeimplementation.htm (accessed 20 April 2004).

Tracy, James D., "Introduction," in James D. Tracy (ed.) *The Political Economy of Merchant Empires*, pp. 1–21, Cambridge, UK: Cambridge University Press, 1991.

"Trade Policy Review [World Trade Organization]: Southern African Customs Union," 25 April 2003. Online. Available at: www.wto.org/english/tratop_e/pr_/tp213_e.htm (accessed 18 June 2004).

Treaty Establishing the European Community as Amended by Subsequent Treaties, Rome, 25 March 1957. Online. Available at: www.tufts.edu/departments/fletcher/multi/texts/BH343.txt (accessed 20 March 2000).

Treaty of Amsterdam. Part One, Substantive Amendments. Article 1. Online. Available at: www.ue.eu.int/Amsterdam/en/amsteroc/en/treaty/Partone/amst04.htm; (accessed 23 August 1999).

Tribe, Laurence H. and Dorf, Michael C., *On Reading the Constitution*, Cambridge, Massachusetts, and London, England: Harvard University Press, 1991.

Tuma, Elias H., *European Economic History: Tenth Century to the Present*, New York: Harper & Row, 1971.

Turner, Mark, "Africa's first world war," *Financial Times* Weekend, 14/15 November 1998, I.

—— "CFA emerges relatively unscathed," in "African Banking," Special Survey, *Financial Times*, 21 May 1999, 23.

Ungerer, Horst, *A Concise History of European Monetary Integration: From EPU to EMU*, Westport, Connecticut: Quorum Books, 1997.

U.S. Customs and Border Protection, Department of Homeland Security, "What is Money Laundering?" Online. Available at: www.cbp.gov/xp/cgov/enforcement/ice/investigations/financial_investigations/money (accessed 6 March 2004).

"U.S.-SACU Free Trade Agreement." Online. Available at: www.ustr.gov/new/fta/sacu.htm (accessed 18 June 2004).

"Viewpoint by Kenya's President Mwai Kibaki on the East African Common Market," 5 November 2003. Online. Available at: www.statehouse.go.ke/commentary.htm (accessed 5 April 2004).

Vogel, Jr., Thomas T., "In a hurricane's wake, private sector grabs the reins of rescue," *The Wall Street Journal*, 20 November 1998, A1 and A8.

Voyle, Susanna, "DeBeers hopes small print will give an edge in diamond market," *Financial Times*, 4 March 1998, 1.

Walton, Gary M. and Robertson, Ross M., *History of the American Economy*, 5th edn, New York: Harcourt Brace Jovanovich, Inc., 1983.

Walton, Gary M. and Rockoff, Hugh, *History of the American Economy*, 8th edn, Fort Worth, Texas: Dryden Press, 1998.

Warn, Ken and Fidler, Stephen, "Argentina studies dollar blueprint," *Financial Times*, 22 January 1999, 1.

Warn, Ken, "Menem forces dollar plan to top of political agenda," *Financial Times*, 15 March 1999, 3.

Wartzman, Rick, "In the wake of Nafta, a family firm sees business go south," *The Wall Street Journal*, 23 February 1999, A1 and A10.

Watkins, Eric, "Free zone at centre of Turk trading hopes," *Financial Times*, 12 October 1994, 8.

Webb, Gary, *Dark Alliance: the CIA, the Contras, and the Crack Cocaine Explosion*, 1st edn, New York: Seven Stories Press, 1998.

Weber, Thomas E., "Web's Vastness foils even best search engines," *The Wall Street Journal*, 3 April 1998, B1.

Weber, Tim, "Assessing the euro assessment," *BBC News*, 9 June 2003. Online. Available at: www.news.bbc.co.uk/1/hi/business/2975790.stm (accessed 8 August 2004).

Weigall, David and Stirk, Peter (eds), *The Origins and Development of the European Community*, Leicester and London: Leicester University Press, 1992.

Weiss, Gary, "Investors beware: chop stocks are on the rise," *Business Week*, 15 December 1997, 112, 114–16, 118, 122, 126, and 128.

—— "The mob is busier than the Feds think," *Business Week*, 15 December 1997, 130.

Wessel, David, "Looking out for globalization's tweeners," *The Wall Street Journal*, 28 July 2005, A2.

"What is NAFTA?" *Financial Times*, 17 November 1993, 6.

"When east meets west: a survey of EU enlargement," *The Economist*, 22 November 2003.

Wickins, Peter L., *An Economic History of Africa from the Earliest Times to Partition*, Capetown: Oxford University Press, 1981.

Wolff, Richard D., *The Economics of Colonialism: Britain and Kenya, 1870–1930*, New Haven and London: Yale University Press, 1974.

"World trade," Special Survey, *Financial Times*, 29 November 1999.

"World trade blocs: NAFTA," *BBC News*, 3 September 2003. Online. Available at: www.news.bbc.co.uk/1/hi/business/3077610.stm (accessed 25 April 2004).

Zeiler, Thomas W., "GATT fifty years ago: U.S. trade policy and imperial tariff preferences," *Business and Economic History*, 26, 2, Winter 1997, 709–17.

—— *Free Trade, Free World: The Advent of GATT*, Chapel Hill: University of North Carolina Press, 1999.

Zizola, Giancarlo, "Secretariats and councils of the Roman Curia," translated by Dinah Livingstone, in Peter Huizing and Knut Walf (eds) *The Roman Curia and the Communion of Churches*, pp. 42–6, New York: Seabury Press, 1979.

Zollverein, in *The Columbia Encyclopedia*, 5th edn., New York: Columbia University Press, 1993. Online. Available at: www.infoplease.com/ce5/CE057153.html (accessed 25 January 1999).

Index